A Closer Walk With God

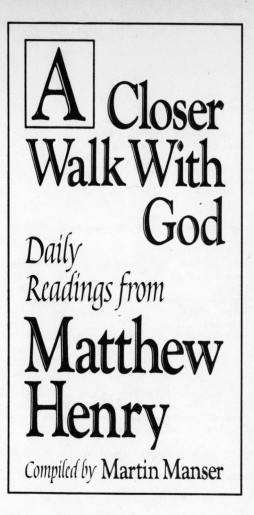

A Closer Walk With God

Daily
Readings from

Matthew Henry

Compiled by Martin Manser

Daybreak Books
Zondervan Publishing House
Grand Rapids, Michigan

A Closer Walk with God
Copyright © 1987 by Marshall Pickering
First published in 1987 by Marshall Morgan and Scott Ltd
Part of the Marshall Pickering Holdings Group
A subsidiary of the Zondervan Corporation

Daybreak Books are published by
Zondervan Publishing House
1415 Lake Dr., S.E.
Grand Rapids, MI 49506

Library of Congress Cataloging-in-Publication Data

Henry, Matthew, 1662–1714.
    A closer walk with God : daily readings from Matthew Henry /
compiled by Martin Manser.
        p.   cm.
    Reprint. Originally published: Basingstoke, Hants, UK :
Marshall Pickering, 1987.
    ISBN 0-310-51700-1
    1. Devotional calendars.   I. Manser, Martin H.   II. Title.
BV4811.H39   1989
242'.2—dc20   89-7932
                                                                          CIP

This Zondervan Edition is by special arrangement with Marshall Pickering.

Printed in the United States of America

89   90   91   92   93   94   95 / DH / 11   10   9   8   7   6   5   4   3   2

Text set in Baskerville by Brian Robinson, Buckingham
Printed in Great Britain by Anchor Brendon Ltd, Tiptree, Essex

Preface

'Every minister ought to read *Matthew Henry* entirely and carefully through once at least,' declared C. H. Spurgeon. George Whitefield is said to have carried the set of *Matthew Henry's Commentary* on all of his travels and read it daily on his knees. And for over two-and-a-half centuries very many people have been enlightened and inspired by Matthew Henry's comments on the scriptures.

Matthew Henry was born at Broad Oak, a Welsh farmhouse at Iscoyd, Clwyd on October 18, 1662. His father, Philip Henry, was a non-conformist minister who, along with two thousand other ministers, had been expelled from the Established Church. At the age of three, Matthew Henry was reading the Bible, and by the time he was nine, he was competent in Latin and Greek.

Matthew Henry was educated at home by his father, and after completing further studies that included the study of law at Gray's Inn in London, he was ordained at the age of 25 and served a Presbyterian congregation in Chester. He held the pastorate there from 1687 to 1712.

In 1704, he began writing his *Notes on the Old Testament*. In 1712 he moved to Hackney, London. He continued to fulfil the duties of the pastorate and at the same time wrote his *Commentary*. Before he died in 1714 he had completed writings through all the Old Testament and up to the Acts of the Apostles in the New Testament. After his death, several of his pastor friends collected his notes and sermons and completed the *Commentary* from Romans to Revelation.

Many abridgments and edited versions of *Matthew Henry's Commentary* have been published; in the present one some archaic expressions have been modernized while retaining the 'flavour' of the original. The Bible version quoted is the Authorized (King James) Version.

This compilation of readings has been edited with a view to not only providing a daily source of encouragement and instruction, but also opening up the rich treasury of Matthew Henry's devotional comments to a wider audience. Indeed, some readers might find their appetites whetted and be encouraged to turn to the abridged one-volume version or even the original six-volume edition of the *Commentary*.

This book of daily readings has been compiled with the hope that Matthew Henry's pastoral and practical notes will lead readers to a deeper understanding of the scriptures and so to a closer walk with the living God.

Martin H. Manser
October 1986

January 1

To live is Christ

Philippians 1:21

We have here an account of the life and death of Paul: his life was Christ, and his death was gain. It is the undoubted character of every true Christian that to him *to live is Christ*. The glory of Christ ought to be the end of our life, the grace of Christ the principle of our life, and the word of Christ the rule of it. The Christian life is derived from Christ, and directed to him. He is the principle, rule, and end of it.

All those to whom to live is Christ to them to die *will be gain*: it is great gain, a present gain, everlasting gain. Death is a great loss to a carnal worldly man; for he loses all his comforts and all his hopes: but to a true Christian it is gain, for it is the end of all his weakness and misery; it is the perfection of his comforts and accomplishment of his hopes; it delivers him from all the evils of life, and brings him to the possession of the chief good.

Or: *To me to die is gain*; that is, 'to the gospel as well as to myself, which will receive a further confirmation by the seal of my blood, as it had before by the labours of my life.' So Christ would be *magnified by* his death, v.20. Some read the whole expression thus: *To me, living and dying, Christ is gain*; that is, 'I desire no more, neither while I live nor when I die, but to win Christ and be found in him.'

January 2

The faithful witness

Revelation 1:5

The Lord Jesus Christ is *the faithful witness*; he was from eternity a witness to all the counsels of God and he was in time a faithful witness to the revealed will of God. Upon his testimony we may safely depend, for he is a faithful witness, cannot be deceived and cannot deceive us.

He is the *first-begotten* or first-born from the dead, or the first parent and head of the resurrection, the only one who raised himself by his own power, and who will by the same power raise up his people from their graves to everlasting honour; for he has begotten them again to a lively hope by his resurrection from the dead.

He is the Prince of the kings of the earth; from him they have their authority; by him their power is limited and their wrath restrained; by him their counsels are overruled, and to him they are accountable. This is good news to the church, and. it is good evidence of the Godhead of Christ, who is King of kings and Lord of lords. The Lord Jesus Christ is the great friend of his church and people, one who has done great things for them.

January 3

The Alpha and the Omega

Revelation 1:5–8

The Lord Jesus Christ has loved his people, and, pursuing that everlasting love, he has, first, *washed them from their sins in his own blood*. Sins leave a stain upon the soul, a stain of guilt and of pollution. Nothing can remove this stain but the blood of Christ; and, rather than it should not be washed out, Christ was willing to shed his own blood, to purchase pardon and purity for them.

Secondly, the Lord Jesus Christ has made his people *kings and priests to God and his Father*. Having justified and sanctified them, he makes them kings to his Father; that is, in his Father's account, with his approval, and for his glory. As kings, they overcome the world, mortify sin, govern their own spirits, conquer Satan, have power and prevalence with God in prayer, and shall judge the world. He has made them priests, given them access to God, enabled them to enter into the holiest and to offer spiritual and acceptable sacrifices, and has given them an unction suitable to his character; and for these high honours and favours they are bound to ascribe to him dominion and glory for ever.

He will be the judge of the world. Revelation begins and ends with a prediction of the second coming of the Lord Jesus Christ. We should set ourselves to meditate frequently upon the second coming of Christ, and keep it in the eye of our faith and expectation. He is the beginning and the end (v.8); all things are from him and for him; he is the Almighty; he is the same eternal and unchangeable one.

January 4

To you who believe he is precious

1 Peter 2:7

True faith in Jesus Christ is the only way to prevent a man's utter confusion. Three things put a man into great confusion, and faith prevents them all—disappointment, sin, and judgment. Faith has a remedy for each.

'*To you therefore who believe he is precious*, or he is an honour, Christ is the crown and honour of a Christian; you who believe will be so far from being ashamed of him that you will boast of him and glory in him for ever.' As to wicked men, the disobedient will go on to disallow and reject Jesus Christ; but God is resolved that he shall be, despite all opposition, the head of the corner.

Jesus Christ is exceedingly precious to all the faithful. The majesty and grandeur of his person, the dignity of his office, his near relation, his wonderful works, his immense love—every thing engages the faithful to the highest esteem and respect for Jesus Christ.

Disobedient people have no true faith. By disobedient people understand those that are unpersuadable, incredulous, and impenitent. These may have some right notions, but no solid faith. Those that ought to be builders of the church of Christ are often the worst enemies that Christ has in the world. In the Old Testament the false prophets did the most mischief; and in the New Testament the greatest opposition and cruelty that Christ met with were from the scribes, Pharisees, chief priests, and those who pretended to build and take care of the church.

God will carry on his own work, and support the interest of Jesus Christ in the world, in spite of the falseness of pretended friends and the opposition of his worst enemies.

[3]

January 5

Spiritual blessings

Ephesians 1:3

The apostle blesses God for spiritual blessings (v.3), where he styles him *the God and Father of our Lord Jesus Christ*; for, as Mediator, the Father was his God; as God, and the second Person in the blessed Trinity, God was his Father. It speaks of the mystical union between Christ and believers, that the God and Father of our Lord Jesus Christ is their God and Father, and that in and through him. All blessings come from God as the Father of our Lord Jesus Christ. No good can be expected from a righteous and holy God to sinful creatures, but by his mediation.

He hath blessed us with all spiritual blessings. Note, spiritual blessings are the best blessings with which God blesses us, and for which we are to bless him. He blesses us by bestowing such things upon us as make us really blessed. We cannot thus bless God again; but must do it by praising, and magnifying, and speaking well of him on that account. Those whom God blesses with some he blesses with all spiritual blessings; to whom he gives Christ, he freely gives all these things. It is not so with temporal blessings; some are favoured with health, and not with riches; some with riches, and not with health, etc. But, where God blesses with spiritual blessings, he blesses with all.

They are *spiritual blessings in heavenly places*; that is, say some, in the church, distinguished from the world, and called out of it. Or it may be read, *in heavenly things*, such as come from heaven, and are designed to prepare men for it, and to secure their reception into it. So we should learn to mind spiritual and heavenly things as the principal things, spiritual and heavenly blessings as the best blessings, with which we cannot be miserable and without which we cannot but be so.

January 6

Walk in love

Ephesians 5:1–2

Here we have the exhortation to mutual love, or to Christian charity. This puts a great honour upon practical religion, that it is the imitating of God. We must be holy as God is holy, merciful as he is merciful, perfect as he is perfect. But there is no one attribute of God more recommended to our imitation than that of his goodness. Be you imitators of God, or resemble him, in every grace, and especially in his love, in his pardoning goodness.

As dear children, as children usually resemble parents in the distinctive features of their faces and in the dispositions and qualities of their minds; or as becomes the children of God, who are beloved and cherished by their heavenly Father. Children are obliged to imitate their parents in what is good, especially when dearly beloved by them. The character that we bear of God's children obliges us to resemble him, especially in his love and goodness, in his mercy and readiness to forgive.

And walk in love (v.2). This godlike grace should conduct and influence our whole way of life. It should be the principle from which we act; it should direct the ends at which we aim. We should be more careful to give proof of the sincerity of our love one to another.

As Christ also hath loved us. Here the apostle directs us to the example of Christ, whom Christians are obliged to imitate, and in whom we have an instance of the most free and generous love that ever was, that great love with which he has loved us, for *he hath given himself for us.*

He has begun a good work in you

Philippians 1:6

He who planted Christianity in the world will preserve it as long as the world stands. Christ will have a church till the mystery of God will be finished and the mystical body completed. The church is built upon a rock, and the *gates of hell shall not prevail against it.* But it is rather to be applied to particular persons, and then it speaks of the certain accomplishment of the work of grace wherever it is begun.

The work of grace is a good work, a blessed work; for it makes us good, and is an earnest of good to us. It makes us like God, and fits us for the enjoyment of God. That may well be called a good work which does us the greatest good.

Wherever this good work is begun it is of God's beginning: *He has begun a good work in you.* We could not begin it ourselves, for we are by nature dead in trespasses and sins: and what can dead men do towards raising themselves to life; or how can they begin to act till they are enlivened in the same respect in which they are said to be dead?

The work of grace is but begun in this life; it is not finished here; as long as we are in this imperfect state there is something more to be done. If the same God who begins the good work did not undertake the carrying on and finishing of it, it would lie for ever unfinished. He must perform it who began it. We may be confident, or well persuaded, that God not only will not forsake, but that he will finish and crown the work of his own hands.

The work of grace will never be perfected *till the day of Jesus Christ*, the day of his appearance. When he shall come to judge the world, and finish his mediation, then this work will be complete, and the top-stone will be brought forth with shouting.

Christ's gracious invitation

John 7:37

Here is the gospel invitation to come to Christ.

We observe:

(1) when Christ gave this invitation: *On the last day of the* feast of tabernacles, that great day. The eighth day, which concluded that solemnity, was to be a *holy convocation*.

(2) how Christ gave this invitation: *Jesus stood and cried*, which denotes his great earnestness and importunity, and his desire that all might take notice, and take hold of this invitation.

The invitation itself is very general: *If any man* thirst, whoever he be, he is invited to Christ be he high or low, rich or poor, young or old, bond or free, Jew or Gentile. It is also very gracious: *If any man thirst, let him come to me and drink.* If any man desires to be truly and eternally happy, let him apply himself to Christ, and be ruled by Christ, and he will undertake to make him so.

Let him come to me. Let him not go to the ceremonial law, which would neither pacify the conscience nor purify it, and therefore could not make the *comers thereunto perfect*. Nor let him go to the heathen philosophy, which does but beguile men, lead them into a wood, and leave them there; but let him go to Christ, accept his doctrine, submit to his discipline, believe in him; come to him as the fountain of living waters, the giver of all comfort.

Let him come *and drink*, he shall have what he comes for, and abundantly more; he shall have that which will not only refresh, but replenish, a soul that desires to be happy.

Christ's promise of comfort

John 7:38–39

Here is a gospel promise of comfort and happiness in Christ. *He that believeth on me, out of his belly shall flow* . . . See here what it is to come to Christ: It is *to believe on him, as the scripture hath said*; it is to receive him as he is offered to us in the gospel. We must not frame a Christ according to our fancy, but believe in a Christ according to the scripture.

See how thirsty souls, who come to Christ, shall be made to drink. Israel, who believed Moses, drank of the *rock that followed them*, the streams followed; but believers drink of a rock in them, Christ in them; he is in them a well of *living water*. Provision is made not only for their present satisfaction, but for their continual perpetual comfort.

The graces and comforts of the Spirit are compared to *living* (meaning 'running') *water*, because they are the active quickening principles of spiritual life, and the earnests and beginnings of eternal life. The comfort flows in both plentifully and constantly as a river; strong as a stream to bear down the opposition of doubts and fears. There is a fulness in Christ of grace for grace. These flow out *of his belly*, that is, out of his heart or soul, which is the subject of the Spirit's working and the seat of his government.

Here is the evangelist's exposition of this promise, v.39: *This spoke he of the Spirit*: not of any outward advantages accruing to believers (as perhaps some misunderstood him), but of the gifts, graces, and comforts of the Spirit. Observe that it is promised to all that believe on Christ that they shall *receive the Holy Ghost*. Some received his miraculous gifts; all receive his sanctifying graces. The gift of the Holy Ghost is one of the great blessings promised in the new covenant, and, if promised, no doubt performed to all that have an interest in that covenant.

The Spirit dwelling and working in believers is as a *fountain of living* running water, out of which plentiful streams flow, cooling and cleansing as water, mollifying and moistening as water, making them fruitful, and others joyful.

January 10

Life more abundant

John 10:10

Christ, the shepherd, is come to give life to the sheep. In opposition to the design of the thief, which is to kill and destroy (which was the design of the scribes and Pharisees) Christ said, *I am come* among men *that they might have life*. He came to put life into the flock, the church in general, which had seemed rather more like a valley full of dry bones than like a pasture covered over with flocks. Christ came to vindicate divine truths, to purify divine ordinances, to redress grievances, and to revive dying zeal, to seek those of his flock that were lost, to *bind up that which was broken*, and this to his church is as *life from the dead*.

Life is inclusive of all good, and stands in opposition to the death threatened; that *we might have life*, as a criminal has when he is pardoned, as a sick man when he is cured, a dead man when he is raised; that we might be justified, sanctified, and at last glorified.

Christ came that we might have life *more abundant* than that which was lost and forfeited by sin, more abundant than that which was promised by the law of Moses, length of days in Canaan, more abundant than could have been expected or than we are able to ask or think. Christ came to give life and something more, something better, life with advantage; that in Christ we might not only live, but live comfortably, live plentifully, live and rejoice. Life in abundance is eternal life, life without death or fear of death, life and much more.

January 11

The good shepherd

John 10:14

See here the grace and tenderness of the good shepherd: *I am the good shepherd* (v.12). It is matter of comfort to the church, and all her friends, that, however she may be damaged and endangered by the

[9]

treachery and mismanagement of her under-officers, the Lord Jesus is, and will be, as he ever has been, *the good shepherd*.

Christ *knows his sheep*. He knows with a distinguishing eye who are his sheep, and who are not; he knows the sheep under their many infirmities, and the goats under their most plausible disguises. He knows with a favourable eye those that in truth are his own sheep; he is aware of their state, concerns himself for them, has a tender and affectionate regard to them, and is continually mindful of them in the intercession he ever lives to make within the veil; he visits them graciously by his Spirit, and has communion with them; he knows them, that is, he approves of and accepts them.

Christ *is known of them*. He observes them with an eye of favour, and they observe him with an eye of faith. Christ's knowing his sheep is put before their knowing him, for he knew and loved us first, and it is not so much our knowing him as our being known of him that is our happiness. Yet it is the character of Christ's sheep that they know him; know him from all pretenders and intruders; they know his mind, know his voice, know by experience the power of his death. Christ speaks here as if he gloried in being known by his sheep, and thought their respect an honour to him.

January 12

The good shepherd lays down his life for the sheep

John 10:15

Christ's offering up himself for his sheep is another proof of his being a good shepherd, and in this he yet more commended his love. v.15, 17, 18.

He declares his purpose of dying for his flock, v.15: *I lay down my life for the sheep*. He not only ventured his life for them (in such a case, the hope of saving it might balance the fear of losing it), but he actually deposited it, and submitted to a necessity of dying for our redemption; he put it as a pawn or pledge; as purchase-money paid down.

Sheep appointed for the slaughter, ready to be sacrificed, were ransomed with the blood of the shepherd. He laid down his life, not only for the good of the sheep, but in their stead. Thousands of sheep had been offered in sacrifice for their shepherds, as sin-offerings, but here, by a surprising reverse, the shepherd is sacrificed for the sheep.

Christ was perfectly voluntary in his sufferings and death, v.18: 'No one doth or can force my life from me against my will, but I freely *lay it down of myself*, I deliver it as my own act and deed, for I have (which no man has) power to lay it down, and to take it again.'

See here the grace of Christ; since none could demand his life of him by law, or extort it by force, he *laid it down of himself* for our redemption. He offered himself to be the Saviour: 'Lo, I come.'

January 13

They shall never perish

John 10:28–29

The Lord Jesus has provided a happiness for his sheep, suited to them: *I give unto them eternal life*, v.28. The estate settled upon them is rich and valuable; it is life, eternal life. Man has a living soul; therefore the happiness provided is life, suited to his nature. Man has an immortal soul: therefore the happiness provided is eternal life, running parallel with his duration. The manner of conveyance is free: I give it to them; it is not bargained and sold upon a valuable consideration; but given by the free grace of Jesus Christ. The donor has power to give it. He who is the fountain of life, and Father of eternity, has authorized Christ to give eternal life. He gives the assurance of it, the pledge and earnest of it, the first-fruits and foretastes of it, that spiritual life which is eternal life begun, heaven in the seed, in the bud, in the embryo.

The Lord Jesus has undertaken for his people's security and preservation to this happiness. They shall be saved from everlasting perdition. *They shall by no means perish for ever*; so the words are. As there is an eternal life, so there is an eternal destruction; the soul not annihilated, but ruined; its being continued, but its comfort and happiness irrecoverably lost. All believers are saved from this; whatever cross they may come under, they shall not come into condemnation. Shepherds that have large flocks often lose some of the sheep and allow them to perish; but Christ has engaged that none of his sheep will perish, not one.

His people cannot be kept from their everlasting happiness; it is in reserve, but he that gives it to them will preserve them to it. *Neither shall any man pluck them out of my hand.* A mighty contest is here supposed about these sheep. The shepherd is so careful of their welfare that he has them not only within his fold, and under his eye, but in his hand, interested in his special love and taken under his special protection; yet their enemies are so daring that they attempt to pluck them out of his hand—his whose own they are, whose care they are; but they cannot, they shall not, do it.

January 14

Continuing in the faith

Acts 14:22

Let us see what Paul and Barnabas did: they *confirmed the souls of the disciples*; that is, they inculcated that upon them which was proper to confirm them, v.22. Young converts are apt to waver, and a little thing shocks them. Their old acquaintances beg they will not leave them. Those that they look upon to be wiser than themselves set before them the absurdity, indecency, and danger, of a change. All this tempts them to think of making a retreat in time; but the apostles come and tell them that this is the true *grace of God wherein they stand*, and therefore they must stand to it that there is no danger like that of losing their part in Christ, no advantage like that of keeping their hold of him; that, whatever their trials may be, they shall have strength from Christ to pass through them; and, whatever their losses may be, they shall be abundantly recompensed. And this confirms the souls of the disciples; it fortifies their pious resolutions, in the strength of Christ, to adhere to Christ whatever it may cost them.

They exhorted them to continue in the faith; or, as it may be read, *they encouraged them*. They told them it was both their duty and interest to persevere; to abide in the belief of Christ's being the Son of God, and the Saviour of the world. Note, those that are in the faith are concerned to *continue in the faith* in spite of all the temptations they may be under to desert it, from the smiles or frowns of this world. And it is necessary that they should often be exhorted to do so. Those that are continually surrounded with temptations to apostasy

[12]

have need to be continually attended with pressing exhortations to perseverance.

That which they insisted most upon was *that we must through much tribulation enter into the kingdom of God.* Not only *they* must, but *we* must; it must be counted upon that all who will go to heaven must expect tribulation and persecution on their way there.

January 15

The gospel of Jesus Christ

Mark 1:1–2

We may observe here what the New Testament is—the divine testament, to which we adhere above all that is human; the new testament, which we advance above that which was old. It is *the gospel of Jesus Christ the Son of God,* v.1. It is *gospel*; it is God's word, and is faithful and true. It is a good word, and well *worthy of all acceptation*; it brings us glad tidings. It is the *gospel of Jesus Christ,* the anointed Saviour, the Messiah promised and expected. This Jesus is the *Son of God.* That truth is the foundation on which the gospel is built, and which it is written to demonstrate; for if Jesus be not the Son of God, our *faith is vain.*

From the borrowed quotations (v.2,3) from Malachi and Isaiah we may observe:

(1) that Christ, in his gospel, comes among us, bringing with him a treasure of grace, and a sceptre of government.

(2) such is the corruption of the world, that there is something to do to make room for him, and to remove that which gives not only obstruction, but opposition to his progress.

(3) when God sent his Son into the world, he took care, and when he sends him into the heart, he takes care to prepare his way before him, for the designs of his grace shall not be frustrated.

January 16

Children of God

John 1:12–13

Observe here the true Christian's description and property, and that is he *receives Christ, and believes on his name*; the latter explains the former. Note, first, to be a Christian indeed is to *believe on Christ's name*; it is to assent to the gospel discovery, and consent to the gospel proposal, concerning him. His name is 'the Word of God'; 'the King of kings', 'the Lord our righteousness'; 'Jesus a Saviour'. Now to believe on his name is to acknowledge that he is what these great names speak him to be, and to accept it, that he may be so to us. Secondly, believing in Christ's name is *receiving* him as a gift from God.

The true Christian's dignity and privilege are twofold: first, the privilege of adoption, which takes them into the number of God's children: *To them gave he power to become the sons of God.* Up to that time, the adoption pertained to the Jews only but now, by faith in Christ, Gentiles are the children of God. They have power—authority, a right; to them gave he this pre-eminence. This power have all the saints. The privilege of adoption is entirely owing to Jesus Christ; he gave this power to them that believe on his name.

Secondly, the privilege of regeneration, v.13: *which were born.* Note, all the children of God are born again; all that are adopted are regenerated. Wherever God confers the dignity of children, he creates the nature and disposition of children. Men cannot do so when they adopt. Now here we have an account of the origin of this new birth. It is not propagated by natural generation from our parents—it is *not of blood, nor of the will of the flesh*, nor of corruptible seed,—nor is it produced by the natural power of our own will, but it is of *God*. This new birth is owing to the word of God as the means, and to the Spirit of God as the great and sole author. True believers are *born of God*.

January 17

Hold fast!

Hebrews 10:23

The apostle exhorts believers to hold fast the profession of their faith, v.23. Here observe the duty itself—to hold fast the profession of our faith, to embrace all the truths and ways of the gospel, to lay fast hold of them, and to keep that hold against all temptation and opposition. Our spiritual enemies will do what they can to wrest our faith, and hope, and holiness, and comfort, out of our hands, but we must hold fast our religion as our best treasure.

Notice, too, the manner in which we must do this—without wavering, without doubting, without disputing, without dallying with temptation to apostasy. Having once settled these great things between God and our souls, we must be steadfast and immovable. Those who begin to waver in matters of Christian faith and practice are in danger of falling away.

The motive or reason enforcing this duty is this: *He is faithful that hath promised.* God has made great and precious promises to believers, and he is a faithful God, true to his word; there is no falseness or fickleness with him, and there should be none with us. His faithfulness should excite and encourage us to be faithful, and we must depend more upon his promises to us than upon our promises to him, and we must plead with him the promise of his grace that is sufficient.

January 18

What is faith?

Hebrews 11:1

Here we have a description of the grace of faith. Faith *is the substance of things hoped for.* Faith and hope go together; and the same things that are the object of our hope are the object of our faith. It is a firm persuasion and expectation that God will perform all that he has promised to us in Christ; and this persuasion is so strong that it gives the soul a kind of possession and present fruition of those things, gives them a subsistence in the soul by the first-fruits and foretastes of them, so that believers in the exercise of faith *are filled with joy unspeakable and full of glory*. Christ dwells in the soul by faith, and the soul is filled with the fulness of God, as far as his present measure will admit; he experiences a substantial reality in the object of faith.

Faith is also *the evidence of things not seen*. Faith demonstrates to the eye of the mind the reality of those things that cannot be discerned by the eye of the body. Faith is the firm assent of the soul to the divine revelation and every part of it, and sets to its seal that God is true. It is a full approval of all that God has revealed as holy, just, and good; it helps the soul to make application of all to itself with suitable affections and endeavours; and so it is designed to serve the believer instead of sight, and to be to the soul all that the senses are to the body.

January 19

Seeking God

Hebrews 11:6

Observe what is here said of Enoch's faith, v.6. It is said that *without this faith it is impossible to please God*, without such a faith as helps us to walk with God, an active faith, and that we cannot come to God unless we *believe that he is, and that he is a rewarder of those that diligently seek him*. He must believe that God is, and that he is what he is, what he has revealed himself to be in the scripture, a Being of infinite perfections, subsisting in three Persons, Father, Son, and Holy Ghost. Observe the practical belief of the existence of God, as revealed in the word, would be a powerful awe-band upon our souls, a bridle of restraint to keep us from sin, and a spur of constraint to put us upon all manner of gospel obedience.

That he is a rewarder of those that diligently seek him. Here observe that by the fall we have lost God; we have lost the divine light, life, love, likeness, and communion. God is again to be found of us through Christ, the second Adam; God has prescribed means and ways in which he may be found; namely a strict attention to his oracles, attendance on his ordinances, and ministers duly discharging their office and associating with his people, observing his providential guidance, and in all things humbly waiting his gracious presence.

Those who would find God in these ways of his must *seek him diligently*; they must seek early, earnestly, and perseveringly. *Then shall they seek him, and find him, if they seek him with all their heart*; and when once they have found him, as their reconciled God, they will never repent the pains they have spent in seeking after him.

January 20

Anxious thoughts

Matthew 6:25

There is scarcely any one sin against which our Lord Jesus more largely and earnestly warns his disciples, or against which he arms them with more variety of arguments, than the sin of disquieting, distracting, distrustful cares about the things of this life, which are a bad sign that both the treasure and the heart are on the earth.

Here is (v.25) the prohibition laid down. It is the counsel and command of the Lord Jesus that we *take no thought* about the things of this world; *I say unto you*. He says it as our Lawgiver, and the Sovereign of our hearts; he says it as our Comforter, and the Helper of our joy.

What is it that he says? *Take no thought for your life, not yet for your body* (v.25). *Take no thought, saying, What shall we eat?* (v.31) and again (v.34), *Take no thought—Be not in care*. As against hypocrisy, so against worldly cares, the caution is thrice repeated, and yet no vain repetition: it is a *sin which doth so easily beset us*. It intimates how pleasing it is to Christ, and of how much concern it is to ourselves, that we should live without carefulness. It is the repeated command of the Lord Jesus to his disciples, that they should not divide and pull in pieces their own minds with care about the world.

There is a thought concerning the things of this life, which is not only lawful, but duty, but the thought here forbidden is a disquieting, tormenting thought, which hurries the mind hither and thither, and hangs it in suspense; which disturbs our joy in God, and is a damp upon our hope in him; which breaks the sleep, and hinders our enjoyment of ourselves, of our friends, and of what God has given us.

The thought here forbidden is also a distrustful, unbelieving thought. God has promised to provide for those that are his all things needful for life as well as godliness, the life that now is, food and a covering: not dainties, but necessaries. He never said, 'They shall be feasted,' but, *'Verily, they shall be fed.'*

January 21

Trusting God

Matthew 6:25

One would think the command of Christ was enough to restrain us from this foolish sin of disquieting, distrustful care, independently of the comfort of our own souls, which is so nearly concerned; but to show how much the heart of Christ is upon it, and what pleasure he takes in those that hope in his mercy, the command is backed with the most powerful arguments. If reason may but rule us, surely we shall ease ourselves of these thorns. To free us from anxious thoughts and to expel them, Christ here suggests to us comforting thoughts, that we may be filled with them. It will be worth while to take pains with our own hearts, to argue them out of their disquieting cares, and to make ourselves ashamed of them. They may be weakened by right reason, but it is by an active faith only that they can be overcome.

Is not the life more than meat, and the body than raiment? v.25. Yes, no doubt it is; so he says who had reason to understand the true value of present things, for he made them, he supports them, and supports us by them; and the thing speaks for itself.

This is an encouragement to us to trust God for *food* and *raiment*, and so to ease ourselves of all perplexing cares about them. God has given us life, and given us the body; it was an act of power, it was an act of favour, it was done without our care: what cannot he do for us, who did that?—what will he not? If we take care about our souls and eternity, which are more than the body, and its life, we may leave it to God to provide for us food and raiment, which are less.

January 22

The birds of the air

Matthew 6:26

Behold the fowls of the air. Here is an argument taken from God's providence towards the inferior creatures, and their dependence, according to their capacities, upon that providence. Look upon the fowls, and learn to trust God for food (v.26), and disquiet not yourselves with thoughts of *what you shall eat.*

Observe the providence of God concerning them. Look upon them and receive instruction. There are various sorts of fowls; they are numerous, some of them ravenous, but they are all fed; it is rare that any of them perish for want of food, even in winter. The fowls, as they are least as service to man, so they are least within his care; men often feed upon them, but seldom feed them; yet they are fed, we know not how, and some of them fed best in the hardest weather; and it is *your heavenly Father that feeds them.*

But that which is especially observed here is, that they are fed without any care or project of their own; *they sow not, neither do they reap, nor gather into barns.* The ant indeed does, and the bee, and they are set before us as examples of prudence and industry; but the fowls of the air do not; they make no provision for the future themselves, and yet every day, as duly as the day comes, provision is made for them, and their *eyes wait on God.*

Improve this for your encouragement to trust in God. *Are ye not much better than they?* Yes, certainly you are. The heirs of heaven are much better than the fowls of heaven; nobler and more excellent beings, and, by faith, they soar higher; they are of a better nature and nurture. You are dearer to God, and nearer, though they fly in the open firmament of heaven. He is their Maker and Lord, their Owner and Master; but besides all this, he is your Father, and in his account *ye are of more value than many sparrows*; you are his children, his first-born; now he that feeds his birds surely will not starve his babes. They trust your Father's providence, and will not you trust it?

The lilies of the field

Matthew 6:28–30

Consider the lilies of the field. Consider how frail the lilies are; they are the *grass of the field*. Lilies, though distinguished by their colours, are still but grass. This grass *today is*, and *tomorrow is cast into the oven*.

Consider how free from care the lilies are: they *toil not* as men do, to earn clothing; *neither do they spin*, as women do, to make clothing. It does not follow that we must therefore neglect, or do carelessly, the proper business of this life. Idleness tempts God, instead of trusting him; but he that provides for the inferior creatures, without their labour, will much more provide for us, by blessing our labour, which he has made our duty. And if we should, through sickness, be unable to toil and spin, God can furnish us with what is necessary for us.

Consider what the lilies grow to. Out of that obscurity in a few weeks they come to be so very fair and fine *that even Solomon, in all his glory, was not arrayed like one of these*. The array of Solomon was very splendid and magnificent, yet he comes far short of the beauty of the lilies, and a bed of tulips outshines him.

All this teaches us to cast the care of our necessary clothing upon God—Jehovah-jireh (the Lord will provide); trust him that clothes the lilies, to provide for you what you shall *put on*. If he gives such fine clothes to the grass, much more will he give fitting clothes to his own children. He shall much more clothe you: for you are nobler creatures, of a more excellent being; if so he clothe the short-lived grass, much more will he clothe you that are made for immortality.

January 24

Your father knows

Matthew 6:32

Your heavenly Father knows ye have need of all these things; these necessary things, food and raiment. He knows our wants better than we do ourselves, though he is in heaven, and his children on earth, he observes what the least and poorest of them has occasion for.

You think, if such a good friend did but know your wants and difficulties, you would soon have relief: your God knows them; and he is your Father that loves you and pities you, and is ready to help you; your heavenly Father, who has the wherewithal to supply all your needs.

Away, therefore, with all disquieting thoughts and cares; go to your Father; tell him, he knows that you need such things. Tell him whether you have or not. Though he knows our wants, he wants to know them from us; and when we have opened them to him, let us cheerfully direct ourselves to his wisdom, power, and goodness, for our supply. Therefore we should ease ourselves of the burden of care, by casting it upon God, because it is he *that careth for us*. If he cares, why should we care?

January 25

Seek first God's kingdom

Matthew 6:33

Seek first the kingdom of God—mind religion as your great and principal concern. Our duty is to seek; to desire, pursue, and aim at these things. Aim at the kingdom of heaven; press towards it; give diligence to make it sure; seek for this glory, honour, and immortality; prefer heaven and heavenly blessings far before earth and earthly delights.

And the happiness of this kingdom, seek the *righteousness* of it; God's righteousness, the righteousness which he requires to be brought about in us and by us, such as exceeds that of the scribes and Pharisees; we must follow peace and holiness.

Seek first the kingdom of God. Let you care for your souls and another world take the place of all other cares: and let all the concerns of this life be made subordinate to those of the life to come: we must seek the things of Christ more than our own things; and if ever they come in competition, we must remember to which we are to give the preference. Seek these things first; first in thy days: let the morning of youth be dedicated to God. Seek this first every day; let waking thoughts be of God.

Observe the gracious promise: *all these things*, the necessary supports of life, *shall be added unto you*. You shall have what you seek, the *kingdom of God and his righteousness*, for never any sought in vain, that sought in earnest; and besides that, you shall have food and raiment.

O what a blessed change would it make in our hearts and lives, if we but firmly believed this truth, that the best way to be comfortably provided for in this world is to be most intent upon another world!

January 26

Living one day at a time

Matthew 6:34

We must not perplex ourselves inordinately about future events, because every day brings along with it its own burden of cares and grievances. So we are told that thoughtfulness for the morrow is needless: *Let the morrow take thought for the things of itself.* The saints have a Friend that is their arm every morning, and gives out fresh supplies daily, according as the business of every day requires, and so he keeps his people in a constant dependence upon him. Let us refer it therefore to the morrow's strength, to do the morrow's work, and bear the morrow's burden. Tomorrow, and the things of it, will be provided for without us; why need we thus anxiously care for that which is so wisely cared for already?

This does not forbid a prudent foresight, and preparation accordingly, but a perplexing solicitude, and a prepossession of difficulties and calamities, which may perhaps never come, or if they do, may be easily borne, and the evil of them guarded against. The meaning is, let us mind present duty, and then leave events to

God; do the work of the day in its day, and then let tomorrow bring its work along with it.

Thoughtfulness for the morrow is one of those foolish and hurtful lusts, which those that will be rich fall into. *Sufficient unto the day is the evil thereof.* This present day has trouble enough attending it, we need not accumulate burdens by anticipating our trouble, nor borrow perplexities from tomorrow's evils to add to those of this day. It is uncertain what tomorrow's evils may be, but whatever they be, it is time enough to take thought about them when they come.

January 27

The throne of grace

Hebrews 4:16

There is a throne of grace set up, a way of worship instituted, in which God may with honour meet poor sinners, and they may with hope draw night to him, repenting and believing. God might have set up a tribunal of strict and inexorable justice, dispensing death, the wages of sin, to all who were convened before it; but he has chosen to set up a throne of grace.

A throne of grace speaks great encouragement even to the chief of sinners. There grace reigns, and acts with sovereign freedom, power, and bounty. Our business at the throne of grace should be that *we may obtain mercy and find grace to help in time of need.* Mercy and grace are the things we want, mercy to pardon all our sins and grace to purify our souls.

In all our approaches to this throne of grace for mercy, we should come with a humble freedom and boldness, with a liberty of spirit and a liberty of speech; we should ask in faith, nothing doubting; we should come with a Spirit of adoption, as children to a reconciled God and Father. We are indeed to come with reverence and godly fear, but not with terror and amazement; not as if we were dragged before the tribunal of justice, but kindly invited to the mercy-seat, where grace reigns, and loves to exert and exalt itself towards us.

Crucified with Christ

Galatians 2:20

Here the apostle Paul gives us an excellent description of the mysterious life of a believer.

He is crucified, and yet he lives; the old man is crucified, but the new man is living; he is dead to the world, and dead to the law, and yet alive to God and Christ; sin is mortified, and grace quickened.

I live, and yet not I: this is strange; he lives in the exercise of grace; he has the comforts and the triumphs of grace; and yet that grace is not from himself, but from another. Believers see themselves living in a state of dependence.

He is *crucified with Christ*, and yet *Christ lives in him*; this results from his mystical union with Christ, by means of which he is interested in the death of Christ, so as because of that to die unto sin; and yet interested in the life of Christ, so as because of that to live unto God. He *lives in the flesh*, and yet *lives by faith*; to outward appearance he lives as other people do, his natural life is supported as others are; yet he has a higher and nobler principle that supports and actuates him, that of faith in Christ, and especially as eyeing the wonders of his love in giving himself for him. So it is that, though he lives in the flesh, yet he does not live after the flesh.

Those who have true faith live by that faith; and the great thing which faith fastens upon is Christ's loving us and giving himself for us. The great evidence of Christ's loving us is his giving himself for us; and this is that which we are chiefly concerned to mix faith with, for our living to him.

Christt, the true and living bread

John 6:33

Christ here shows that he is the *true bread*; this he repeats again and again, v.33, 35, 48–51. Observe that Christ is *bread*, is that to the soul which bread is to the body, nourishes and supports the spiritual life as does bread the bodily life. The doctrines of the gospel concerning Christ—that he is the Mediator between God and man, that he is our peace, our righteousness, our Redeemer; by these things no men live. Our bodies could better live without food than our souls without Christ.

Christ is the *bread of God* (v.33), divine bread; it is he that is of God (v.46), bread which my Father gives (v.32), which he has made to be the food of our souls, the bread of God's family, his children's bread.

Christ is *the living bread* (v.51). Bread is itself a dead thing, and nourishes not but by the help of the faculties of a living body; but Christ is himself living bread, and nourishes by his own power. Manna was a dead thing; if kept but one night, it putrefied and bred worms; but Christ is ever living, everlasting bread, that never moulds, nor grows old. The doctrine of Christ crucified is now as strengthening and comforting to a believer as ever it was, and his mediation still of as much value and efficacy as ever.

He gives life unto the world (v.33), spiritual and eternal life; the life of the soul in union and communion with God here, and in the vision and fruition of him hereafter; a life that includes in it all happiness. The manna did only preserve and support life, did not preserve and perpetuate life, much less restore it; but Christ *gives* life to those that were dead in sin.

Obedient to the Father

John 6:38

Christ assures us that he came from heaven upon his Father's business (v.38), not to *do his own will, but the will of him that sent him.* He *came from heaven*, which speaks of him as an intelligent active being, who voluntarily descended to this lower world, a long journey, and a great step downward, considering the glories of the world he came from and the calamities of the world he came to.

We may well ask with wonder, 'What moved him to such an expedition?' Here he tells us that he came to do, not *his own will*, but the will of his Father; not that he had any will that stood in competition with the will of his Father, but those to whom he spoke suspected he might.

Christ did not come into the world as a private person that acts for himself only, but under a public character, to act for others as an ambassador, or plenipotentiary, authorized by a public commission; he came into the world as God's great agent and the world's great physician. It was not any private business that brought him here, but he came to settle affairs between parties no less considerable than the great Creator and the whole creation.

Christ, when he was in the world, did not carry on any private design, nor had any separate interest at all, distinct from theirs for whom he acted. The scope of his whole life was to glorify God and do good to men. He therefore never consulted his own ease, safety, or quiet; but, when he was to lay down his life, though he had a human nature which startled at it, he set aside the consideration of that, and resolved his will as man into the will of God: *Not as I will, but as thou wilt.*

January 31

What is heaven like?

John 17:24

Heaven is to be where Christ is: *Where I am*; in the paradise to where Christ's soul went at death; in the third heaven to where his soul and body went at his ascension. In this world we are but on our passage; there we truly are where we are to be for ever; so Christ reckoned, and so must we.

Heaven is to be with him where he is; this is no tautology, but intimates that we shall not only be in the same happy place where Christ is, but that the happiness of the place will consist in his presence; this is *the fulness of its joy*. The very heaven of heaven is to be with Christ, there in company with him, and communion with him.

Heaven is to behold his glory, which the Father has given him. The glory of the Redeemer is the brightness of heaven. That glory before which angels cover their faces was his glory. Christ will *come in the glory of his Father, for he is the brightness of his glory*. God shows his glory there, as he does his grace here, through Christ.

The happiness of the redeemed consists very much in the beholding of this glory; they will have the immediate view of his glorious person. They will have a clear insight into his glorious undertaking, as it will be then accomplished; they will see into those springs of love from which flow all the streams of grace; they shall have an appropriating sight of Christ's glory, and an assimilating sight: they shall be *changed into the same image, from glory to glory*.

February 1

The unsearchable riches of Christ

Ephesians 3:8

The apostle Paul here informs the Ephesians how he was employed by God as an apostle to the Gentiles, and to all men. With respect to the Gentiles, he preached to them *the unsearchable riches of Christ*, v.8.

Observe how humbly the apostle speaks of himself: *I am less than the least of all saints.* St Paul, who was the chief of the apostles, calls himself less than the least of all saints: he means on account of his having been formerly a persecutor of the followers of Christ. He was, in his own esteem, as little as could be. What can be less than the least?

Notice that those whom God advances to honourable employments he humbles and makes low in their own eyes; and, where God gives grace to be humble, there he gives all other grace. You may also observe in what a different manner the apostle speaks of himself and of his office. While he magnifies his office, he debases himself. A faithful minister of Christ may be very humble, and think very meanly of himself, even when he thinks and speaks very highly and honourably of his sacred function.

Observe how highly the apostle speaks of Jesus Christ: *the unsearchable riches of Christ.* There is a mighty treasury of mercy, grace, and love laid up in Christ Jesus, and that both for Jews and Gentiles. Or the riches of the gospel are here spoken of as the riches of Christ: the riches which Christ purchased for, and bestows upon, all believers. And they are unsearchable riches, which we cannot find the bottom of, which human sagacity could never have discovered and men could not otherwise reach the knowledge of but by revelation.

February 2

Coming into God's presence

Hebrews 10:19

Here the apostle sets forth the privileges that Christ has secured for believers, that, while they take the comfort, they may give him the glory of all. Believers have boldness to enter into the holiest. They have access to God, light to direct them, liberty of spirit and of speech to conform to the direction; they have a right to the privilege and a readiness for it, assistance to use it and assurance of acceptance and advantage. They may enter into the gracious presence of God in his holy oracles, ordinances, providences, and covenant, and so into communion with God, where they receive communications from him, till they are prepared to enter into his glorious presence in heaven. Believers have a high priest over the house of God, even Jesus.

The apostle tells us the way and means by which Christians enjoy such privileges, and declares it to be *by the blood of Jesus*, by the merit of that blood which he offered up to God as an atoning sacrifice: he has purchased for all who believe in him free access to God in the ordinances of his grace here and in the kingdom of his glory. This blood, being sprinkled on the conscience, chases away slavish fear, and gives the believer assurance both of his safety and his welcome into the divine presence.

February 3

The new and living way

Hebrews 10:20

The apostle, having given this general account of the way by which we have access to God, now enters further into the particulars of it, v.20.

It is the *only* way; there is no way left but this. The first way to the tree of life is, and has been, long shut up. It is a *new* way, both in opposition to the covenant of works and to the antiquated dispensation of the Old Testament; it is the last way that will ever be opened to men. Those who will not enter in this way exclude themselves for ever. It is a way that will always be effectual.

It is a *living* way. It would be death to attempt to come to God in the way of the covenant of works; but this way we may come to God, and live. It is by a living Saviour, who, though he was dead, is alive; and it is a way that gives life and lively hope to those who enter into it.

It is a way that Christ has *consecrated for us through the veil, that is, his flesh*. The veil in the tabernacle and temple signified the body of Christ; when he died, the veil of the temple was rent asunder, and this was at the time of the evening sacrifice, and gave the people a surprising view into the holy of holies, which they never had before. Our way to heaven is by a crucified Saviour; his death is to us the way of life. To those who believe this he will be precious.

February 4

Drawing near to God

Hebrews 10:22

The apostle now proceeds to show the Hebrews the duties binding upon them on account of the privileges. They must *draw near* to God in a right manner. Since such a way of access and return to God is opened, it would be the greatest ingratitude and contempt of God and Christ still to keep at a distance from him. They must draw near:

With a true heart—without any allowed guile or hypocrisy. God is the searcher of hearts, and he requires truth in the inward parts. Sincerity is our gospel perfection, though not our justifying righteousness.

In full assurance of faith, with a faith grown up to a full persuasion that when we come to God by Christ we shall have acceptance. We should lay aside all sinful distrust. Without faith it is impossible to please God; and the stronger our faith is, the more glory we give to God.

Having our hearts sprinkled from an evil conscience, by a believing application of the blood of Christ to our souls. They may be cleansed from guilt, from filth, from sinful fear and torment, from all aversion to God and duty, from ignorance, and error, and superstition, and whatever evils the consciences of men are subject to by reason of sin.

Our bodies washed with pure water, that is, with the water of baptism (by which we are recorded among the disciples of Christ, members of his mystical body), or with the sanctifying virtue of the Holy Spirit, reforming and regulating our outward conversation as well as our inward frame, cleansing from the filthiness of the flesh as well as of the spirit. There must be a due preparation for making our approaches to God.

Pride and humility

James 4:6

We are taught here to observe the difference God makes between pride and humility. *God resisteth the proud, but giveth grace unto the humble*, v.6. Two things are here to be observed:

(1) The disgrace cast upon the proud: God resists them; the original word signifies, God's setting himself as in battle array against them; and can there be a greater disgrace than for God to proclaim a man a rebel, an enemy, a traitor to his crown and dignity, and to proceed against him as such?

The proud resists God; in his understanding he resists the truths of God; in his will he resists the laws of God; in his passions he resists the providence of God; and therefore no wonder that God sets himself against the proud. Let proud spirits hear this and tremble—*God resists them*. Who can describe the wretched state of those who make God their enemy? He will certainly fill with shame (sooner or later) the faces of such as have filled their hearts with pride. We should therefore resist pride in our hearts, if we would not have God resist us.

(2) The honour and help God gives to the humble. Grace, as opposed to disgrace, is honour; this God gives to the humble; and, where God gives grace to the humble, there he will give all other graces, and, as in the beginning of this sixth verse, he will *give more grace*. Wherever God gives true grace, he will give more; for to him that has, and uses what he has rightly, more shall be given. He will especially give more grace to the humble, because they see their need of it, will pray for it and be thankful for it; and such shall have it.

February 6

Full submission

James 4:7

We are taught here to submit ourselves entirely to God: *Submit yourselves therefore to God. Resist the devil, and he will flee from you*, v.7. Christians should forsake the friendship of the world, and watch against that envy and pride which they see prevailing in natural men, and should by grace learn to glory in their submissions to God. 'Submit yourselves to him as subjects to their prince, in duty, and as one friend to another, in love and interest. Submit your understandings to the truths of God; submit your wills to the will of God, the will of his precept, the will of his providence. Submit yourselves to God, as considering how many ways you are bound to this, and as considering what advantage you will gain by it; for God will not hurt you by his dominion over you, but will do you good.'

Now, as this subjection and submission to God are what the devil most industriously strives to hinder, so we ought with great care and steadiness to resist his suggestions. If he would represent a tame yielding to the will and providence of God as what will bring calamities, and expose to contempt and misery, we must resist these suggestions of fear. If he would represent submission to God as a hindrance to our outward ease, or worldly preferments, we must resist these suggestions of pride and sloth. If he would tempt us to lay any of our miseries, and crosses, and afflictions, to the charge of Providence, so that we might avoid them by following his directions instead of God's, we must resist these provocations to anger, not fretting ourselves in any wise to do evil. Let not the devil, in these or the like attempts, prevail upon you; but *resist him and he will flee from you*. If we basely yield to temptations, the devil will continually follow us; but if we *put on the whole armour of God*, and stand out against him, he will be gone from us. Resolution shuts and bolts the door against temptation.

Draw nigh to God

James 4:8–9

In verses 8 and 9 we are directed how to act towards God in our becoming submissive to him.

Draw nigh to God. The heart that has rebelled must be brought to the foot of God; the spirit that was distant and estranged from a life of communion and converse with God must become acquainted with him; '*Draw nigh to God*, in his worship and institutions, and in every duty he requires of you.'

Cleanse your hands. He who comes unto God must have clean hands: hands free from blood, and bribes, and every thing that is unjust or cruel, and free from every defilement of sin. The hands must be cleansed by faith, repentance, and reformation, or it will be in vain for us to draw nigh to God in prayer, or in any of the exercises of devotion.

Those who halt between God and the world are here meant by the *double-minded*. To *purify the heart* is to be sincere, and to act upon this single aim and principle, rather to please God than to seek after anything in this world: hypocrisy is heart-impurity; but those who submit themselves to God in the right way will purify their hearts as well as cleanse their hands.

Be afflicted and mourn, and weep. Be afflicted when afflictions are sent upon you, and do not despise them; or be afflicted in your sympathies with those who are so, and in laying to heart the calamities of the church of God. Mourn and weep for your own sins and the sins of others. *Let your laughter be turned to mourning and your joy to heaviness.* This may be taken either as a prediction of sorrow or a prescription of seriousness. Let men think to set grief at defiance, yet God can bring it upon them; none laugh so heartily but he can turn their laughter into mourning.

God will draw nigh to us

James 4:10

Humble yourselves in the sight of the Lord. Let the inward acts of the soul be suitable to all those outward expressions of grief, affliction, and sorrow, mentioned in verses 8 and 9. Humility of spirit is here required, as in the sight of him who looks principally at the spirits of men. Let there be a thorough humiliation in bewailing everything that is evil; let there be great humility in doing that which is good: *Humble yourselves.*

We have great encouragement to act in this way towards God: *He will draw nigh to those that draw nigh to him,* v.8, and *he will lift up* those who humble themselves in his sight, v.10. Those that draw nigh to God in a way of duty shall find God drawing nigh to them in a way of mercy. Draw nigh to him in faith, and trust, and obedience, and he will draw nigh to you for your deliverance. If there be not a close communion between God and us, it is our fault, and not his.

If we be truly penitent and humble under the marks of God's displeasure, we shall in a little time know the advantages of his favour; he will lift us up out of trouble, or he will lift us up in our spirits and comforts under trouble; he will lift us up to honour and safety in the world, or he will lift us up in our way to heaven, so as to raise our hearts and affections above the world.

God will revive the spirit of the humble; he will hear the desire of the humble, and he will at last lift them up to glory. Before honour is humility. The highest honour in heaven will be the reward of the greatest humility on earth.

February 9

Let brotherly love continue

Hebrews 13:1

The apostle calls the believing Hebrews to the performance of many excellent duties, in which it becomes Christians to excel. He calls them to *brotherly love*, v.1, by which he does not only mean a general affection to all men, as our brethren by nature, all made of the same blood, nor that more limited affection which is due to those who are of the same immediate parents, but that special and spiritual affection which ought to exist among the children of God.

It is here supposed that the Hebrews had this love one for another. Though, at this time, that nation was miserably divided and distracted among themselves, both about matters of religion and the civil state, yet there was true brotherly love left among those of them who believed on Christ; and this appeared in a very eminent manner presently after the shedding forth of the Holy Ghost, when they had all things in common, and sold their possessions to make a general fund of subsistence to their brethren. The spirit of Christianity is a spirit of love. Faith works by love. The true religion is the strongest bond of friendship; if it be not so, it has its name for nothing.

This brotherly love was in danger of being lost, and that in a time of persecution, when it would be most necessary; it was in danger of being lost by those disputes that were among them concerning the respect they ought still to have to the ceremonies of the Mosaic law. Disputes about religion too often produce a decay of Christian affection; but this must be guarded against, and all proper means used to preserve brotherly love. Christians should always love and live as brethren, and the more they grow in devout affection to God their heavenly Father the more they will grow in love to one another for his sake.

February 10

Showing hospitality

Hebrews 13:2

The apostle calls his readers to hospitality: *Be not forgetful to entertain strangers* for his sake, v.2. Here observe the duty required—*to entertain strangers*, both those that are strangers to the commonwealth of Israel, and strangers to our persons, especially those who know themselves to be strangers here and are seeking another country, which is the case of the people of God, and was so at this time: the believing Jews were in a desperate and distressed condition. But he seems to speak of strangers as such; though we know not who they are, nor whence they come, yet, seeing they are without any certain dwelling place, we should allow them room in our hearts and in our houses, as we have opportunity and ability.

Notice too, the motive: *Thereby some have entertained angels unawares*; as Abraham and Lot did, and one of those that Abraham entertained was the Son of God; and, though we cannot suppose this will ever be our case, yet what we do to strangers, in obedience to him, he will reckon and reward as done to himself. God has often bestowed honours and favours upon his hospitable servants, beyond all their thoughts, *unawares*.

February 11

Sympathy and purity

Hebrews 13:3–4

The apostle goes on to call his readers to Christian sympathy: *Remember those that are in bonds*, v.3. Here observe the duty—to *remember those that are in bonds* and in *adversity*. God often orders it so that while some Christians and churches are in adversity others enjoy peace and liberty. Those that are themselves at liberty must sympathize with those that are in bonds and adversity, as if they were bound with them in the same chain: they must feel the sufferings of their brethren.

The reason of the duty is this: *As being yourselves in the body*; not only in the body natural, and so liable to the like sufferings, and you should sympathize with them now that others may sympathize with you when your time of trial comes; but in the same mystical body, under the same head, *and if one member suffer all the rest suffer with it.*

The readers are also called to purity and chastity, v.4. Here you have a recommendation of God's ordinance of marriage, that it is *honourable in all*, and ought to be so esteemed by all, and not denied to those to whom God has not denied it. It is honourable, for God instituted it for man in paradise, knowing it was not good for him to be alone. He married and blessed the first couple, the first parents of mankind, to direct all to look unto God in the great concern, and to marry in the Lord.

Here, too, is a dreadful but just censure of impurity and lewdness: *Whoremongers and adulterers God will judge.* God knows who are guilty of such sins, no darkness can hide them from him. He will call such sins by their proper names, not by the names of love and gallantry, but of whoredom and adultery, whoredom in the single state and adultery in the married state. He will bring them into judgment, he will judge them, either by their own consciences here, or he will set them at his tribunal at death, and in the last day.

February 12

True contentment

Hebrews 13:5–6

The apostle urges the Hebrews to Christian contentment, v.5,6. Here observe the sin that is contrary to this grace and duty—*covetousness*, an over-eager desire of the wealth of this world, envying those who have more than we. This sin we must allow no place in our conduct; for, though it be a secret lust lurking in the heart, if it be not subdued it will enter into our way of life and be seen in our manner of speaking and acting. We must take care not only to keep this sin down, but to root it out of our souls.

The duty and grace that is contrary to covetousness means being satisfied and pleased *with such things as we have*; present things, for past things cannot be recalled, and future things are only in the hand of God. What God gives us from day to day we must be content with, though it falls short of what we have enjoyed up to this time, and though it does not come up to our expectations for the future. We must be content with our present lot.

The apostle shows what reason Christians have to be contented with their lot: *God hath said, I will never leave thee, nor forsake thee*, v.5,6. This was said to Joshua, but belongs to all the faithful servants of God. Old Testament promises may be applied to New Testament saints. This promise contains the sum and substance of all the promises. *I will never*, no, *never leave thee*, nor ever *forsake thee*. Here are no fewer than five negatives heaped together, to confirm the promise; the true believer shall have the gracious presence of God with him in life, at death, and for ever.

From this comprehensive promise believers may assure themselves of help from God: *So that we may boldly say, The Lord is my helper; I will not fear what man shall do unto me*, v.6. Men can do nothing against God, and God can make all that men do against his people to turn to their good.

February 13

Day by day

2 Corinthians 4:16–17

Though our outward man perish, our inward man is renewed day by day, v.16. Every one of us has an outward and an inward man, a body and a soul. If the outward man perish, there is no remedy, it must and will be so, it was made to perish. It is our happiness if the decays of the outward man contribute to the renewing of the inward man, if afflictions outwardly are gain to us inwardly, if when the body is sick, weak, and perishing, the soul is vigorous and prosperous. The best of men have need of further renewing of the inward man, even day by day. Where the good work is begun there is more work to be done, for carrying it forward. And as in wicked men things grow every day worse and worse, so in godly men they grow better and better.

The prospect of eternal life and happiness kept the believers from fainting. The apostle and his fellow-sufferers saw their afflictions working towards heaven, and that they would end at last (v.17).

They then weighed things in the balance of the sanctuary; they put as it were the heavenly glory in one scale and their earthly sufferings in the other; and, pondering things in their thoughts, they found afflictions to be light, and the glory of heaven to be *a far more exceeding weight*. What sense was ready to pronounce heavy and long, grievous and tedious, faith perceived to be light and short, and but for a moment.

February 14

The eye of faith

2 Corinthians 4:18

The prospect of eternal life and happiness was a mighty support and comfort to the believers. Their faith enabled them to make this right judgment of things: *We look not at the things which are seen, but at the things which are not seen*, v.18. It is by faith that we see God, who is invisible, and by this we look to an unseen heaven and hell, and faith is the *evidence of things not seen*.

There are unseen things, as well as things that are seen. There is this vast difference between them: unseen things are eternal, seen things but temporal, or temporary only.

By faith we not only discern these things, and the great difference between them, but by this also we take our aim at unseen things, and chiefly regard them, and make it our end and scope, not to escape present evils, and obtain present good, both of which are temporal and transitory, but to escape future evil and obtain future good things, which, though unseen, are real, and certain, and eternal; and faith is *the substance of things hoped for*, as well as the evidence of things not seen.

February 15

Knowing and living

Colossians 1:9–10

The apostle proceeds in these verses to pray for the Christians at Colosse. He heard that they were good, and he prayed that they might be better. He was constant in this prayer: *We do not cease to pray for you*. It may be he could hear of them but seldom, but he constantly prayed for them.

He begs of God that they might be knowing, intelligent Christians: *filled with the knowledge of his will, in all wisdom and spiritual understanding*. The knowledge of our duty is the best knowledge. A mere empty notion of the greatest truths is insignificant. Our knowledge of the will of God must be always practical: we must know it, in order to do it. Christians should endeavour to be filled with knowledge; not only to know the will of God, but to know more of it, and to *increase in the knowledge of God*, v.10, and to *grow in grace, and in the knowledge of our Lord and Saviour*.

The apostle also prays that their conduct might be good. Good knowledge without a good life will not profit. Our understanding is then a spiritual understanding when we exemplify it in our way of living: *That you may walk worthy of the Lord unto all pleasing*, v.10, that is, as becomes the relation we stand in him and the profession we make of him. *Being fruitful in every good work*. This is what we should aim at. Good words will not do without good works. We must abound in good works, and in every good work: not in some only, which are more easy, and suitable, and safe, but in all, and every instance of them. There must be a regular, uniform regard to all the will of God. And the more fruitful we are in good works the more we shall *increase in the knowledge of God*.

Strong in God's power

Colossians 1:11

The apostle continues his prayer for the Colossian Christians: that they might be *Strengthened with all might, according to his glorious power*, v.11. It is a great comfort to us that he who undertakes to give strength to his people is a God of power and of glorious power. Where there is spiritual life there is still need of spiritual strength, strength for all the actions of the spiritual life.

To be strengthened is to be furnished by the grace of God for every good work, and fortified by that grace against every evil one: it is to be enabled to do our duty, and still to hold fast our integrity.

The blessed Spirit is the author of this strength; for we are *strengthened with might by his Spirit in the inner man*. The word of God is the means of it, by which he conveys it; and it must be brought in by prayer. It was in answer to earnest prayer that the apostle obtained sufficient grace. In praying for spiritual strength we are not restricted in the promises, and therefore should not be restricted in our own hopes and desires.

Observe Paul's prayer for *all might*. It seems unreasonable that a creature should be strengthened with all might, for that is to make him *almighty*; but he means, with all that might which we have occasion for, to enable us to discharge our duty or preserve our innocence, that grace which is sufficient for us in all the trials of life and able to help us in time of need.

It is *according to his glorious power*. He means, according to the grace of God: but the grace of God in the hearts of believers is the power of God; and there is a glory in this power; it is an excellent and sufficient power.

The special use of this strength was for undergoing work: *That you may be strengthened unto all patience and longsuffering with joyfulness*. He prays not only that they may be supported under their troubles, but strengthened for them.

Coming to Jesus

Matthew 11:28

We are here invited to Christ as our Priest, Prince, and Prophet, to be saved, and, for that, to be ruled and taught by him.

We must come to Jesus Christ as our rest, *Come unto me, all ye that labour*, v.28. Observe the character of the persons invited: *all that labour, and are heavy laden*, a word in season to him that is weary. This burden is to be understood as the burden of sin, both the guilt and the power of it. Note, all those, and those only, are invited to rest in Christ, that are aware of sin as a burden, and groan under it; that are not only convinced of the evil of sin, of their own sin, but are contrite in soul for it; that are really sick of their sins, weary of the service of the world and of the flesh; that see their state sad and dangerous by reason of sin, and are in pain and fear about it. This is a necessary preparation for pardon and peace.

Come unto me. That glorious display of Christ's greatness which we have in v.27, as Lord of all, might frighten us from him, but see here how he holds out *the golden sceptre*, that we may touch the top of it and may live. It is the duty and interest of weary *and heavy laden* sinners to *come to Jesus Christ.* Renouncing all those things which stand in opposition to him, or in competition with him, we must accept him, as our Physician and Advocate, and give up ourselves to his conduct and government; freely willing to be saved by him, in his own way, and upon his own terms. Come and cast that burden upon him, under which you are heavy laden. This is the gospel call.

Rest for the weary

Matthew 11:29

The blessing is promised to those that do come: *I will give you rest.* Jesus Christ will give assured rest to those weary souls that by a lively faith come to him for it; *rest* from the terror of sin, in a well-grounded peace of conscience; *rest* from the power of sin, in a regular order of the soul; a *rest* in God, and a tranquillity of soul, in his love.

We must come to Jesus Christ as our ruler, and submit ourselves to him, v.29. *Take my yoke upon you.* This must go along with the former, for Christ is exalted to be both a Prince and a Saviour, a *Priest upon his throne.* The *rest* he promises is a release from the drudgery of sin, not from the service of God, but an obligation to the duty we owe to him. Note, Christ has a *yoke* for our necks, as well as a crown for our heads, and this yoke he expects we should take upon us and draw in. To call those who are weary and heavy laden to *take a yoke upon* them looks like adding affliction to the afflicted; but the relevance of it lies in the word *my*: 'You are under a yoke which makes you weary: shake that off and try mine, which will make you easy.' To take Christ's yoke upon us is to put ourselves into the relation of servants and subjects to him, and then to conduct ourselves accordingly, in a conscientious obedience to all his commands, and a cheerful submission to all his assignments.

February 19

Learning from Christ

Matthew 11:29

We must come to Jesus Christ as our teacher, and set ourselves to learn of him, v.29. Christ has erected a great school, and has invited us to be his scholars. We must enter ourselves, associate with his scholars, and daily attend the instructions he gives by his word and Spirit. We must converse much with what he said, and have it ready to use upon all occasions; we must conform to what he did and follow his steps.

Two reasons are given why we must *learn of Christ*:

(1) *I am meek and lowly in heart*, and therefore fit to teach you. He is *meek*, and can have compassion on the ignorant, whom others would be in a passion with. Many able teachers are hot and hasty, which is a great discouragement to those who are dull and slow; but Christ knows how to bear with such, and to open their understandings.

He is lowly in heart. He condescends to teach poor scholars, to teach novices; he chose disciples, not from the court, nor the schools, but

[43]

from the seaside. He teaches the first principles, such things as are milk for babes; he stoops to the lowliest capacities.

(2) *You shall find rest to your souls.* The only way, and a sure way to find rest for our souls is, to sit at Christ's feet and hear his word. The way of duty is the way of rest. The understanding finds rest in the knowledge of God and Jesus Christ, and is there abundantly satisfied, finding that wisdom in the gospel which has been sought for in vain throughout the whole creation.

February 20

My yoke is easy

Matthew 11:30

To take Christ's yoke upon us is to obey the gospel of Christ, to yield ourselves to the Lord: it is Christ's yoke. We are yoked to work, and therefore must be diligent; we are yoked to submit, and therefore must be humble and patient: we are yoked together with our fellow-servants, and therefore must keep up the communion of saints. Now this is the hardest part of our lesson, and therefore it is qualified, v.30. *My yoke is easy and my burden is light*; you need not be afraid of it.

The yoke of Christ's commands is an *easy yoke*; it is not only easy, but gracious, so the word signifies; it is sweet and pleasant; there is nothing in it to make sore the yielding neck, nothing to hurt us, but, on the contrary, much to refresh us. It is a yoke that is lined with love. Such is the nature of all Christ's commands, so reasonable in themselves, so profitable to us, and all summed up in one word, and that a sweet word, love.

The burden of Christ's cross is a *light burden*, very light: afflictions from Christ, which come to us as men; afflictions for Christ, which come to us as Christians; the latter are especially meant. The burden in itself is not joyous, but grievous; yet as it is Christ's, it is light. God's presence, Christ's sympathy, and especially the Spirit's aids and comforts make suffering for Christ light and easy. Let this reconcile us to the difficulties, and help us over the discouragements we may meet with, both in doing work and suffering work; though we may lose for Christ, we shall not lose by him.

[44]

February 21

The Word of God

John 1:1

Augustine says that his friend Simplicius told him he had heard a Platonic philosopher say that these first verses of St John's gospel were 'worthy to be written in letters of gold'. Let us enquire what there is in those strong lines. The evangelist here lays down the great truth he is to prove, that Jesus Christ is God, one with the Father.

Observe of whom he speaks—the Word. The evangelist in v.18 plainly tells us why he calls Christ the Word—*because he is the only begotten Son, who is in the bosom of the Father, and has declared him.*

Word is two-fold: word conceived, and word uttered. There is the *word conceived*, that is, thought, which is the first and only immediate product and conception of the soul (all the operations of which are performed by thought), and it is one with the soul. And thus the second Person in the Trinity is fitly called the Word; for he is the *first-begotten of the Father*, that eternal essential Wisdom which the Lord possessed, as the soul does its thought.

There is the *word uttered*, and this is speech, the chief and most natural indication of the mind. And thus Christ is the Word, for by him God has in *these last days spoken to us.* He has made known God's mind to us, as a man's word or speech makes known his thoughts, as far as he pleases, and no further. He is the Word speaking from God to us, and to God for us.

February 22

In the beginning with God

John 1:1–2

Christ's existence in the beinning: *In the beginning was the Word.* This speaks of his existence, not only before his incarnation, but before all time. The beginning of time, in which all creatures were produced and brought into being, found this eternal Word in being.

The world was *from* the beginning, but the Word was *in* the beginning. Eternity is usually expressed by being *before the foundation of the world*. The Word had a being before the world had a beginning. He that was in the beginning never began, and therefore was ever—without beginning of time.

The evangelist asserts here the Word's co-existence with the Father: *The Word was with God, and the Word was God.* Let none say that when we invite them to Christ we would draw them from God, for Christ is *with God* and *is God*; it is repeated in v.2: *the same*, the very same that we believe in and preach, was *in the beginning with God*, that is, he was so from eternity. In the beginning the world was from God, as it was created by him; but the Word was with God, as ever with him. He that undertook to *bring us to God*, was himself from eternity *with God*; so that this grand concern of man's reconciliation to God was concerted between the Father and Son from eternity, and they understand one another perfectly well in it.

February 23

Life and light

John 1:3-4

The evangelist goes on to assert the work of the Word in making the world, v.3. *All things were made by him.* He was with God, not only so as to be acquainted with the divine counsels from eternity, but to be active in the divine operations in the beginning of time. By Christ, the Word, not as a subordinate instrument, but as a co-ordinate agent, God *made the world*, not as the workman cuts by his axe, but as the body sees by the eye.

The contrary is denied: *Without him was not any thing made that was made*, from the highest angel to the meanest worm. God the Father did nothing without him in that work.

This proves that the Word is God; for he that built all things is God. This shows how well qualified he was for the work of our redemption and salvation. Help was laid upon one that was mighty indeed; for it was laid upon him that made all things; and he is appointed the author of our bliss who was the author of our being.

Here is recorded that the origin of life and light is in him: *In him was life*, v.4. This further proves that he is God, and every way qualified for his undertaking; for he has *life in himself*; not only the *true God*, but the *living God*.

Creatures endowed with the faculty of reason have their light from him; that *life* which is *the light of men* comes from him. Life in man is something greater and nobler than it is in other creatures; it is *rational*, and not merely animal. From whom may we better expect the light of divine revelation than from him who gave us the light of human reason? And if, when God gave us natural life, that life was in his Son, how readily should we receive the gospel-record, that he has given us *eternal* life, and *that life* too is *in his Son*!

February 24

The light shines in the darkness

John 1:5

It might be objected, if this eternal Word was all in all in the creation of the world, how is it that he has been so little taken notice of and regarded? To this the evangelist answers, v.5, *The light shines, but the darkness comprehends it not*.

Here we see the discovery of the eternal Word to the lapsed world, even before he was manifested in the flesh: *The light shineth in darkness.* Light is self-evidencing, and will make itself known; this light, whence the light of men comes, hath shone, and doth shine.

The eternal Word, as God, shines in the darkness of natural conscience. Though men by the fall are become darkness, yet that which may be known of God is manifested in them. Something of the power of the divine Word, both as creating and as commanding, all mankind have an innate sense of; were it not for this, earth would be a hell, a place of *utter darkness*; blessed be God, it is not so yet.

We observe too the disability of the degenerate world to receive this discovery: *The darkness comprehended it not*; most men received the grace of God in these discoveries in vain. The world of mankind *comprehended not* the natural light that was in their understandings, but became *vain in their imaginations* concerning the eternal God and the eternal Word. The darkness of error and sin overpowered and quite eclipsed this light. The Jews, who had the light of the Old Testament, yet did not comprehend Christ in it. As there was a veil upon Moses' face, so there was upon the people's hearts.

February 25

God has spoken

Hebrews 1:1

Here we see the way in which God communicated himself and his will to men under the Old Testament. We have here an account of the persons by whom God delivered his mind under the Old Testament; they were *the prophets*, that is, persons chosen of God, and qualified by him, for that office of revealing the will of God to men. No man takes this honour to himself, unless called; and whoever are called of God are qualified by him.

Notice the persons to whom God spoke by the prophets: *To the fathers*, to all the Old Testament saints who were under that dispensation. God favoured and honoured them with much clearer light than that of nature, under which the rest of the world were left.

Observe the order in which God spoke to men in those times that went before the gospel, those past times: he spoke to his ancient people *at sundry times and in divers manners. At sundry times*, or 'by several parts', as the word signifies, which may refer either to the several ages of the Old Testament dispensation or to the several gradual openings of his mind concerning the Redeemer, *in divers manners*, according to the different ways in which God thought fit to communicate his mind to his prophets.

February 26

God's final word

Hebrews 1:1–2

Observe here God's method of communicating his mind and will under the New Testament dispensation, these *last days* as they are called, that is, either towards the end of the world, or the end of the Jewish state. The times of the gospel are the last times, the gospel revelation is the last we are to expect from God. There was first the natural revelation; then the patriarchal, by dreams, visions, and voices; then the Mosaic, in the law given forth and written down;

then the prophetic, in explaining the law, and giving clearer discoveries of Christ: but now we must expect no new revelation, but only more of the Spirit of Christ to help us better to understand what is already revealed.

The excellency of the gospel revelation above the former consists in two things.

It is the final, the finishing revelation, given forth in the last days of divine revelation, to which nothing is to be added, but the canon of scripture is to be settled and sealed: so that now the minds of men are no longer kept in suspense by the expectation of new discoveries, but they rejoice in a complete revelation of the will of God, so far as is necessary for them to know in order to their direction and comfort. For the gospel includes a discovery of the great events that shall come to the church of God to the end of the world.

It is a revelation which God has made by his Son, the most excellent messenger that was ever sent into the world, far superior to all the ancient patriarchs and prophets, by whom God communicated his will to his people in former times.

February 27

The glory of Jesus

Hebrews 1:2–3

Here we have an excellent account of the glory of our Lord Jesus Christ. The glory of his office, and that in three respects:

God hath appointed him to be heir of all things. As God, he was equal to the Father; but, as God-man and Mediator, he was appointed by the Father to be the heir of all things, the sovereign Lord of all, the absolute disposer, director, and governor of all persons and of all things.

By him God made the worlds, both visible and invisible, the heavens and the earth; not as an instrumental cause, but as his essential word and wisdom.

He upholds all things by the word of his power: he keeps the world from dissolving. By him all things consist. The weight of the whole creation is laid upon Christ: he supports the whole and all the parts.

The apostle passes to the glory of the person of Christ, who was able to execute such an office: *He was the brightness of his Father's glory,*

[49]

and the express image of his person, v.3. This is a high and lofty description of the glorious Redeemer, this is an account of his personal excellency. He is, in person, the Son of God, the only begotten Son of God, and as such he must have the same nature. The person of the Son is the glory of the Father, shining forth with a truly divine splendour. The person of the Son is the true image and character of the person of the Father; being of the same nature, he must bear the same image and likeness. In beholding the power, wisdom, and goodness, of the Lord Jesus Christ, we behold the power, wisdom, and goodness, of the Father.

February 28

The pathway to exaltation

Hebrews 1:3

From the glory of the person of Christ the apostle proceeds to mention the glory of his grace; his condescension itself was truly glorious. The sufferings of Christ had this great honour in them, to be a full satisfaction for the sins of his people: *By himself he purged our sins*, that is, by the proper innate merit of his death and bloodshed, by their infinite intrinsic value; as they were the sufferings of himself, he has made atonement for sin.

From the glory of Christ's sufferings we are at length led to consider the glory of his exaltation: *When by himself he had purged our sins, he sat down at the right hand of the Majesty on high*, at his Father's right hand. As Mediator and Redeemer, he is invested with the highest honour, authority, and activity, for the good of his people; the Father now does all things by him, and receives all the services of his people from him. Having assumed our nature, and suffered in it on earth, he has taken it up with him to heaven, and there it has the high honour to be next to God, and this was the reward of his humiliation.

Increasing in wisdom and favour

Luke 2:51-52

Jesus returned with his parents to Nazareth. He did not urge his parents either to come and settle at Jerusalem or to settle him there, though that was the place of improvement and preferment, and where he might have the best opportunities of showing his wisdom, but very willingly retired into his obscurity at Nazareth. Here we are told, that he improved, and came on, to admiration, v.52: *He increased in wisdom and stature.* In the perfection of his divine nature there could be no increase; but this is meant of his human nature, his body increased in stature and bulk, he grew in the growing age; and his soul increased in wisdom, and in all the endowments of a human soul. Though the eternal Word was united to the human soul from his conception, yet the divinity that dwelt in him manifested itself to his humanity by degrees, in proportion to his capacity; as the faculties of his human soul grew more and more capable, the gifts it received from the divine nature were more and more communicated.

And he increased in *favour with God and man*, that is, in all those graces that rendered him acceptable to God and man. In this, Christ accommodated himself to his estate of humiliation, that as he condescended to be an infant, a child, a youth, so the image of God shone brighter in him when he grew up to be a youth, than it did, or could, while he was an infant and a child. Young people, as they grow in stature, should grow in wisdom, and then, as they grow in wisdom, they will grow in favour *with God and man*.

March 1

The baptism of Jesus

Matthew 3:16–17

In Christ's baptism, we observe how solemnly heaven was pleased to grace the baptism of Christ with a special display of glory, v.16,17: *Jesus when he was baptized, went up straightway out of the water.* Others that were baptized *confessed their sins*, v.6; but Christ having no sins to confess, *went up* immediately *out of the water*, as one that entered upon his work with the utmost cheerfulness and resolution; he would lose no time.

Now, when he was coming up out of the water, and all the company had their eye upon him, *Lo! the heavens were opened unto him.* This was to encourage him to go on in his undertaking, with the prospect of the glory and *joy that were set before him.*

He saw the Spirit of God descending like a dove, or *as a dove, and* coming or *lighting upon him.* In the beginning of the old world, *the Spirit of God moved upon the face of the waters,* hovered as a bird upon the nest. So here, in the beginning of this new world, Christ, as God, needed not to receive the Holy Ghost, but it was foretold that *the Spirit of the Lord should rest upon him,* and here he did so; for he was to be a Prophet; and prophets always spoke by the Spirit of God, who came upon them.

March 2

This is my beloved son

Matthew 3:17

At Jesus' baptism the Holy Spirit *descended on him like a dove;* whether it was a real, living dove, or, as was usual in visions, the representation or facsimile of a dove, is uncertain.

The Spirit of Christ is a dove-like spirit, innocent dove, without bitterness. *The Spirit descended,* not in the shape of an eagle, which is, though a royal bird, yet a bird of prey, but in the shape of a dove: no creature is more harmless and inoffensive than a dove. Such was the

[52]

Spirit of Christ; such must Christians be, *harmless as doves*.

To explain and complete this solemnity, there came *a voice from heaven*, which, we have reason to think, was heard by all that were present. The Holy Spirit manifested himself in the likeness of a *dove*, but God the Father by *a voice*.

See here how God owns our Lord Jesus: *This is my beloved Son*. Jesus Christ is the Son of God, by eternal generation, as he was *begotten of the Father before all worlds*, and by supernatural conception, yet this is not all; he is the Son of God by special designation to the work and office of the world's Redeemer.

Observe the affection the Father had for him; he *is my beloved Son* and see here how ready he is to own us in him: He *is my beloved Son*, not only *with* whom, but *in* whom, I *am well pleased*. He is pleased with all that are in him, and are united to him by faith. Up to this time God had been displeased with the children of men, but now his anger is turned away, and he has made us *accepted in the beloved*.

March 3

The authority of Christ

Matthew 7:28–29

In these verses, we are told what impressions Christ's discourse made upon the audience. It was an excellent sermon; and it is probable that he said more than is here recorded.

They were *astonished at his doctrine*; it is to be feared that few of them were brought by it to follow him: but for the present, they were filled with wonder. It is possible for people to admire good preaching, and yet to remain in ignorance and unbelief; to be astonished, and yet not sanctified.

The reason was because he taught them *as one having authority, and not as the scribes*. The scribes pretended to have as much authority as any teachers whatsoever, and were supported by all the external advantages that could be obtained, but their preaching was mean, and flat, and jejune: they spoke as those that were not themselves masters of what they preached: the word did not come from them with any life or force; they delivered it as a schoolboy says his lesson; but Christ delivered his discourse, as a judge gives his charge. He did indeed deliver his discourses with a tone of authority; his lessons were laws; his word a word of command. Christ, upon the mountain, showed more true authority than the scribes in Moses' seat. Thus when Christ teaches by his Spirit in the soul, he teaches with authority. He says, *Let there be light, and there is light.*

March 4

Christ's gracious encouragement

Matthew 9:2

The first event after Christ's return to Capernaum, as recorded in these verses, was the cure of the man sick of the palsy. Here we may observe the favour of Christ, in what he said to him; *Son, be of good cheer, thy sins be forgiven thee.* We read not of anything said to Christ; probably the poor sick man could not speak for himself, and they that brought him chose rather to speak by actions than words; they set him before Christ; that was enough. It is not in vain to present ourselves and our friends to Christ as the objects of his pity. Misery cries as well as sin, and mercy is no less quick of hearing than justice.

Christ addressed him kindly: *Son.* Christ gave him a gracious encouragement: '*Be of good cheer.* Have a good heart on it; cheer up thy spirits.' Probably the poor man, when let down among them all in his bed, was disconcerted in countenance, was afraid of a rebuke for being brought in so rudely: but Christ does not stand upon ceremony; he bids him *be of good cheer*; and then cures him.

Christ gives good reason for that encouragement: *Thy sins are forgiven thee.* Now this may be considered as an introduction to the cure of his bodily ailment: 'Thy sins are *pardoned*, and therefore thou shalt be healed' or as a reason of the command to *be of good cheer*, whether he were cured of his disease or not.

The way, the truth, and the life

John 14:6

Christ is *the way*: Christ was his own way, for by *his own blood he entered into the holy place*, and he is our way, for we enter by him. By his doctrine and example he teaches us our duty, by his merit and intercession he procures us our happiness, and so he is the way. In him God and man meet, and are brought together.

He is *the truth*. As truth is opposed to figure and shadow, Christ is the substance of all the Old Testament types, which are therefore said to be *figures of the true*. As truth is opposed to falsehood and error, the doctrine of Christ is true doctrine. When we enquire for truth, we need to learn no more than the truth as it is in Jesus. As truth is opposed to fallacy and deceit; he is true to all that trust in him, as true as truth itself.

He is *the life*; for we are *alive unto God* only in and *through Jesus Christ*. Christ in us is to our souls what our souls are to our bodies. Christ is *the resurrection and the life*.

Christ is *the way, the truth, and the life*; He is the beginning, the middle, and the end. In him we must set out, go on, and finish. As the truth, he is the guide of our way; as the life, he is the end of it. He is *the true and living way*; there are truth and life in the way, as well as at the end of it. He is the true way to life, the only true way; other ways may seem right, but the end of them is *the way of death*.

No man cometh to the Father, but by me. Fallen man must come to God as a Judge, but cannot come to him as a Father, otherwise than by Christ as Mediator. We cannot perform the duty of coming to God, by repentance and the acts of worship, without the Spirit and grace of Christ, nor obtain the happiness of coming to God as our Father without his merit and righteousness; he is the *high priest of our profession*, our advocate.

March 6

Poor in spirit

In verses 8-12, our Saviour gives us eight characters of blessed people; which represent to us the principal graces of a Christian. On each of them a present blessing is pronounced: *Blessed are* they; and to each a future blessedness is promised.

The poor in spirit are happy, v.3. There is a poor-spiritedness that is so far from making men blessed that it is a sin and a snare—cowardice and base fear, and a willing subjection to the lusts of men. But this poverty of spirit is a gracious disposition of soul, by which we are emptied of self, in order to our being filled with Jesus Christ.

To be poor in spirit is:

(1) to be contentedly poor, willing to be empty of worldly wealth, if God orders that to be our lot; to bring our mind to our condition, when it is a low condition.

(2) to be humble and lowly in our eyes. To be poor in spirit is to think meanly of ourselves, of what we are, and have, and do; the poor are often taken in the Old Testament for the humble and self-denying, as opposed to those that are at ease, and the proud.

(3) to come down from all confidence in our own righteousness and strength, that we may depend only upon the merit of Christ for our justification, and the spirit and grace of Christ for our sanctification. That *broken and contrite spirit* with which the publican cried for mercy to a poor sinner is this poverty of spirit.

Theirs is the kingdom of heaven. The kingdom of grace is composed of such; they only are fit to be members of Christ's church; the kingdom of glory is prepared for them. Those who thus humble themselves, and comply with God when he humbles them, shall be thus exalted.

March 7

Blessed are the meek

Matthew 5:5

The meek are happy, v.5: *Blessed are the meek*. The meek are those who quietly submit themselves to God, to his word and to his rod, who follow his directions, and comply with his designs, and are *gentle towards all men*; who can bear provocation without being inflamed by it; are either silent, or return a soft answer; and who can show their displeasure when there is occasion for it, without being transported into any indecencies; who can be cool when others are hot; and in their patience keep possession of their own souls, when they can scarcely keep possession of anything else. They are the meek, who are rarely and hardly provoked, but quickly and easily pacified; and who would rather forgive twenty injuries than revenge one, having the rule of their own spirits.

These meek ones are here represented as happy, even in this world. They are *blessed*, for they are like the blessed Jesus; they are like the blessed God himself, who is Lord of his anger, and in whom fury is not. They are blessed, for they have the most comfortable, undisturbed enjoyment of themselves, their friends, their God; they are fit for any relation, any condition, any company; fit to live, and fit to die.

They shall inherit the earth; it is almost the only express temporal promise in all the New Testament. Not that they shall always have much of the earth; but this branch of godliness has, in a special manner, the promise of the life that now is. Meekness, however ridiculed and run down, has a real tendency to promote our health, wealth, comfort, and safety, even in this world. The meek and quiet are observed to live the most easy lives, compared with the perverse and turbulent.

March 8

Hungering and thirsting for righteousness

Matthew 5:6

They that hunger and thirst after righteousness are happy, v.6. Some understand this as an instance of outward poverty, and a low condition in this world, which not only exposes men to injury and wrong, but makes it in vain for them to seek to have justice done them. Yet, *blessed are they*, if they suffer these hardships for and with a good conscience; let them hope in God, who will see justice done, right take place, and will deliver the poor from their oppressors.

But this verse is certainly to be understood spiritually: righteousness is here put for all spiritual blessings. These we must hunger and thirst after. We must truly and really desire them, as one who is hungry and thirsty desires food and drink, who cannot be satisfied with anything but food and drink, and will be satisfied with them, though other things be wanting.

Hunger and thirst are appetites that return frequently and call for fresh satisfaction; so these holy desires rest not in anything attained, but are carried out towards renewed pardons, and daily fresh supplies of grace.

Those who thus *hunger and thirst* after spiritual blessings are blessed in those desires and *shall be filled* with those blessings. They shall be filled with those blessings. God will give them what they desire to their complete satisfaction. It is God only who can fill a soul, whose grace and favour are adequate to its just desires; and he will fill those with grace for grace, who, in a sense of their own emptiness, have recourse to his fulness.

Blessed are the merciful

Matthew 5:7

The *merciful* are happy, v.7. This, like the rest, is a paradox; for the merciful are not taken to be the wisest, nor are likely to be the richest; yet Christ pronounces them blessed. Those are the merciful, who are piously and charitably inclined to pity, help, and aid people in misery. A man may be truly merciful, who has not the resources to be bountiful or liberal; and then God accepts the willing mind.

We must not only bear our own afflictions patiently, but we must, by Christian sympathy, partake of the afflictions of our brethren; pity and tender mercies must be shown; and, being put on, they must put forth themselves in contributing all we can for the assistance of those who are any way in misery. We must have compassion on the souls of others, and help them; pity the ignorant, and instruct them; the careless, and warn them; those who are in a state of sin, and snatch them from the fire. We must have compassion on those who are melancholy and in sorrow, and comfort them; on those whom we have an advantage against, and not be rigorous and severe with them; on those who are in want, and supply them; which if we refuse to do, whatever we pretend, we shut up our hearts from them.

They shall obtain mercy; mercy with men, when they need it; we know not how soon we may stand in need of kindness, and therefore should be kind; but especially mercy with God, for *with the merciful he will show himself merciful.*

The pure in heart

Matthew 5:8

The *pure in heart* are happy, v.8: *Blessed are the pure in heart, for they shall see God.* This is the most comprehensive of all the beatitudes; here holiness and happiness are fully described and put together.

Here is the most comprehensive character of the blessed; they are the *pure in heart*. True religion consists in heart-purity. Those who are inwardly pure show themselves to be under the power of *pure and undefiled* religion. True Christianity lies in the heart, in the purity of the heart; the washing of that from wickedness. The heart must be kept pure from fleshly lusts, all unchaste thoughts and desires; and from worldly lusts; from all filthiness of flesh and spirit, all that which comes out of the heart, and defiles the man. *Create in me such a clean heart, O God!*

Here is the most comprehensive comfort of the blessed; *They shall see God.* It is the perfection of the soul's happiness to *see* God; seeing him, as we may by faith in our present state, is a heaven upon earth; and seeing him as we shall in the future state, is the heaven of heaven.

The happiness of seeing God is promised to those, and those only, who are *pure in heart.* None but the pure are capable of seeing God, nor would it be something happy to the impure. What pleasure could an unsanctified soul take in the vision of a holy God? As *he* cannot endure to look upon their iniquity, so *they* cannot endure to look upon his purity.

March 11

Our Father in heaven

Matthew 6:9

The preface of our Lord's prayer: *Our Father who art in heaven.* Before we come to our business, there must be a solemn address to him with whom our business lies: *Our Father.* This intimates that we must pray, not only alone and for ourselves, but with and for others; for we are members one of another, and are called into fellowship with each other. We are here taught to whom to pray, to God only, and not to saints and angels, for they are ignorant of us, are not to have the honours we give in prayer, nor can give the favours we expect.

We must address ourselves to him as *our Father*, and must call him so. He is a common Father to all mankind by creation. He is in a special manner a Father to the saints, by adoption and regeneration; and an unspeakable privilege it is. If he is our Father, he will pity us in our weaknesses and infirmities, will spare us, and will deny us nothing that is good for us.

He is our Father in heaven: so in heaven as to everywhere else, for the heavens cannot contain him; yet so in heaven as there to manifest his glory, for it is his throne, and it is to believers a throne of grace: to such a throne we must direct our prayers. Heaven is a place of perfect purity, and we must therefore lift up pure hands, must study to sanctify his name, who is the Holy One, and dwells in that holy place.

March 12

His name and kingdom

Matthew 6:9-10

Hallowed be thy name. It is the same word that in other places is translated *sanctified.* In these words:

(1) we give glory to God; it may be taken not as a petition, but as an adoration; as that, the Lord be magnified, or glorified, for God's holiness is the greatness and glory of all his perfection.

We must begin our prayers with praising God, and it is very fit he should be first served, and that we should give glory to God, before we expect to receive mercy and grace from him. Let him have the praise of his perfection, and then let us have the benefit of them.

(2) we fix our end, and it is the right end to be aimed at, and ought to be our chief and ultimate end in all our petitions, that God may be glorified; all our other requests must be in subordination to this, and in pursuance of it.

Thy kingdom come. This petition has plainly a reference to the doctrine which Christ preached at this time, which John Baptist had preached before, and which he afterwards sent his apostles out to preach—*the kingdom of heaven is at hand.* The kingdom of your Father who is in heaven, the kingdom of the Messiah, this is at hand, pray that it may come. '*Let thy kingdom come,* let the gospel be preached to all and embraced by all; let all be brought to subscribe to the record God has given in his word concerning his Son, and to embrace him as their Saviour and Sovereign. Let the bounds of the gospel-church be enlarged, the kingdom of the world be made Christ's kingdom, and all men become subjects to it, and live as becomes their character.'

Thy will be done

Matthew 6:10

Thy will be done in earth, as it is in heaven. We pray that God's kingdom being come, we and others may be brought into obedience to all the laws and ordinances of it. By this let it appear that Christ's kingdom is come, *let God's will be done*; and by this let it appear that it is come as a *kingdom of heaven*, let it introduce a heaven upon earth.

Observe the thing prayed for, *thy will be done*; 'Enable me to do what is pleasing to thee; give me that grace that is necessary to the right knowledge of thy will, and an acceptable obedience to it. Let thy will be done conscientiously by me and others, not our own will, the will of the flesh or the mind, not the will of men, much less Satan's will, that we may neither displease God in anything we do, nor be displeased at any thing God does.'

Notice the pattern of what is prayed for, that it may be *done on earth*, in this place of our trial and probation, *as it is done in heaven*, the place of rest and joy. We pray that earth may be made more like heaven by the observance of God's will, and that saints may be made more like the holy angels in their devotion and obedience.

Our daily bread

Matthew 6:11

Give us this day our daily bread. Because our natural being is necessary to our spiritual well-being in this world, therefore, after the things of God's glory, kingdom and will, we pray for the necessary supports and comforts of this present life, which are the gifts of God, and must be asked of him.

Every word here has a lesson in it: We ask for *bread*; that teaches us sobriety and temperance; we ask for bread, not dainties, not superfluities; but that which is wholesome. We ask for *our* bread; that teaches us honesty and industry: we do not ask for the bread out of other people's mouths. We ask for our *daily* bread; which teaches us not to take thought for the morrow (v.34), but constantly to depend upon divine Providence. We beg of God to *give* it us, not sell it us, nor lend it us, but give it. The greatest of men must be under obligation to the mercy of God for their daily bread. We pray, 'Give is to *us*; not to me only, but to others in common with me.' This teaches us charity, and a compassionate concern for the poor and needy. It intimates also that we ought to pray with our families; we and our households eat together, and therefore ought to pray together. We pray that God would give it us *this day*; which teaches us to renew the desire of our souls towards God, as the wants of our bodies are renewed; as duly as the day comes, we must pray to our heavenly Father, and reckon we could as well go a day without food, as without prayer.

March 15

Confessing and forgiving
Matthew 6:12–13

Father in heaven, *forgive us our debts*, our debts to thee. Our sins are our debts; there is a debt of duty, which, as creatures, we owe to our Creator. Our hearts' desire and prayer to our heavenly Father every day should be that he would *forgive us our debts*; that the obligation to punishment may be cancelled and vacated, that we may not come into condemnation; that we may be discharged, and have the comfort of it. In petitioning for the pardon of our sins, the great plea we have to rely upon is the satisfaction that was made to the justice of God for the sin of man, by the dying of the Lord Jesus.

As we forgive our debtors: this is not a plea of merit, but a plea of grace. Those that come to God for the forgiveness of their sins against him must make conscience of forgiving those who have offended them, else they curse themselves when they say the Lord's prayer.

And lead us not into temptation, but deliver us from evil. This petition is expressed negatively: *Lead us not into temptation*. Having prayed that the guilt of sin may be removed, we pray, as is fit, that we may never return again to folly, that we may not be tempted to it. 'Lord, do not lay stumbling-blocks and snares before us, nor put us into circumstances that may be an occasion of falling.'

Their petition is also expressed positively: *But deliver us from evil; from the evil one*, the devil, the tempter; 'Keep us, that either we may not be assaulted by him, or we may not be overcome by those assaults;' or *from the evil thing*, sin, the worst of evils; an evil, an only evil; that evil thing which God hates, and which Satan tempts men to and destroys them by.

March 16

Turning prayer to praise

Matthew 6:13

We come to the conclusion of our Lord's prayer: it is a plea to enforce the foregoing petitions. It is our duty to plead with God in prayer, to fill our mouth with arguments, not to move God, but to affect ourselves; to encourage our faith, to excite our fervency, and to evidence both. '*Thine is the kingdom*; thou hast the government of the world, and the protection of the saints, thy willing subjects in it.' '*Thine is the power*, to maintain and support that kingdom, and to make good all thine engagements to thy people.' '*Thine is the glory*, as the end of all that is given to, and done for, the saints, in answer to their prayers.'

The best pleading with God is praising of him; it is the way to obtain further mercy, as it qualifies us to receive it. In all our addresses to God it is right that praise should have a considerable share, for praise is befitting to the saints; they are to be to our God *for a name and for a praise*. It is just and equal; we praise God, and give him glory, not because he needs it—he is praised by a world of angels, but because he deserves it; and it is our duty to give him glory, in compliance with his design in revealing himself to us. *The kingdom, and the power, and the glory*, it is all thine. A true saint never thinks he can speak honourably enough of God: here there should be a gracious fluency, and this *for ever. Amen*. So be it.

Saying 'no' to ourselves

Luke 9:23–24

We must accustom ourselves to all instances of self-denial and patience. We must live a life of self-denial, mortification, and contempt of the world; we must not indulge our ease and appetite, for then it will be hard to bear toil, and weariness, and want, for Christ. We are daily subject to affliction, and we must accommodate ourselves to it, and acquiesce in the will of God in it, and must learn to endure hardship. We frequently meet with crosses in the way of duty; and, though we must not pull them upon our own heads, yet, when they are laid for us, we must *take them up*, carry them after Christ, and make the best of them.

We must prefer the salvation and happiness of our souls before any secular concern whatsoever. That he who to preserve his liberty, his power of preferment, or to save his life, denies Christ and his truths, wilfully wrongs his conscience, and sins against God, will be, not only not a saver, but an unspeakable loser, in the issue, when profit and loss come to be balanced. *He that will save his life* upon these terms *will lose it*, will lose that which is of infinitely more value, his precious soul.

We must firmly believe also that, if we lose our life for cleaving to Christ and our religion, we shall *save* it to our unspeakable advantage; for we shall be abundantly recompensed in the resurrection of the just, when we shall have it again a new and an eternal life.

The cost of discipleship

Luke 14:25–26

Here Christ tells the multitudes what the worst is that they must count upon, much the same with what he had gone through before them and for them. He takes it for granted that they had a mind to be his disciples, that they might be qualified for his kingdom. They expected that he should say, 'If any man come to me, and be my disciple, he shall have wealth and honour in abundance; let me alone to make him a great man.' But he tells them quite the contrary.

They must be willing to leave that which was very dear, and therefore must come to him thoroughly weaned from all their creature-comforts, and dead to them, so as cheerfully to part with them rather than leave their interest in Christ, v.26. A man cannot be Christ's disciple but he must *hate father, and mother, and his own life*. He is not sincere, he will not be constant and persevering, unless he loves Christ better than anything in this world, and be willing to part with that which he may and must leave, either as a sacrifice, when Christ may be glorified by our parting with it or as a temptation, when by our parting with it we are put into a better capacity of serving Christ.

Every good man loves his relations; and yet, if he be a disciple of Christ, he must comparatively *hate* them, must love them less than Christ. Not that their persons must be in any degree hated, but our comfort and satisfaction in them must be lost and swallowed up in our love to Christ. When our duty to our parents comes in competition with our evident duty to Christ, we must give Christ the preference.

March 19

Counting the cost

Luke 14:28–32

Christ bids the people count the cost of bearing the cross. Our Saviour here illustrates the necessity of this by two comparisons, the former showing that we must consider the expenses of our religion, the latter that we must consider the perils of it.

When we take upon ourselves a profession of religion we are like a man that undertakes to built a tower, and therefore must consider the expense of it (v.28–30). Let him compare the charge with what he has, lest he make himself to be laughed at, by *beginning to build* what he is *not able to finish*. Those that intend to build this tower must *sit down and count the cost*. Let them consider that it will cost them the mortifying of their sins, even the most beloved lusts; it will cost them a life of self-denial and watchfulness, and a constant course of holy duties; it may perhaps, cost them their reputation among men and all that is dear to them in this world, even life itself.

When we undertake to be Christ's disciples we are like a man that *goes to war*, and therefore must consider the hazard of it, and the difficulties that are to be encountered, v.31,32. A king that declares war against a neighbouring prince considers whether he has strength with which to make his part good, and, if not, he will lay aside his thoughts of war. Is not the Christian life a warfare? We have many passes in our way that must be disputed with the sword; we must fight every step we go, so restless are our spiritual enemies in their opposition.

March 20

The Lamb of God

John 1:29

Here is John's testimony to Christ on the first day that he saw him coming from the wilderness; and here he witnessed that he is *the Lamb of God, which taketh away the sin of the world*, v.29. Let us learn here that Jesus Christ is the Lamb of God, which speaks of him as the great sacrifice, by which atonement is made for sin, and man reconciled to God. Of all the legal sacrifices he chooses to allude to the lambs that were offered, not only because a lamb is an emblem of meekness, and Christ must be led as a lamb to the slaughter, but with a special reference to the daily sacrifice and to the paschal lamb, the blood of which, being sprinkled upon the door-posts, secured the Israelites from the stroke of the destroying angel. He is the Lamb of God; he is appointed by him, he was devoted to him, and he was accepted with him; in him he was well pleased. Christ, who was to make atonement for sin, is called the *Lamb of God*.

March 21

He takes away the sin of the world

John 1:29

Jesus Christ, *the Lamb of God takes away sin.* He, being Mediator between God and man, takes away that which is, above anything, offensive to the holiness of God, and destructive to the happiness of man. He came, first, to take away the guilt of sin by the merit of his death, to vacate the judgment, and reverse the consequences of the punishment which mankind lay under, by an act of indemnity, of which all penitent obedient believers may claim the benefit. He came, secondly, to take away the power of sin by the Spirit of his grace, so that it shall not have dominion over us.

He takes away the *sin of the world*; purchases pardon for all those that repent, and believe the gospel, of whatever country, nation, or language. This is encouraging to our faith; if Christ takes away the sin of the world, then why not my sin?

It is our duty, with an eye of faith, to *behold* the Lamb of God thus taking away the *sin of the world.* See him taking away sin, and let that increase our hatred of sin, and resolutions against it. Let not us hold that fast which the Lamb of God came to take away: for Christ will either take our sins away or take us away. Let it increase our love to Christ, *who loved us, and washed us from our sins in his own blood.*

March 22

God so loved the world

John 3:16

Jesus Christ came to save us by pardoning us, that we might not die by the sentence of the law, v.16,17. Here is gospel indeed, good news, the best that ever came from heaven to earth.

Here is God's love, in giving his Son for the world, v.16. The great gospel mystery is revealed: *God so loved the world that he gave his only begotten Son.* Jesus Christ is the only begotten Son of God. This magnifies his love in giving him for us, in giving him to us; now we know that he loves us, when he has given his only begotten Son for us, which expresses not only his dignity in himself, but his dearness to his Father.

In order to gain the redemption and salvation of man, it pleased God to *give his only begotten Son*. He *gave him*, that is, he gave him up to suffer and die for us, as the great propitiation or expiatory sacrifice.

In this God has commended his love to the world: God so *loved the world*, so really, so richly. Behold and wonder that the great God should love such a worthless world! That the holy God should love such a wicked world with a love of goodwill, when he could not look upon it with any complacency. This was a time of love indeed.

March 23

God's rescue operation

John 3:16–17

Here is the great gospel duty, and that is to *believe in Jesus Christ*, to accept the gift, and answer the intention of the giver. We must yield an unfeigned assent and consent to the record God has given in his word concerning his Son. God having given him to us to be our Prophet, Priest, and King, we must give up ourselves to be ruled, and taught, and saved by him.

Here is the great gospel benefit: *That whosoever believes in Christ shall not perish*. It is the unspeakable happiness of all true believers, for which they are eternally indebted to Christ, that they are saved from the miseries of hell, delivered from going down to the pit; they *shall not perish*. God has taken away their sin, they shall not die—a pardon is purchased. They are entitled to the joys of heaven: they shall *have everlasting life*. The convicted traitor is not only pardoned, but preferred, and made a favourite, and treated as one whom the King of kings delights to honour.

Here is God's design in sending his Son into the world: it was *that the world through him might be saved*. He did not come to *condemn the world*. He had reason enough to expect that he should, for it is a guilty world. He came *that the world through him might be saved*, that a door of salvation might be opened to the world, and whoever would might enter in by it. God was in Christ *reconciling the world to himself*.

This is good news to a convinced conscience, healing to broken bones and bleeding wounds, that Christ, our Judge, came not to condemn, but to save.

March 24

The suffering of Christ

1 Peter 3:18

Jesus Christ himself was not exempted from sufferings in this life, though he had no guilt of his own and could have declined all suffering if he had pleased. The reason or meritorious cause of Christ's suffering was the sins of men: *Christ suffered for sins*. The sufferings of Christ were a true and proper punishment; this punishment was suffered to expiate and to make an atonement for sin; and it extends to all sin.

In the case of our Lord's suffering, it was the just that suffered for the unjust; he substituted himself in our stead and bore our iniquities. He that knew no sin suffered instead of those that knew no righteousness. The merit and perfection of Christ's sacrifice were such that for him to suffer *once* was enough. The legal sacrifices were repeated from day to day, and from year to year; but the sacrifice of Christ, once offered, purgeth away sin.

The end or design of our Lord's sufferings was to *bring us to God*, to reconcile us to God, to give us access to the Father, to render us and our services acceptable, and to bring us to eternal glory.

The issue and event of Christ's suffering, as to himself, were these, he was put to death in his human nature, but he was quickened and raised again by the Spirit.

Now, if Christ was not exempted from sufferings, why should Christians expect it? If he suffered to expiate sins, why should not we be content when our sufferings are only for trial and correction, but not for expiation? If he, though perfectly just, why should not we, who are all criminals? If he once suffered, and then entered into glory, shall not we be patient in trouble, since it will be but a little time and we shall follow him to glory?

[70]

This is my body

We have here the institution of the great gospel ordinance of the Lord's supper, which was received of the Lord. In this ordinance, the body of Christ is signified and represented by bread.

Christ *took bread*. His taking the bread was a solemn action, and was probably done in such a manner as to be observed by them that sat with him, that they might expect something more than ordinary to be done with it. *He blessed it*; set it apart for this use by prayer and thanksgiving.

His breaking of the bread denotes the breaking of Christ's body *for* us, that it might be fitted *for* our use—*He was bruised for our iniquities* and the breaking of Christ's body *to* us, as the father of the family breaks the bread to the children.

He gave it to his disciples, as the Master of the family, and the Master of this feast; it is not said, he gave it to the apostles, though they were so, and had been often called so before this, but to the disciples, because all the disciples of Christ have a right to this ordinance.

He said, *Take, eat; this is my body*, v.26. He here tells them to accept Christ as he is offered, to receive the atonement, approve of it, consent to it, submit to his grace and to his government.

This is my body, this eating and drinking. Believing carries all the efficacy of Christ's death to our souls. *This is my body*, spiritually and sacramentally, 'this signifies and represents my body.' The bread is not changed into the substance of Christ's body. We partake of the sun, not by having the bulk and body of the sun put into our hands, but the beams of it darted down upon us; so we partake of Christ by partaking of his grace, and the blessed fruits of the breaking of his body.

This is my blood

Matthew 26:27–28

In the Lord's supper, the blood of Christ is signified and represented by the wine. *He took the cup* and *gave thanks*, to teach us, not only in every ordinance, but in every part of the ordinance, to have our eyes up to God.

This cup he gave to the disciples with a command: *Drink ye all of it*—thus he welcomes his guests to his table, obliges them all to drink of his cup—and with an explanation: *For this is my blood of the new testament.* Therefore drink it with appetite, delight, because it is so rich a cordial. Up to that time the blood of Christ had been represented by the blood of beasts, real blood: but, after it was actually shed, it was represented by the blood of grapes, metaphorical blood.

Now observe what Christ said of his blood represented in the sacrament: *It is my blood of the new testament.* The old testament was confirmed by the blood of bulls and goats, but the new testament with the blood of Christ, which is here distinguished from that. The covenant God is pleased to make with us, and all the benefits and privileges of it, are owing to the merits of Christ's death.

It is shed for many. The blood of the old testament was shed for a few. The atonement was made only *for the children of Israel*: but Jesus Christ is a propitiation *for the sins of the whole world.*

It is shed for the remission of sins, that is, to purchase remission of sins for us. The redemption which we have through his blood, is *the forgiveness of sins.* The new covenant which is procured and ratified by the blood of Christ is a charter of pardon, an act of indemnity, for a reconciliation between God and man.

March 27

Overwhelmed with sorrow

Matthew 26:38

Here we have the story of Christ's agony in the garden of Gethsemane. This was the beginning of sorrows to our Lord Jesus. *He began to be sorrowful and very heavy*, v.37. In Luke's account it is called an agony, a conflict. It was not any bodily pain or torment that he was in, nothing occurred to hurt him; but, whatever it was, it was from within; he troubled himself.

But what was the cause of all this? What was it that put him into this agony? Certainly, it was nothing of despair or distrust of his Father, much less any conflict or struggle with him. As the Father loved him because he laid down his life for the sheep, so he was entirely subject to his Father's will in it.

He engaged in an encounter with the powers of darkness: *This is your hour, and the power of darkness; the prince of this world cometh*. Now is the close engagement in single combat between Michael and the dragon, hand to hand; *now is the judgment of this world*; the great cause is now to be determined, and the decisive battle fought, in which the *prince of this world* will certainly be beaten and *cast out*.

Christ was now *bearing the iniquities* which the Father laid upon him, and, by his sorrow and amazement, he accommodated himself to his undertaking. The sufferings he was entering upon were for our sins; they were all made to meet upon him, and he knew it.

He had a full and clear prospect of all the sufferings that were before him. He foresaw the treachery of Judas, the unkindness of Peter, the malice of the Jews, and their base ingratitude. He knew that he should now in a few hours be scourged, spat upon, crowned with thorns, nailed to the cross: death in its most dreadful appearances, death in pomp, attended with all its terrors, looked him in the face; and this made him sorrowful, especially because it was the wages of our sin, which he had undertaken to satisfy for.

Man of sorrows

Matthew 26:38

Finding himself seized by his suffering, Christ goes to his disciples, v.38, and, acquaints them with his condition: *My soul is exceedingly sorrowful, even unto death.* It gives some little ease to a troubled spirit, to have a friend ready to unbosom itself to, and give vent to its sorrows. Christ here tells them that it was his soul that was now in an agony. This proves that Christ had a true human soul; for he suffered, not only in his body, but in his soul.

Christ also tells them the degree of his sorrow. He was *exceedingly sorrowful*. It was sorrow in the highest degree, even unto death; it was a killing sorrow, such sorrow as no mortal man could bear and live. He was ready to die for grief; they were sorrows of death. His sorrow would continue even unto death. 'My soul will be sorrowful as long as it is in this body; I see no outlet but death.' He now *began* to be sorrowful, and never ceased to be so till he said, *It is finished*; that grief is now finished, which began in the garden. It was prophesied of Christ, that he should be *a Man of sorrows*.

Christ engages their company and attendance: *Tarry ye here, and watch with me.* Surely he was destitute indeed of help, when he entreated theirs, who, he knew, would be but miserable comforters; but he would hereby teach us the benefit of the communion of saints. It is good to have, and therefore good to seek, the assistance of our brethren, when at any time we are in an agony; *for two are better than one.* What he said to them, he saith to all, *Watch.* Not only watch for him, in expectation of his future coming, but watch with him, in application to our present work.

Thy will be done

Matthew 26:39

Here we observe what passed between Christ and his Father when he was in this agony: *Being in agony, he prayed.* Prayer is never out of season, but it is especially seasonable in an agony.

He fell on his face; his lying prostrate denotes the agony he was in, the extremity of his sorrow, and his humility in prayer.

We may observe three things in his prayer:

(1) The title he gives to God: *O my Father.* Thick as the cloud was, he could see God as a Father through it. Note, in all our addresses to God we should eye him as a Father, as our Father; and it is in a special manner comfortable to do so, when we are in an agony.

(2) The favour he begs: *If it be possible, let this cup pass from me.* He calls his sufferings a cup; not a river, not a sea, but a cup, which we shall soon see the bottom of. When we are under troubles, we should make the best, the least, of them, and not aggravate them. He begs that this cup might *pass from him*, that is, that he might avoid the sufferings now at hand; or, at least, that they might be shortened. This intimates no more than that he was really and truly Man, and as a Man he could not but be averse to pain and suffering.

But observe the proviso: *If it be possible.* If God may be glorified, man saved, and the ends of his undertaking answered, without his drinking of this bitter cup, he desires to be excused; otherwise not.

(3) His entire submission to, and acquiescence in, the will of God. Nevertheless, not as I will, but as thou wilt. The reasons of Christ's submission to his sufferings, was, his Father's will: *as thou wilt*, v.39. In conformity to this example of Christ, we must drink of the bitter cup which God puts into our hands, be it ever so bitter; though nature struggle, grace must submit.

Let him be crucified!

Matthew 27:22–23

Here we see the people pressing earnestly to have Jesus crucified. Pilate, being amazed at their choice of Barabbas, was willing to hope that it was rather from a fondness for him than from an enmity to Jesus; and therefore he puts it to them, *'What shall I do then with Jesus?* Shall I release him likewise, for the greater honour of your feast, or will you leave it to me?' 'No,' *they all said, 'Let him be crucified.'* That death they desired he might die, because it was looked upon as the most scandalous and ignominious; and they hoped thereby to make his followers ashamed to own him.

Now as to this demand we are further told how Pilate objected against it: *Why, what evil hath he done?* A proper question to ask before we censure any in common discourse, much more for a judge to ask before he pass a sentence of death. It is much for the honour of the Lord Jesus, that, though he suffered as an evil-doer, yet neither his judge nor his prosecutors could find that he had done any evil. Had he done any evil against God? No, he *always did those things that pleased him.* Had he done any evil against the civil government? No, as he did himself, so he taught others, to *render to Caesar the things that were Caesar's.* This repeated assertion of his unspotted innocence plainly intimates that he died to satisfy for the sins of others.

See how the people insisted upon it: *They cried out the more, Let him be crucified.* They do not go about to show any evil he had done, but, right or wrong, he must be crucified. Quitting all pretensions to the proof of the premises, they resolve to hold the conclusion, and what was wanting in evidence to make up in clamour.

March 31

Why hast thou forsaken me?

Matthew 27:46

We have here the crucifixion of our Lord Jesus. *My God, my God, why hast thou forsaken me?* A strange complaint to come from the mouth of our Lord Jesus, who, we are sure, was *God's elect, in whom his soul delighted,* and one in whom he was always well pleased.

Our Lord Jesus was, in his sufferings, for a time, forsaken by his Father. Not that the union between the divine and human nature was in the least weakened or shocked; no, he was *now by the eternal Spirit offering himself*: nor as if there were any abatement of his Father's love to him, or his to his Father, but his Father forsook him; that is, first, he delivered him up into the hands of his enemies, and did not appear to deliver him out of their hands. He let loose the powers of darkness against him, and suffered them to do their worst. Secondly, he withdrew from him the present comfortable sense of his pleasure in him. When *his soul* was first *troubled,* he had a voice from heaven to comfort him; when he was in his agony in the garden, there appeared an angel from heaven strengthening him; but now he had neither the one nor the other. God hid his face from him. Thirdly, he let out upon his soul an afflicting sense of his wrath against man for sin. Christ was made *sin* for us, a *curse* for us; and therefore, though God loved him as a Son, he frowned upon him as a surety.

Our Lord Jesus, even when he was thus forsaken of his Father, kept hold of him as his God, nevertheless: *My God, my God*; though forsaking me, yet *mine*.

April 1

Christ's atoning death

Colossians 1:14,20

The work of redemption lies in two things:

(1) in the remission of sin: *In whom we have redemption, even the forgiveness of sins,* v.14. It was sin which sold us, sin which enslaved

us: if we are redeemed, we must be redeemed from sin; and this is by forgiveness, or remitting the obligation to punishment.

(2) in reconciliation to God: *God by him reconciled all things to himself*, v.20. He is the Mediator of reconciliation, who procures peace as well as pardon for sinners, who brings them into a state of friendship and favour at present, and will bring all holy creatures, angels as well as men, into one glorious and blessed society at last: *things in earth, or things in heaven.*

Observe how the redemption is procured: it is *through his blood*, v.14; he has *made peace through the blood of his cross*, v.20, and it is *in the body of his flesh through death*, v.22. It was the *blood which made an atonement, for the blood is the life; and without the shedding of blood there is no remission.* There was such a value in the blood of Christ that, on account of Christ's shedding it, God was willing to deal with men upon new terms to bring them under a covenant of grace, and for his sake, and in consideration of his death upon the cross, to pardon and accept to favour all who comply with them.

April 2

Seeking Jesus

Matthew 28:5

At dawn on the first day of the week, the angel encourages the women against their fears, v.5. To come near to graves and tombs, especially in silence and solitude, has something in it frightful, much more was it so to those women, to find an angel at the sepulchre; but he soon makes them easy with the words, '*Fear not ye*. Let not the news I have to tell you be any surprise to you, for you were told before that your Master would rise; let it be no terror to you, for his resurrection will be your consolation; fear not any hurt, that I will do you, nor any evil tidings I have to tell you. *Fear not ye, for I know that ye seek Jesus.* I know you are friends to the cause. I do not come to frighten you, but to encourage you.'

Those that seek Jesus have no reason to be afraid; for, if they seek him diligently they shall find him, and shall find him their bountiful rewarder. All our believing enquiries after the Lord Jesus are observed, and taken notice of in heaven: *I know that ye seek Jesus*; and shall certainly be answered, as these were, with good words, and comfortable words.

Ye seek Jesus that was crucified. He mentioned his being crucified, the more to commend their love to him; 'You seek him still, though *he was crucified*; you retain your kindness for him nevertheless.' True believers love and seek Christ, not only *though* he was crucified, but *because* he was so.

April 3

He is risen!

Matthew 28:6

The angel assures the women of the resurrection of Christ; and there was enough in that to silence their fears, v.6: *He is not here, for he is risen.* To be told *He is not here* would have been no welcome news to those who sought him, if it had not been added, *He is risen.* We must not hearken to those who say, *Lo, here is Christ, or, Lo, he is there,* for he is not *here,* he is not *there,* he is *risen.* In all our enquiries after Christ, we must remember that he is risen; and we must seek him as one risen.

We must seek him not with any gross carnal thoughts of him. There were those that *knew Christ after the flesh;* but now from this time forward we know him so no more. It is true, he had a body; but it is now a *glorified body.* They that make pictures and images of Christ forget that *he is not here, he is risen;* our communion with him must be spiritual, by faith in his word.

We must seek him with great reverence and humility, and an awful regard to his glory, for *he is risen.* God has *highly exalted him,* and *given him a name above every name,* and therefore every knee and every soul must *bow before him.*

We must seek him with a *heavenly mind;* when we are ready to make this world our home, and to say, *It is good to be here,* let us remember our Lord Jesus *is not here, he is risen,* and therefore let not our hearts be here, but let them rise too, and *seek the things that are above.*

Go quickly!

Matthew 28:7

The angel directs the women to go carry the tidings to the disciples, v.7: *Go quickly, and tell his disciples.* It was good to be there, but they have other work appointed them; this is the day of good tidings, and though they have the first taste of the comfort, yet they must not have the monopoly of it, must not hold their peace. They must go and *tell the disciples.* Public usefulness to others must be preferred before the pleasure of secret communion with God ourselves; for *it is more blessed to give than to receive.*

The disciples of Christ must first be *told the news*; not, 'Go, tell the chief priests and the Pharisees, that they may be confounded;' but, 'Tell the disciples, that they may be *comforted.*' God anticipates the joy of his friends more than the shame of his enemies, though the perfection of both is reserved for hereafter.

Tell his disciples; it may be they will believe your report, however, tell them that they may encourage themselves under their present sorrows and that they may enquire further into it themselves.

The women are sent to tell it to them, and so are made, as it were, the apostles of the apostles. This was an honour put upon them, and a recompense for their constant affectionate adherence to him, at the cross, and in the grave, and a rebuke to the disciples who forsook him.

The women were bid to *go quickly* upon this errand. Why, what haste was there? Would not the news keep cold, and be welcome to them at any time? Yes, but they were now overwhelmed with grief, and Christ would have this cordial news hastened to them.

Fear and great joy

Matthew 28:8

Here is the women's departure from the sepulchre, to bring notice
to the disciples, v.8. Observe what frame and temper of spirit they
were in: they *departed with fear and great joy*; a strange mixture, fear
and joy at the same time, in the same soul. To hear that Christ was
risen, was matter of joy; but to be led into his grave, and to see an
angel, and talk with him about it, could not but cause fear. It was
good news, but they were afraid that it was too good to be true. But
observe, it is said of their joy, it was *great joy*; it is not said so of their
fear. Holy fear has joy attending it. They that serve the Lord with
reverence, serve him with gladness. Spiritual joy is mixed with
trembling, it is only perfect love and joy that will cast out all fear.

Notice what haste they made: *They did run*. The fear and joy
together quickened their pace, and added wings to their motion; the
angel bid them *go quickly*, and they *ran*. Those that are sent on God's
errand must not loiter, or lose time; where the heart is enlarged with
the glad tidings of the gospel, the feet will *run the way of God's
commandments*.

Observe what errand they went upon: they ran, to *bring his
disciples word*. Not doubting but it would be joyful news to them,
they ran, to comfort them with the same comforts with which they
themselves were comforted of God. The disciples of Christ should be
forward to communicate to each other their experiences of sweet
communion with heaven; should tell others what God has done for
their souls, and spoken to them. Joy in Christ Jesus, like the
ointment of the right hand, will betray itself, and fill all places
within the lines of its communication with its odours.

If there is no resurrection . . . (1)

1 Corinthians 15:13–17

It seems from verse 12 and the course of the argument that there were some among the Corinthians who thought the resurrection an impossibility. *If there be no resurrection of the dead, then Christ has not risen*, v.13; and again, '*If the dead rise not*, cannot be raised or recovered to life, *then is Christ, not raised*, v.16. And yet it was foretold in ancient prophecies that he should rise; and it has been proved by multitudes of eye-witnesses that he has risen. And will you say, will any among you dare to say, that is not, cannot be, which God long ago said should be, and which is now undoubted matter of fact?'

It would follow from this that the preaching and faith of the gospel would be vain: *If Christ be not risen, then is our preaching vain, and your faith vain*, v.14. This supposition would destroy the principal evidence of Christianity; and so:

(1) make preaching vain: 'We apostles should *be found false witnesses of God*, v.15; we pretend to be God's witnesses for this truth, and to work miracles by his power in confirmation of it, and are deceivers, liars for God, if in his name, and by power received from him, we go forth, and proclaim and assert a thing false in fact, and impossible to be true. If Christ be not raised, the gospel is a jest; it is chaff and emptiness.'

(2) make the faith of Christians vain, as well as the labours of ministers: *If Christ be not raised, your faith is vain; you are yet in your sins*, v.17, still under the guilt and condemnation of sin, because it is through his death and sacrifice for sin alone that forgiveness is to be had. *We have redemption through his blood, the forgiveness of sins.*

If there is no resurrection . . . (2)

1 Corinthians 15:18–19

Another absurdity following from supposing the resurrection to be an impossibility is that *those who have fallen asleep in Christ have perished.* If there be no resurrection, they cannot rise, and therefore are lost, even those who have died in the Christian faith, and for it.

It would also follow that Christ's ministers and servants are *of all men most miserable*, as having *hope in him in this life only*, v.19. Their condition who hope in Christ would be worse than that of other men.

All who believe in Christ have hope in him; all who believe in him as a Redeemer hope for redemption and salvation by him; but if there is no resurrection, or state of future recompense, their hope in him must be limited to this life: and, if all their hopes in Christ lie within the compass of this life, they are in a much worse condition than the rest of mankind, especially at that time, and under those circumstances, in which the apostles wrote; for then they had no countenance nor protection from the rulers of the world, but were hated and persecuted by all men.

It would be a gross absurdity in a Christian to admit the supposition of no resurrection or future state. It would leave no hope beyond this world, and would frequently make his condition the worst in the world. Indeed, the Christian is by his religion crucified to this world, and taught to live upon the hope of another. Carnal pleasures are insipid to him in a great degree; and spiritual and heavenly pleasures are those which he assumes and pants after. How sad is his case indeed, if he must be dead to worldly pleasures and yet never hope for any better!

April 8

The trumpet shall sound

1 Corinthians 15:51–53

The apostle here tells the Corinthians what had been concealed from or unknown to them till then—that all the saints would not die, but all would be changed. Those that are alive at our Lord's coming will be caught up into the clouds, without dying. But it is plain from this passage that it will not be without changing from corruption to incorruption. The frame of their living bodies shall be thus altered, as well as those that are dead; and this *in a moment, in the twinkling of an eye*, v.52. This is the mystery which the apostle shows the Corinthians: *Behold, I show you a mystery*; or bring into open light a truth dark and unknown before.

The Lord himself shall descend with a shout, with the voice of the archangel, and with the trump of God, so here, *the trumpet must sound*. It is the loud summons of all the living and all the dead, to come and appear at the tribunal of Christ. At this summons the graves shall open, the dead saints shall rise incorruptible, and the living saints be changed to the same incorruptible state, v.52.

The reason for this change is this, v.53: *For this corruptible must put on incorruption, and this mortal must put on immortality.* How otherwise could the man be a fit inhabitant of the incorruptible regions, or be fitted to possess the eternal inheritance? This corruptible body must be made incorruptible, this mortal body must be changed into immortal, that the man may be capable of enjoying the happiness designed for him.

April 9

The triumph of the resurrection

1 Corinthians 15:54–55

The apostle lets us know what will follow upon this change of the living and dead in Christ: *Then shall be brought to pass that saying, Death is swallowed up in victory.* Death shall be perfectly subdued and conquered, and saints for ever delivered from its power. Such a conquest shall be obtained over it that it shall for ever disappear in those regions to which our Lord will bear his risen saints. And therefore the saints will sing their song of triumph on this. Then, when this mortal shall have put on immortality, will death be for ever swallowed up. Upon this destruction of death will they break out into a song of triumph.

They will glory over death as a vanquished enemy, and insult this great and terrible destroyer: '*O death! where is thy sting?* Where is now thy sting, thy power to hurt? We are dead; but behold we live again, and shall die no more. Thou art vanquished and disarmed, and we are out of the reach of thy deadly dart. Where now is thy fatal artillery? We fear no further mischiefs from thee, nor heed thy weapons, but defy thy power, and despise thy wrath.'

'And, *O grave! where is thy victory?* What has become of it; Once we were thy prisoners, but the prison-doors are burst open, the locks are bolts have been forced to give way, our shackles are knocked off, and we are for ever released. Captivity is taken captive. Thy triumphs, grave, are at an end. The bonds of death are loosed, and we are at liberty, and are never more to be hurt by death, nor imprisoned in the grave.'

April 10

Thanks be to God!

1 Corinthians 15:56–57

The sting of death is sin; but Christ, by dying, has taken out this sting. He has made atonement for sin; he has obtained remission of it. It may hiss therefore, but it cannot hurt. *The strength of sin is the law*; but the curse of the law is removed by our Redeemer's *becoming a curse for us.* So that sin is deprived of its strength and sting, though Christ, that is, by his incarnation, suffering, and death. Death may seize a believer, but cannot sting him, cannot hold him in his power.

It is altogether owing to the grace of God in Christ that sin is pardoned and death disarmed. The law puts arms into the hand of death, to destroy the sinner; but pardon of sin takes away this power from the law, and deprives death of its strength and sting.

It is no wonder, therefore that this triumph of the saints over

[85]

death should issue in thanksgiving to God: *Thanks be to God, who giveth us the victory through our Lord Jesus Christ*, v.57. The way to sanctify all our joy is to make it flow into the praise of God. Then only do we enjoy our blessings and honours in a holy manner when God has his revenue of glory out of it, and we are free to pay it to him. And this really improves and exalts our satisfaction. We are conscious at once of having done our duty and enjoyed our pleasure. And what can be more joyous in itself than the saints' triumph over death, when they shall rise again? With what acclamations will saints rising from the dead applaud him! How will the heaven of heavens resound his praises for ever! *Thanks be to God* will be the burden of their song; and angels will join the chorus, and declare their consent with a loud Amen, Hallelujah.

April 11

Walking in the light

1 John 1:7

But, if we walk in the light, we have fellowship one with another, and the blood of Jesus Christ his Son cleanseth us from all sin. As the blessed God is the eternal boundless light, and the Mediator is, from him, the light of the world, so the Christian institution is the great luminary that appears in our sphere, and shines here below. A conformity to this in spirit and practice demonstrates fellowship or communion with God.

Those that so walk show that they know God, that they have received of the Spirit of God, and that the divine impress or image is stamped upon their souls. *Then we have fellowship one with another*, they with us and we with them, and both with God, in his blessed communications to us. And this is one of the communications to us—that his Son's *blood* or death is applied or imputed to us: *The blood of Jesus Christ his Son cleanseth us from all sin.*

The eternal life, the eternal Son, has put on flesh and blood, and so became Jesus Christ. Jesus Christ has shed his blood for us, or died to wash us from our sins in his own blood. His blood applied to us discharges us from the guilt of all sin, both original and actual, inherent and committed: and so far we stand righteous in his sight; and not only so, but his blood procures for us those sacred influences by which sin is to be subdued more and more, till it is wholly abolished.

[86]

April 12

If we confess our sins

1 John 1:8–10

If we say, We have no sin, we deceive ourselves, and the truth is not in us, v.8. We must beware of deceiving ourselves in denying or excusing our sins. The more we see them the more we shall esteem and value the remedy.

If we say, We have not sinned, we make him a liar, and his word is not in us, v.10. The denial of our sin not only deceives ourselves, but reflects dishonour upon God. It challenges his veracity. He has abundantly testified of, and testified against, the sin of the world.

The apostle then instructs the believer in the way to the continued pardon of his sin. Here we have the believer's duty: *If we confess our sins,* v.9. Penitent confession and acknowledgment of sin are the believer's business, and the means of his deliverance from his guilt.

Here is also the assurance of the happy outcome. This is the veracity, righteousness, and clemency of God, to whom he makes such confession: *He is faithful and just to forgive us our sins, and to cleanse us from all unrighteousness,* v.9.

God is faithful to his covenant and word, in which he has promised forgiveness to penitent believing confessors. He is just to himself and his glory who has provided such a sacrifice, by which his righteousness is declared in the justification of sinners. He is just to his Son who has not only sent him for such service, but promised to him that those who come through him shall be forgiven on his account. He is merciful and gracious also, and so will forgive, to the contrite confessor, all his sins, cleanse him from the guilt of all unrighteousness, and in due time deliver him from the power and practice of it.

The God of peace

Hebrews 13:20

The apostle offers up his prayers to God for the Hebrew believers, being willing to do for them as he desired they should do for him: *Now the God of peace* . . . , v.20. In this excellent prayer observe:

(1) the title given to God—*the God of peace*, who has found a way for peace and reconciliation between himself and sinners, and who loves peace on earth and especially in his churches.

(2) the great work ascribed to him: He has *brought again from the dead our Lord Jesus* . . . Jesus raised himself by his own power; and yet the Father was concerned in it, attesting thereby that justice was satisfied and the law fulfilled. He rose again for our justification; and that divine power by which he was raised is able to do everything for us that we stand in need of.

(3) the titles given to Christ—*our Lord Jesus*, our Sovereign, our Saviour, and the *great shepherd of the sheep*. Ministers are under-shepherds, Christ is the great shepherd. This denotes his interest in his people. They are the flock of his pasture, and his care and concern are for them. He feeds them, and leads them, and watches over them.

Through Jesus Christ

Hebrews 13:20

Observe here the way and method in which God is reconciled, and Christ raised from the dead: *Through the blood of the everlasting covenant*. The blood of Christ satisfied divine justice, and so procured Christ's release from the prison of the grave, as having paid our debt, according to an eternal covenant or agreement between the Father and the Son; and this blood is the sanction and seal of an everlasting covenant between God and his people.

Notice the mercy prayed for: *Make you perfect in every good work* . . . , v.21. The perfection of the saints in every good work is the great thing desired by them and for them, that they may here have a perfection of integrity, a clear mind, a clean heart, lively affections, regular and resolved wills, and suitable strength for every good work to which they are called now, and at length a perfection of degrees to fit them for the employment and felicity of heaven.

The way in which God makes his people perfect is by *working in them always what is pleasing in his sight,* and that *through Jesus Christ, to whom be glory for ever.* There is no good thing effected in us but it is the work of God; he works in us, before we are fit for any good work. No good thing is effected in us by God, but through Jesus Christ, for his sake and by his Spirit. And therefore eternal glory is due to him, who is the cause of all the good principles effected in us and all the good works done by us. To this everyone should say, *Amen.*

The Lamb of God

Revelation 5:6–7

The apostle beholds the book taken into the hands of the Lord Jesus Christ, for it to be unsealed and opened by him. Here Christ is described by his place and position: *In the midst of the throne and of the four beasts, and of the elders.* He was on the same throne with the Father; he was nearer to him than either the elders or ministers of the churches. Christ, as man and Mediator, is subordinate to God the Father, but is nearer to him than all the creatures: *for in him all the fulness of the Godhead dwells bodily.* The ministers stand between God and the people. Christ stands as Mediator between God and both ministers and people.

Here Christ is also described in the form in which he appeared. Before he is called *a lion,* v.5; here he appears *as a lamb slain.* He is a lion to conquer Satan, a lamb to satisfy the justice of God. He appears with the marks of his sufferings upon him, to show that he intercedes in heaven in the virtue of his satisfaction. He appears as a *lamb, having seven horns and seven eyes,* perfect power to execute all the will of God and perfect wisdom to understand it all and to do it in the most effectual manner: *for he hath the seven Spirits of God,* he has received the Holy Spirit without measure, in all perfection of light, and life, and power, by which he is able to teach and rule all parts of the earth.

Christ is described by his act and deed: *He came, and took the book out of the right hand of him that sat on the throne*, v.7, not by violence, nor by fraud, but he prevailed to do it (as v.5), he prevailed by his merit and worthiness, he did it by authority and by the Father's appointment. God very willingly and justly put the book of his eternal counsels into the hand of Christ, and Christ as readily and gladly took it into his hand; for he delights to reveal and to do the will of his Father.

April 16

Thou art worthy

Revelation 5:8–10

The church begins the song of praise, as being more immediately concerned in it, v.8, the four living creatures, and the *four and twenty elders*, the Christian people, under their minister, lead up the chorus.

Observe the object of their worship—*the Lamb*, the Lord Jesus Christ; it is the declared will of God that all men *should honour the Son as they honour the Father*; for he has the same nature. They *fell down before him*, gave him not an inferior sort of worship, but the most profound adoration. *The harps* were the instruments of praise, *the vials* were full of odours or incense, which signify *the prayers of the saints*: prayer and praise should always go together.

In their new song they acknowledge the infinite fitness and worthiness of the Lord Jesus for this great work of opening and executing the counsel and purposes of God, v.9: *Thou art worthy to take the book, and to open the seals thereof*, every way sufficient for the work and deserving of the honour. They insist upon the merit of his sufferings, which he had endured for them: '*Thou wast slain*, slain as a sacrifice, thy blood was shed.' The fruits of his sufferings are redemption to God and high exaltation: Thou *hast made us to our God kings and priests, and we shall reign on the earth*, v.10.

Worthy is the Lamb

Revelation 5:11–14

The doxology, begun by the church, is carried on by the angels; they are the attendants on the throne of God and guardians to the church; though they did not need a Saviour themselves, yet they rejoice in the redemption and salvation of sinners, and they agree with the church in acknowledging the infinite merits of the Lord Jesus as dying for sinners, that he is *worthy to receive power, and riches, and wisdom, and strength, and honour, and glory, and blessing.*

This doxology, begun by the church and carried on by the angels, is resounded and echoed by the whole creation, v.13. *By him all things consist*; and all the creatures, had they sense and language, would adore that great Redeemer who delivers the creation from that bondage under which it groans, through the corruption of men, and the just curse denounced by the great God upon the fall; that part which is made for the whole creation is a song of *blessing, and honour, and glory, and power to him that sits on the throne*—to God as God, or to God the Father, as the first Person in the Trinity and the first in the plan of our salvation—and *to the Lamb*, as the second Person in the Godhead and the Mediator of the new covenant. We worship and glorify one and the same God for our creation and for our redemption.

We see how the church that began the heavenly anthem, finding heaven and earth join in the concert, closes all with their *Amen*, and end as they began, with a low prostration before the eternal and everlasting God.

Risen with Christ

Colossians 3:1-2

If you then have risen with Christ. It is our privilege that we have risen with Christ; that is, have benefit by the resurrection of Christ, and because of our union and communion with him are justified and sanctified, and shall be glorified.

So the apostle infers that we must *seek those things which are above.* We must mind the concerns of another world more than the concerns of this. We must make heaven our scope and aim, seek the favour of God above, keep up our communion with the upper world by faith, and hope, and holy love, and make it our constant care and business to secure our title to and qualifications for the heavenly bliss. And the reason is because *Christ sits at the right hand of God.* He who is our best friend and our head is advanced to the highest dignity and honour in heaven, and has gone before to secure to us the heavenly happiness; and therefore we should seek and secure what he has purchased at so vast an expense, and is taking so much care about.

The apostle explains this duty, v.2: *Set your affection on things above, not on things on the earth.* To seek heavenly things is to set our affections upon them, to love them and let our desires be towards them. We must acquaint ourselves with them, esteem them above all other things, and be attentive in preparation for the enjoyment of them. *Things on earth* are here set in opposition to *things above.* We must not dote upon them, nor expect too much from them, that we may set our affections on heaven; for heaven and earth are contrary one to the other, and a supreme regard to both is inconsistent; and the prevalence of our affection to one will proportionably weaken and abate our affection to the other.

April 19

Mortification

Colossians 3:5–7

Since it is our duty to set our affections upon heavenly things, it is our duty to mortify our *members which are upon the earth*, and which naturally incline us to the things of the world. Kill them, suppress them, as you do weeds or vermin which spread and destroy all about them.

He specifies the lusts of the flesh, for which they were before so very remarkable: *fornication, uncleanness, inordinate affection, evil concupiscence*—the various workings of the carnal appetites and fleshly impurities—and the love of the world: *and covetousness, which is idolatry*. Observe, covetousness is spiritual idolatry: it is the giving of that love and regard to worldly wealth which are due to God only, and carries a greater degree of malignity in it, and is more highly provoking to God, than is commonly thought.

He proceeds to show how necessary it is to mortify sins, v.6,7, because, if we do not kill them, they will kill us: *For which things' sake the wrath of God cometh on the children of disobedience*, v.6. See what we are all by nature more or less: *we are children of disobedience*: not only disobedient children, but under the power of sin and naturally prone to disobey. We should mortify these sins because they have lived in us: *In which you also walked some time, when you lived in them*, v.7. The consideration that we have formerly lived in sin is a good argument why we should now forsake it.

April 20

The new man

Colossians 3:8–10

So we are to mortify inordinate passions, v.8: *But now you also put off all these, anger, wrath, malice*; for these are contrary to the design of the gospel, as well as grosser impurities; and, though they are more spiritual wickedness, have not less malignity in them.

Anger and wrath are bad, but malice is worse, because it is more rooted and deliberate; it is anger heightened and settled. And, as the corrupt principles in the heart must be cut off, so the product of them in the tongue; as *blasphemy*, which seems there to mean, not much speaking ill of God as speaking ill of men, giving ill language to them, or raising ill reports of them, and injuring their good name by any evil arts; *filthy communication*, that is, all lewd and wanton discourse, which comes from a polluted mind in the speaker and propagates the same defilements in the hearers; and lying: *Lie not one to another*, v.9, for it is contrary both to the law of truth and the law of love, it is both unjust and unkind, and naturally tends to destroy all faith and friendship among mankind.

Seeing you have put off the old man with his deeds, and have put on the new man, v.10. Those who have put off the old man have put it off with its deeds; and those who have put on the new man must put on all its deeds—not only espouse good principles but perform them in good conduct.

The new man is said to be *renewed in knowledge*, because an ignorant soul cannot be a good soul. The grace of God works upon the will and affections by renewing the understanding.

April 21

Love and compassion

Colossians 3:12

The apostle proceeds to exhort to mutual love and compassion. We must not only put off anger and wrath, as v.8, but we must put on compassion and kindness, v.12; not only cease to do evil, but learn to do well; not only not do hurt to any, but do what good we can to all.

The argument here used to enforce the exhortation is very moving: *Put on, as the elect of God, holy and beloved*. Those who are the elect of God, holy and beloved, ought to conduct themselves in every thing as becomes them, and so as not to lose the credit of their holiness, nor the comfort of their being chosen and beloved. It becomes those who are holy towards God to be lowly and loving towards all men.

Observe what we must put on in particular: *compassion* towards the miserable; *kindness* towards our friends, and those who love us. A courteous disposition becomes the elect of God; for the design of the gospel is not only to soften the minds of men, but to sweeten them, and to promote friendship among men as well as reconciliation with God.

We are also to put on a *humbleness of mind*, in submission to those above us, and condescension to those below us. There must not only be a humble demeanour, but a humble mind.

April 22

Mutual love

Colossians 3:12–13

The apostle continues to encourage mutual love. We must put on:

(1) *meekness* towards those who have provoked us, or been any way injurious to us. We must not be transported into any indecency by our resentment of indignities and neglects: but must prudently bridle our own anger, and patiently bear the anger of others.

(2) *longsuffering* towards those who continue to provoke us. Many can bear a short provocation who are weary of bearing when it grows long. But we must suffer long both the injuries of men and the rebukes of divine Providence.

(3) mutual forbearance, in consideration of the infirmities and deficiencies under which we all labour: *Forbearing one another*. We have all of us something which needs to be borne with, and this is a good reason why we should bear with others in what is disagreeable to us.

(4) a readiness to forgive injuries: *Forgiving one another, if any man have a quarrel against any*. While we are in this world, where there is so much corruption in our hearts, and so much occasion of difference and contention, quarrels will sometimes happen, even among the elect of God, who are holy and beloved.

And the reason is: *Even as Christ forgave you, so also do you*. The consideration that we are forgiven by Christ so many offences is a good reason why we should forgive others.

April 23

Put on love

Colossians 3:14-15

In order to undertake these precepts, we are exhorted here to do several things. We are to clothe ourselves with love, v.14: *Above all things put on charity*. Let this be the upper garment, the robe, the livery, the mark of our dignity and distinction. He lays the foundation in faith, and the top-stone in charity, *which is the bond of perfectness*, the cement and centre of all happy society. Christian unity consists of unanimity and mutual love.

We are to submit ourselves to the government of the *peace of God*, v.15: *Let the peace of God rule in your hearts*, that is, God's being at peace with you, and the comfortable sense of his acceptance and favour: or, a disposition to peace among yourselves, a peaceable spirit, that keeps the peace, and makes peace. This is called the *peace of God*, because it is of his working in all who are his.

To which you are called in one body: We are called to this peace, to peace with God as our privilege and peace with our brethren as our duty. Being united in one body, we are called to be at peace with one another, as the members of the natural body; for we are the body of Christ. To preserve in us this peaceable disposition, we must be *thankful*. The work of thanksgiving to God is such a sweet and pleasant work that it will help to make us sweet and pleasant towards all men.

April 24

The word of Christ

Colossians 3:16-17

We are to let the *word of Christ dwell in us richly*, v.16. The gospel is the word of Christ, which has come to us; that is, be always ready and at hand to us in everything, and have its due influence and use. Many have the word of Christ dwelling in them, but it dwells in them but poorly; it has no mighty force and influence upon them.

Then the soul prospers when the word of God *dwells in us richly*, when we have abundance of it in us, and are full of the scriptures and of the grace of Christ. And this *in all wisdom*. The proper office of wisdom is to apply what we know to ourselves, for our own direction.

We are to *teach and admonish one another*. This would contribute very much to our furtherance in all grace; for we sharpen ourselves by quickening others, and improve our knowledge by communicating it for their edification. We must *admonish one another in psalms and hymns*. The singing of psalms is a gospel ordinance;—the Psalms of David, and spiritual hymns and odes, collected out of the scripture. But, when we sing psalms, we make no melody unless we sing with grace in our hearts, unless we are suitably affected with what we sing and go along in it with true devotion and understanding.

All must be done in the name of Christ, v.17: *And whatsoever you do in word or deed, do all in the name of the Lord Jesus*, according to his command and in compliance with his authority, by strength derived from him, with an eye to his glory, and depending upon his merit for the acceptance of what is good and the pardon of what is amiss, *Giving thanks to God and the Father by him*. We must give thanks in all things; whatsoever we do, we must still give thanks; the Lord Jesus must be the Mediator of our praises as well as of our prayers.

April 25

You shall know the truth

John 8:31–32

In what he said to the Jews, we have two things, which he says to all that should at any time believe:

(1) the character of a true disciple of Christ: *If you continue in my word, then are you my disciples indeed*. When they believed on him, as the great Prophet, they gave up themselves to be his disciples. Now, at their entrance into his school, he lays down this for a rule, that he would own none for his disciples but those that *continued in his word*. Those who seem willing to be Christ's disciples ought to be told that they had as good never come to him, unless they come with resolution by his grace to abide by him.

(2) the privilege of a true disciple of Christ. Here are two precious promises made to those who thus approve themselves disciples indeed, v.32. '*You shall know the truth*, shall know all that truth which it is needful and profitable for you to know, and shall be more confirmed in the belief of it, shall know the certainty of it.'

The truth shall make you free. The knowing and believing of this truth does actually make us free, free from prejudices, mistakes, and false notions, free from the dominion of lust and passion; and restores the soul to the government of itself, by reducing it into obedience to its Creator. The mind, by admitting the truth of Christ in the light and power, is vastly enlarged, and has scope and compass given it, is greatly elevated and raised above things of sense, and never acts with so true a liberty as when it acts under a divine command.

April 26

I am the resurrection

John 11:25–26

I am the resurrection and the life, the fountain of life, and the head and author of the resurrection. It is an unspeakable comfort to all good Christians that Jesus Christ is the resurrection and the life, and will be so to them.

Observe to whom these promises are made—to those that believe in Jesus Christ, to those that consent to, and confide in, Jesus Christ as the only Mediator of reconciliation and communion between God and man, that receive the record God has given in his word concerning his Son, sincerely comply with it, and answer all the great intentions of it.

Observe what the promises are, v.25: *Though he die, yet shall he live*, nay, *he shall never die*, v.26. Man consists of body and soul, and provision is made for the happiness of both. For the *body*; here is the promise of a blessed resurrection. Though the body be dead because of sin (there is no remedy but it will die), yet it *shall live again*: the body shall be raised a glorious body. For the *soul*; here is the promise of a blessed immortality. He that lives and believes, who, being united to Christ by faith, lives spiritually because of that union, he will never die. That spiritual life will never be extinguished, but perfected in eternal life.

Christ asks Martha, '*Believest thou this?* Do you assent to it with application? Do you take my word for it?' When we have read or heard the word of Christ concerning the great things of the other world, we should seriously put it to ourselves, 'Do we believe this, this truth in particular, this which is attended with so many difficulties, this which is suited to my case? Does my belief of it make it real to me, and give my soul an assurance of it?'

April 27

Let not your hearts be troubled

John 14:1

Many things happened to trouble the disciples now. Christ had just told them of the unkindness he should receive from some of them, and this troubled them all. He had just told them of his own departure from them, that he should not only go away, but go away in a cloud of sufferings. They will think themselves shamefully disappointed; for they thought that he would be the one to deliver Israel, and should have set up his kingdom in secular power and glory. They will think themselves sadly deserted and exposed. Now, in reference to all these, *Let not your hearts be troubled.* Here are three words, upon any of which the emphasis may significantly be laid.

First, upon the word *troubled*: 'Be not so troubled as to be put into a hurry and confusion; be not cast down and disquieted.' Secondly, upon the word *heart*: 'Though the nation and city be troubled, though your little family and flock be troubled, yet *let not your heart be troubled*. Keep possession of your own souls when you can keep possession of nothing else. The heart is the main fort; whatever you do, keep trouble from this, keep this with *all diligence*. Thirdly, upon the word *your*: 'You that are my disciples and followers, my redeemed, chosen, sanctified ones, however others are overwhelmed with the sorrows of this present time, be not you so, for you know better.

Believe in God

John 14:1

The remedy Christ prescribes against this trouble of mind, which he saw ready to prevail over them is *believe*. Some read it in both parts imperatively, '*Believe in God*, and his perfections and providence, *believe also in me*, and my mediation. Built with confidence upon the great acknowledged principles of natural religion: that there is a God, that he is most holy, wise, powerful, and good; that he is the governor of the world, and has the sovereign disposal of all events; and comfort yourselves likewise with the particular doctrines of that holy religion which I have taught you.' But, we read the former as an acknowledgment that they did believe in God, for which he commends them: 'But, if you would effectually provide against a stormy day, *believe also in me.*'

Those that rightly believe in God will believe in Jesus Christ, whom he has made known to them; and believing in God through Jesus Christ is an excellent means of keeping trouble from the heart. The joy of faith is the best remedy against the griefs of sense.

April 29

My Father's house

John 14:2

Here is a particular direction to act with faith upon the promise of eternal life. He had directed them to trust to God, and to trust in him; but what must they trust God and Christ for? Trust them for a happiness to come when this body and this world shall be no more, and for a happiness to last as long as the immortal soul and the eternal world shall last.

Believe and consider that really there is such a happiness: *In my Father's house there are many mansions; if it were not so, I would have told you*, v.2. Heaven is *a house not made with hands, eternal in the heavens.* It is *my Father's house*; and his Father is our Father, to whom

he was now ascending; so that in right of their elder brother all
true believers shall be welcome to that happiness as to their home.
There are *many* mansions, for there are many sons to be brought to
glory, and Christ exactly knows their number, nor will be
restricted for room by the coming of more company than he
expects.

See what assurance we have of the reality of the happiness itself,
and the sincerity of the proposal of it to us: '*If it were not so, I would
have told you.*' He loves us too well, and is too well disposed towards
us to disappoint the expectations of his own raising, or to leave those
to be of all men most miserable who have been of him most
observant.

April 30

I go and prepare a place for you

John 14:3

The design of Christ's going away was to prepare a place in heaven
for his disciples. 'You are grieved to think of my going away,
whereas I go on your errand, as the forerunner; I am to enter for
you.' He went to prepare a place for us. Heaven would be an
unready place for a Christian if Christ did not go there before.

Believe and consider that therefore he would certainly come again
in due time, to take them to that blessed place which he was now
going to possess for himself and prepare for them, v.3: '*If I go and
prepare a place for you*, if this be the errand of my journey, you may be
sure, when everything is ready, *I will come again, and receive you to
myself*, so that you shall follow me, *that where I am there you may be also.*'
These are comfortable words indeed.

Jesus Christ will come again. The belief in Christ's second
coming, of which he has given us the assurance, is an excellent
preservative against trouble of heart.

He will come again to receive all his faithful followers to himself.
He sends for them privately at death, and gathers them one by one;
but they are to make their public entry in solemn state all together at
the last day, and then Christ himself will come to receive them, to
conduct them in the abundance of his love. He will hereby testify
the utmost respect and endearment imaginable.

That where he is, there they shall be also. This intimates what many other scriptures declare, that the quintessence of heaven's happiness is being with Christ *there*. Christ speaks of his being there as now present, *that where I am*; where I am to be shortly, where I am to be eternally; there you shall be shortly, there you shall be eternally: not only there, in the same place; but there, in the same state: not only spectators of his glory, as the three disciples on the mount, but sharers in it.

May 1

I am the true vine

John 15:1

Jesus Christ is the vine, *the true vine*. It is an instance of the humility of Christ that he is pleased to speak of himself under low and humble comparisons. He that is *the Sun of righteousness*, and *the bright and morning Star*, compares himself to a vine.

He is *the vine*, planted in the vineyard, and not a spontaneous product; planted in the earth, for he is the *Word made flesh*. The vine is a spreading plant, and Christ will be known as *salvation to the ends of the earth*. He is *the true vine*, as truth is opposed to pretence and counterfeit; he is really a fruitful plant, a plant of renown.

Believers are branches of this vine, which supposes that Christ is the root of the vine. The root is unseen, and our *life is hid with Christ*; the root bears the tree, diffuses sap to it, and is all in all to its flourishing and fruitfulness; and in Christ are all supports and supplies. The branches of the vine are many, some on one side of the house or wall, others on the other side; yet, meeting in the root, are all but one vine; thus all true Christians, though in place and opinion distant from each other, yet meet in Christ, the centre of their unity.

The Father is the husbandmen—the land-worker. Though *the earth is the Lord's* it yields him no fruit unless he work it. God has a care of the vine and all the branches. He has an eye upon all the branches, and prunes them, and watches over them, that nothing will hurt them. Never was any husbandman so wise, so watchful, about his vineyard, as God is about his church, which therefore must prosper.

May 2

Bearing fruit

John 15:2

The duty taught us by this comparison is to *bring forth fruit*, and, in order to do this, to *abide* in Christ.

We must be fruitful. From a vine we look for grapes, and from a Christian we look for Christianity; this is the *fruit*, a Christian temper and disposition, a Christian life and conversation, Christian devotions and Christian designs.

In verse 2 it is intimated that there are many who pass for *branches* in Christ who yet do *not bear fruit*: the unfruitful are *taken away*. Were they really united to Christ by faith, they would bear fruit; but being only tied to him by the thread of an outward profession, though they seem to be branches, they will soon be seen to be dry ones.

Observe the promise made to the fruitful: *He purgeth them, that they may bring forth more fruit*. Further fruitfulness is the blessed reward of forward fruitfulness. The first blessing was, *Be fruitful*; and it is still a great blessing. Note that even fruitful branches, in order to bear further fruitfulness, have need of purging or pruning; he takes away that which is superfluous and luxuriant, which hinders its growth and fruitfulness. The best have in them something that is sinful, which should be taken away; some notions or passions that want to be purged away, which Christ has promised to do by his word, and Spirit, and providence. The purging of fruitful branches, in order to bear greater fruitfulness, is the care and work of the great husbandman, for his own glory.

May 3

Abiding in Christ

John 15:4–5

In order to be fruitful we must abide in Christ, must keep up our
union with him by faith, and do all we do in religion in the virtue of
that union. *Abide in me, and I in you*, v.4. It is the great concern of all
Christ's disciples constantly to keep up a dependence upon Christ and
communion with him, habitually to adhere to him, and actually to
derive supplies from him. Those that have come to Christ must abide
in him: '*Abide in me*, by faith; *and I in you*, by my Spirit; *abide in me*,
and then fear not that I will *abide in you*;' for the communion between
Christ and believers never fails on his side. We must abide in Christ's
word by a regard to it, and it in us as a *light to our feet*. '*You cannot bring
forth fruit, except you abide in me*; but, if you do, you *bring forth much fruit*;
for, in short, *without me*, or separate from me, *you can do nothing*.'

Abiding in Christ is necessary in order to do *much* good. He that is
constant in the exercise of faith in Christ and love to him, that lives
upon his promises and is led by his Spirit, *bringeth forth much fruit*, he is
of great service to God's glory, and his own account in the great day.

Abiding in Christ is also necessary to our doing *any* good. It is not
only a means of cultivating and increasing what good there is already
in us, but it is the root and spring of all good: '*Without me you can do
nothing*: not only no great thing, *heal the sick, or raise the dead*, but
nothing.' *Without Christ we can do nothing* aright, nothing that will be
fruit pleasing to God or profitable to ourselves.

May 4

Withered branches

John 15:6

Observe the fatal consequences of forsaking Christ, v.6: *If any man
abide not in me, he is cast forth as a branch*. This is a description of the
fearful state of hypocrites that are *not in Christ*, and of apostates that
abide not in Christ. They are cast forth as dry and withered branches,

which are plucked off because they burden the tree. Those should have no benefit of Christ who think they have no need of him; those who reject him should be rejected by him. Those that abide not in Christ will be abandoned by him.

They are withered, as a branch broken off from the tree. Those that abide not in Christ, though they may flourish awhile in a plausible, at least a passable profession, yet in a little time wither and come to nothing. Their parts and gifts wither; their zeal and devotion wither; their credit and reputation wither; their hopes and comforts wither.

Men gather them. Satan's agents and emissaries pick them up, and make an easy prey of them. Those that fall off from Christ presently fall in with sinners; and the sheep that wander from Christ's fold, the devil stands ready to seize them for himself.

They *cast them into the fire*, that is, they are cast into the fire; and those who seduce them and draw them to sin do in effect cast them there; for they *make them children of hell*. Fire is the fittest place for withered branches, for they are good for nothing else. *They are burned*; this follows of course, but it is here added very emphatically, and makes the threatening very terrible. They will not be consumed in a moment, but they are burning for ever in a fire, which not only cannot be quenched, but will never spend itself.

May 5

Glory to the Father

John 15:7-8

In verse 7 we see the blessed privilege which those have that *abide in Christ*: *If my words abide in you, you shall ask what you will* of my Father in my name, *and it shall be done.* Our union with Christ is maintained by the word: *If you abide in me*; he had said before, *and I in you*; here he explains himself, *and my words abide in you*; for it is in the word that Christ is set before us and offered to us. It is in the word that we receive and embrace him; and so where the *word of Christ dwells richly* there Christ dwells. If the word is our constant guide and monitor if it is in us as at home, then we abide in Christ, and he in us.

Our communion with Christ is maintained by prayer: *You shall ask what you will, and it shall be done to you.* And what can we desire more than to have what we will for the asking? Those that abide in Christ as their heart's delight shall have, through Christ, their heart's desire. If we have Christ, we shall lack nothing that is good for us.

Observe the glory that will redound to God by our fruitfulness, with the comfort and honour that will come to ourselves, by it, v.8. If we *bear much fruit*, our Father will be glorified. The fruitfulness of the apostles, as such, in the diligent discharge of their office, would be to the glory of God in the conversion of souls, and the offering of them up to him. The fruitfulness of all Christians is to the glory of God.

So shall we be Christ's disciples indeed, approving ourselves so, and making it to appear that we are really what we call ourselves. So shall we both show our discipleship and adorn it, and be to our Master *for a name and a praise*, and a glory, that is, disciples indeed.

May 6

I have overcome the world

John 16:33

That in him they might have peace. It is the will of Christ that his disciples should have peace within, whatever their troubles may be outside themselves. Peace in Christ is the only true peace, and in him alone believers have it. Through him we have peace with God, and so in him we have peace in our own minds.

Though the disciples were sent to proclaim *peace on earth*, and *goodwill towards men*, they must expect trouble on earth, and ill-will from men. In the midst of the tribulations of this world it is the duty and interest of Christ's disciples to be of good cheer, to keep up their delight in God whatever is pressing, and their hope in God whatever is threatening.

I have overcome the world. Christ's victory is a Christian's triumph. Christ overcame the prince of this world, disarmed him, and cast him out; and still treads Satan under our feet. Never was there such a conqueror of the world as Christ was, and we ought to be encouraged by it, because Christ has overcome the world before us; so that we may look upon it as a conquered enemy, and because he has conquered it for us, as the captain of our salvation. We are interested in his victory; by his cross the world is *crucified to us*, which speaks of it as being completely conquered and put into our possession; all is yours, even *the world*.

May 7

Be strong in the Lord

Ephesians 6:10–11

Here is a general encouragement to constancy in our Christian way, and to courage in our Christian warfare. Is not our life a warfare? It is so; for we struggle with the common calamities of human life. Is not our religion much more a warfare? It is so; for we struggle with the opposition of the powers of darkness, and with many enemies who would keep us from God and heaven.

If Christians are soldiers of Jesus Christ, they must see that they are *strong in the Lord*. Those who have so many battles to fight, and who, in their way to heaven, must dispute every pass, by means of the sword, have need of a great deal of courage. Be strong for service, strong for suffering, strong for fighting. Let a soldier be ever so well armed externally, if he does not have within a good heart, his armour will stand him in little stead.

Be strong in the Lord. We have no sufficient strength of our own. Our natural courage is as perfect cowardice, and our natural strength as perfect weakness; but all our sufficiency is of God.

'*Put on the whole armour of God*, v.11, make use of all the proper defences and weapons for repelling the temptations and stratagems of Satan—get and exercise all the Christian graces, *the whole armour*, that no part be naked and exposed to the enemy.'

It is called the *armour of God*, because he both prepares and bestows it. We have no armour of our own that will be armour of proof in a trying time. Nothing will stand us in stead but his armour. This armour is prepared for us, but we must *put it on*.

The reason why the Christian should be completely armed is *that he may be able to stand against the wiles of the devil*—that he may be able to hold out, and to overcome in spite of all the devil's assaults, all the deceits he puts upon us, all the snares he lays for us, and all his machinations against us.

May 8

Our enemy

Ephesians 6:12

The apostle here shows what our danger is, and what need we have to put on this whole armour, considering what sort of enemies we have to deal with—the devil and all the powers of darkness: *For we wrestle not against flesh and blood . . .* , v.12. The combat for which we are to be prepared is not against ordinary human enemies, not barely against men compounded of *flesh and blood*, nor against our own corrupt natures singly considered, but against the several ranks of devils, who have a government which they exercise in this world.

We have to do with a subtle enemy, an enemy who uses wiles and stratagems, as v.11. He has a thousand ways of beguiling unstable souls: hence he is called a serpent for subtlety, experienced in the art and trade of tempting.

He is a powerful enemy: *Principalities*, and *powers*, and *rulers*. They are numerous, they are vigorous.

They are spiritual enemies: *Spiritual wickedness in high places*, or wicked spirits, as some translate it. The devil is a spirit, a wicked spirit; and our danger is the greater from our enemies because they are unseen, and assault us before we are aware of them. The devils are wicked spirits, and they chiefly annoy the saints with, and provoke them to, spiritual wickednesses, pride, envy, malice, etc. These enemies are said to be *in high places*, or in heavenly places, so the word is, taking heaven for the whole spreading-out of the air between the earth and the stars, the air being the place from which the devils assault us.

Our enemies strive to prevent our ascent to heaven, to deprive us of heavenly blessings and to obstruct our communion with heaven. They assault us in the things that belong to our souls, and labour to deface the heavenly image in our hearts; and therefore we have need to be on our guard against them.

May 9

Standing our ground

Ephesians 6:13

Observe what our duty is: to take and put on the whole armour of God, and then to stand our ground, and withstand our enemies.

We must *withstand*, v.13. We must not yield to the devil's allurement and assaults, but oppose them. Satan is said to stand up against us so we must stand against him; set up and keep up an interest in opposition to the devil. Satan is the wicked one, and his kingdom is the kingdom of sin: to stand against Satan is to strive against sin. *That you may be able to withstand in the evil day*, in the day of temptation or of any sore affliction.

We must stand our ground: *And, having done all, to stand.* We must resolve, by God's grace, not to yield to Satan. Resist him, and he will flee. If we give way, he will gain ground. If we distrust our cause, our leader, or our armour, we give him advantage. Our present business is to withstand the assaults of the devil, and to stand it out; and then, having done all that is incumbent on the good soldier of Jesus Christ, our warfare will be accomplished, and we shall be finally victorious.

May 10

Truth and righteousness

Ephesians 6:14

We must stand armed; and this is here most enlarged upon. Here is a Christian in complete armour: and the armour is divine: *the armour of God*. The apostle specifies the particulars of this armour, both offensive and defensive. It is observable that, among them all, there is none for the back; if we turn our back upon the enemy, we lie exposed.

Truth is our girdle, v.14. It was prophesied of Christ that *righteousness should be the girdle of his loins and faithfulness the girdle of his reins*. That which Christ was girded with all Christians must be girded with. God desires truth, that is, sincerity, in the inward parts. This is the strength of our loins; and it girds on all other pieces of our armour, and therefore is first mentioned. Some understand it as the doctrine of the truths of the gospel: they should cleave to us as the girdle does to the loins. This will restrain from libertinism and licentiousness, as a girdle restrains and keeps in the body. This is the Christian soldier's belt: ungirded with this he is unblessed.

Righteousness must be our breastplate. The breastplate secures the vital parts, shelters the heart. The righteousness of Christ imputed to us is our breastplate against the arrows of divine wrath. The righteousness of Christ implanted in us is our breastplate to fortify the heart against the attacks which Satan makes against us. The apostle explains this in 1 Thessalonians 5:8, *Putting on the breastplate of faith and love.* Faith and love include all Christian graces; for by faith we are united to Christ and by love to our brethren.

May 11

Peace, faith, and salvation

Ephesians 6:15-17

Resolution must be as the soldier's shoes to our legs: *And their feet shod with the preparation of the gospel of peace.* v.15. *The preparation of the gospel of peace* signifies a prepared and resolved frame of heart, to adhere to the gospel and abide by it, which will enable us to walk with a steady pace in the way of religion, in spite of the difficulties and dangers that may be in it. It is styled *the gospel of peace* because it brings all sorts of peace, peace with God, with ourselves, and with one another.

Faith must be our shield: *Above all*, or chiefly, *taking the shield of faith*, v.16. This is more necessary than any of them. Faith is all in all to us in an hour of temptation. We are to be fully persuaded of the truth of all God's promises and threatenings, such a faith being of great use against temptations. Faith, as receiving Christ and the benefits of redemption, so deriving grace from him, is like a shield, a sort of universal defence.

Our enemy the devil is here called *the wicked one.* His temptations are called *darts*, because of their swift and undiscerned flight, and the deep wounds that they give to the soul. Violent temptations, by which the soul is set on fire of hell, are the darts which Satan shoots at us. Faith is the shield with which we must quench these fiery darts, and so render them ineffectual, that they may not hit us, or at least that they may not hurt us.

Salvation must be *our helmet*, v.17; that is, hope, which has salvation for its object; as 1 Thessalonians 5:8. The helmet secures the head. A good hope of salvation, well founded and well built, will both purify the soul and keep it from being defiled by Satan, and it will comfort the soul and keep it from being troubled and tormented by Satan. He would tempt us to despair; but good hope keeps us trusting in God and rejoicing in him.

May 12

The word of God and prayer

Ephesians 6:17–18

The word of God is *the sword of the Spirit*. The sword is a very necessary and useful part of a soldier's equipment. The word of God is very necessary and of great use to the Christian, in order to maintain his spiritual warfare and succeed in it. It is called *the sword of the Spirit*, because it is of the Spirit's expression and he renders it efficacious and powerful, and *sharper than a two-edged sword*.

Prayer must buckle on all the other parts of our Christian armour, v.18. We must join prayer with all these graces, for our defence against these spiritual enemies, imploring help and assistance of God, as the case requires: and we must pray *always*. Not as though we were to do nothing else but pray, for there are other duties of religion and of our respective positions in the world that are to be done in their place and season; but we should keep up constant times of prayer, and be constant to them.

We must pray *with all prayer and supplication*, with all kinds of prayer: public, private, and secret, social and solitary, solemn and sudden; with all the parts of prayer: confession of sin, petition for mercy, and thanksgivings for favours received.

We must pray *in the Spirit*; our spirits must be employed in the duty and we must do it by the grace of God's good Spirit.

We must *watch thereunto*, endeavouring to keep our hearts in a praying frame, and taking all occasions, and improving all opportunities, for the duty.

This we must do *with all perseverance*. We must abide by the duty of prayer, whatever change there may be in our outward circumstances; and we must continue in it as long as we live in the world. We must likewise persevere in particular requests in spite of discouragements and repulses.

And we must pray *with supplication*, not for ourselves only, but *for all saints*; for we are members one of another.

May 13

Don't be afraid

Matthew 14:26–27

When the disciples saw him walking on the sea, they were troubled, saying, It is a spirit. These disciples said, *It is a spirit*; when they should have said, *It is the Lord*; it can be no other. A little thing frightens us in a storm. When there are fightings outside us, it is no wonder that within are fears. Perhaps the disciples thought it was some evil spirit that raised the storm.

We are told how these fears were silenced, v.27. He *straightway* relieved them, by showing them their mistake; when they were wrestling *with the waves*, he delayed his help for some time; but he hastened his help against their fright, as much the more dangerous; he straightway caused that storm to subside with his word, *Be of good cheer; it is I; be not afraid.*

He rectified their mistake, by making himself known to them: *It is I*. True believers know his name. A right knowledge opens the door to true comfort, especially the knowledge of Christ.

He encouraged them against their fright; *It is I*, and therefore '*Be of good cheer*; pluck up your spirits and be courageous.' If Christ's disciples are not cheerful in a storm, it is their own fault. '*Be not afraid* of the tempest, of the winds and waves, though noisy and very threatening; fear them not, while I am so near you. I am he that concerns himself for you, and will not stand by and see you perish.' Nothing needs be a terror to those that have Christ near them, and know he is theirs; no, not death itself.

May 14

All things work together for good

Romans 8:28

The apostle shows the privilege to which true Christians are entitled: the working together of all providences for the good of those that are Christ's, v.28.

Observe here:

(1) the character of the saints: *They love God.* This includes all the outgoings of the soul's affections towards God as the chief good and highest end. Those that love God make the best of all he does, and take all in good part. They are *the called according to his purpose*, effectually called according to the eternal purpose. The call is effectual, not according to any merit or desert of ours, but according to God's own gracious purpose.

(2) the privilege of the saints, that *all things work together for good to them*, that is, all the providences of God that concern them. All that God performs he performs for them. Their sins are not of his performing, therefore not intended here, though his permitting sin is made to work for their good. But all the providences of God are theirs—merciful providences, afflicting providences, personal, public. They are all for good; perhaps for temporal good, as Joseph's troubles; at least, for spiritual and eternal good. Either directly or indirectly, every providence has a tendency to the spiritual good of those that love God, breaking them off from sin, bringing them nearer to God, weaning them from the world, fitting them for heaven.

Work together. They work, as medicine works upon the body in various ways according to the intention of the physician; but all for the patient's good. *They work together*, as several ingredients in a medicine concur to answer the intention.

He worketh all things together for good; so some read it. It is not from any specific quality in the providences themselves, but from the power and grace of God working in, with, and by, these providences. All this *we know*—know it for a certainty, from the word of God, from our own experience, and from the experience of all the saints.

[113]

May 15

The God of all comfort

The object of the apostle's thanksgiving, to whom he offers up praise, is the blessed God, whom he describes by several glorious titles:

The God and Father of our Lord Jesus Christ God is the Father of Christ's divine nature by eternal generation, of his human nature by miraculous conception in the womb of the virgin, and of Christ as God-man, and our Redeemer, by covenant-relation, and in and through him as Mediator our God and our Father.

The Father of mercies. There is a multitude of tender mercies in God essentially, and all mercies are from God originally: mercy is his genuine offspring and his delight.

The God of all comfort; from him proceedeth the Comforter, the Holy Spirit. He giveth the earnest of the Spirit in our hearts. All our comforts come from God, and our sweetest comforts are in him.

The reasons of the apostle's thanksgivings are these:

(1) the benefits that he himself and his companions had received from God; for God *had comforted* them *in all their tribulation*, v.4. In the world they had trouble, but in Christ they had peace. The apostles met with many tribulations, but they found comfort in them all: their sufferings (which are called *the sufferings of Christ*, v.5, because Christ sympathized with his members when suffering for his sake) did abound, but their consolation by Christ did abound also.

(2) the advantage which others might receive; for God intended that they *should be able to comfort others* in trouble, v.4, by communicating to them their experiences of the divine goodness and mercy. What favours God bestows on us are intended not only to make us cheerful ourselves, but also that we may be useful to others.

Loving God

Matthew 22:36–38

Here we have Christ's answer to the lawyer's question, v.36; it is well for us that such a question was asked him, that we might have his answer.

All the law is fulfilled in one word, and that is, *love*. All obedience begins in the affections, and nothing in religion is done right, that is not done there first. Love is the leading affection, which gives law, and gives ground, to the rest; and therefore that, as the main fort, is to be first secured and garrisoned for God.

Thou shalt love the Lord thy God: the first commandment is: *Thou shalt have no other God*; which implies that we must have him for our God, and that will engage our love to him.

We are directed to love him *with all our heart, and soul, and mind.* Some make these to signify one and the same thing, to love him with all our powers; others distinguish them; the heart, soul, and mind, are the will, affections, and understanding. Our love of God must be a sincere love, and not in word and tongue only, as there are some who say they love him, but their hearts are not with him. It must be a strong love, we must love him in the most intense degree; as we must praise him, so we must love him, *with all that is within us.* It must be a singular and superlative love, we must love him more than anything else; this way the stream of our affections must entirely run. The heart must be united to love God, in opposition to a divided heart. *This is the first and great commandment*; for obedience to this is the spring of obedience to all the rest; which is then only acceptable, when it flows from love.

May 17

Loving our neighbour as ourselves

Matthew 22:39–40

To *love our neighbour as ourselves* is the second great commandment, v.39; it *is like unto that first*; it is inclusive of all the precepts of the second table, as that is of the first. It is *like* it, for it is founded upon it, and flows from it; and a right love to our brother, whom we have seen, is both an instance and an evidence of our *love to God, whom we have not seen.*

It is implied, that we do, and should, love ourselves. There is a self-love which is corrupt, and the root of the greatest sins, and it must be put off and mortified: but there is a self-love which is natural, and the rule of the greatest duty, and it must be preserved and sanctified. We must love ourselves, that is, we must have a due regard to the dignity of our own natures, and a due concern for the welfare of our own souls and bodies.

It is prescribed, that we *love our neighbour as ourselves*. We must honour and esteem all men, and must wrong and injure none; must have a good will to all, and good wishes for all, and, as we have opportunity, must do good to all. We must love our neighbour as ourselves, as truly and sincerely as we love ourselves, and in the same instances; no, in many cases we must deny ourselves for the good of our neighbour, and must make ourselves servants to the true welfare of others, and be willing to spend and be spent for them, to *lay down our lives for the brethren*.

Observe what the weight and greatness of these commandments is, v.40: *On these two commandments hang all the law and the prophets*; that is, this is the sum and substance of all those precepts relating to practical religion which were written in men's hearts by nature, revived by Moses, and backed and enforced by the preaching and writing of the prophets. All hang upon the law of love; take away this, and all falls to the ground, and comes to nothing.

May 18

The demonstration of love

Christ washed his disciples' feet that he might give a proof of that great love with which he loved them.

It is here laid down as an undoubted truth that our Lord Jesus, *having loved his own that were in the world, loved them to the end*, v.1. This is true of the disciples that were his immediate followers, in particular the twelve. These were his own in the world, his family, his school, his bosom friends. Children he had none to call his own, but he adopted them, and took them as his own. These he loved, he called them into fellowship with himself, conversed familiarly with them, was always tender of them, and of their comfort and reputation. He loved them to the end, continued his love to them as long as he lived, and after his resurrection; he never took away his loving kindness.

It is also true of all believers, for these twelve patriarchs were the representatives of all the tribes of God's spiritual Israel. Christ has a warm love for his own that are in the world. He *did* love them with a love of goodwill when he gave himself for their redemption. He *does* love them with a love of satisfaction when he admits them into communion with himself.

Those whom Christ loves *he loves to the end*; he is constant in his love to his people; he rests in his love. He loves with an everlasting love, from everlasting in the counsels of it to everlasting in the consequences of it. Nothing can separate a believer from the love of Christ.

True humility

John 13:3–5

Christ washed his disciples' feet that he might give an instance of his own wonderful humility, and show how lowly and condescending he was, and let all the world know how low he could stoop in love to his own. This is intimated, v.3–5. *Jesus knowing*, and now actually considering, and perhaps discoursing of, his honours as Mediator, and telling his friends that *the Father had given all things into his hand, rises from supper*, and, to the great surprise of the company, who wondered what he was going to do, *washed his disciples' feet*.

Here is the voluntary abasement of our Lord Jesus. *Jesus knowing* his own glory as God, and his own authority and power as Mediator, one would think it should follow, *he rises from supper*, lays aside his ordinary garments, calls for robes, bids them keep their distance, and do him homage; but no, quite the contrary, when he considered this he gave the greatest instance of humility. A well-grounded assurance of heaven and happiness, instead of puffing a man up with pride, will make and keep him very humble. Those that would be found conformable to Christ, and partakers of his Spirit, must study to keep their minds low in the midst of the greatest advancements.

Now that which Christ humbled himself to was to *wash his disciples' feet*. The action itself was mean and servile, and that which servants of the lowest rank were employed in. If he had washed their hands or faces, it had been great condescension; but for Christ to stoop to such a piece of drudgery as this may well excite our admiration. Thus he would teach us to think nothing below us in which we may be of service to God's glory and to the good of our brethren.

May 20

False humility

John 13:8

Christ washed his disciples' feet that he might signify to them spiritual washing, and the cleansing of the soul from the pollutions of sin. Here we may observe, Peter's peremptory refusal to let Christ wash his feet, v.8: *Thou shalt by no means wash my feet; no, never.* So it is in the original. It is the language of a fixed resolution. Here was a show of humility and modesty. Under this show of humility there was a real contradiction to the will of the Lord Jesus: '*I will wash thy feet,*' said Christ; 'But thou never shalt,' said Peter, 'It is not a fitting thing;' so making himself wiser than Christ. It is not humility, but infidelity, to put away the offers of the gospel, as if too rich to be made to us or too good news to be true.

Christ insists upon his offer, and gives a good reason to Peter why he should accept it: *If I wash thee not, thou hast no part with me.* This may be taken as a declaration of the necessity of spiritual washing: '*If I wash not* thy soul from the pollution of sin, *thou hast no part with me*, no interest in me, no communion with me, no benefit by me.'

All those, and those only, that are spiritually washed by Christ, have a part in Christ. It is necessary to our having a part in Christ that he washes us. All those whom Christ owns and saves he justifies and sanctifies, and both are included in his washing them. We cannot partake of his glory if we partake not of his merit and righteousness, and of his Spirit and grace.

May 21

An example to follow

John 13:14

Christ washed his disciples' feet to set before us an example. Observe the lesson that he taught: *You also ought to wash one another's feet*, v.14. Some have understood this literally, but doubtless it is to be understood figuratively; it is an instructive sign, but not sacramental, as the eucharist. This was a parable to the eye; and two things our Master designed to teach us by it:

(1) a humble condescension. We must learn of our Master to be *lowly in heart*, and walk with all lowliness; we must think lowly of ourselves and respectfully of our brethren, and deem nothing below us but sin. Christ had often taught his disciples humility, and they had forgotten the lesson; but now he teaches them in such a way as surely they could never forget.

(2) a condescension to be of service to others. To wash one another's feet is to stoop to the lowliest offices of love, for the real good and benefit one of another, as blessed Paul, who, though free from all, made himself *servant of all*; and the blessed Jesus, who *came not to be ministered unto, but to minister*. We must not grudge to take care and pains, and to spend time, and to diminish ourselves for the good of those to whom we are not under any particular obligations, even of our inferiors, and such as are not in a capacity of making us any requital.

Further, the duty is mutual; we must both accept help from our brethren and afford help to our brethren.

May 22

A new commandment

John 13:34

Our Lord Jesus discourses with his disciples concerning the great duty of brotherly love, v.34,35: *You shall love one another*. Judas had now gone out, and had proved himself a false brother; but they must not therefore harbour such jealousies and suspicions one of another as would be the bane of love: though there was one Judas among them, yet they were not all Judases.

A new commandment I give unto you, v.34. He not only commends it as pleasant, not only counsels it as excellent and profitable, but commands it, and makes it one of the fundamental laws of his kingdom; it goes side by side with the command of believing in Christ. It is the command of our ruler, who has a right to give law to us; it is the command of our Redeemer, who gives us this law in order to the curing of our spiritual diseases and the preparing of us for our eternal bliss.

It is *a new commandment*; that is it is a renewed commandment; it was a commandment from the beginning, as old as the law of nature, it was the second great commandment of the law of Moses; yet this commandment has been so corrupted by the traditions of the Jewish church that when Christ revived it, and set it in a true light, it might well be called a *new commandment*. Laws of revenge and retaliation were so much in vogue, and self-love had so much the ascendant that the law of brotherly love was forgotten as obsolete and out of date; so that as it came from Christ new, it was new to the people. As Christ gives it, it is new. Before it was, *Thou shalt love thy neighbour*; now it is, You shall love *one another*; it is pressed in a more winning way when it is thus pressed as mutual duty owing to one another.

May 23

The badge of discipleship

John 13:35

By this shall all men know that you are my disciples, if you have love one to another, v.35. Brotherly love is the badge of Christ's disciples. By this he knows them, by this they may know themselves, and by this others may know them. This is the livery of his family, the distinguishing character of his disciples; this he would have them noted for, as that in which they excel.

This was what their Master was famous for; all that ever heard of him have heard of his great love. Whereas the way of the world is to be everyone for himself, Christ's disciples should be hearty to one another. He does not say, *By this shall men know* that you are my disciples—if you work miracles, for a worker of miracles is but a cipher without charity; but *if you love one another* from a principle of self-denial and gratitude to Christ. This Christ would have to be the principal note of the true church.

It is the true honour of Christ's disciples to excel in brotherly love. Nothing will be more effectual than this to recommend them to the esteem and respect of others. The adversaries of the early church took notice of it, and said, 'See how these Christians love one another.'

If the followers of Christ do not love one another, they not only cast an unjust reproach upon their profession, but give just cause to suspect their own sincerity. When our brethren stand in need of help from us, and we have an opportunity of being of service to them, when they differ in opinion and practice from us, or are in any way rivals with or provoking to us, and so we have an occasion to condescend and forgive, in such cases as this it will be known whether we have this badge of Christ's disciples.

May 24

The coming of Christ

Matthew 3:11

Here is the dignity and pre-eminence of Christ above John. See how lowly John speaks of himself, that he might magnify Christ, v.11: '*I indeed baptize you with water*, that is the utmost I can do.' But *he that comes after me is mightier than I*. Though John had much power, Christ had more; though John was truly great, great in the sight of the Lord (not a greater was born of woman), yet he thinks himself unworthy to be in the lowliest place of attendance upon Christ, *whose shoes I am not worthy to bear*.

Here, too, is the intention of Christ's appearing, which they were now speedily to expect.

He shall baptize you with the Holy Ghost and with fire. It is Christ's prerogative to baptize *with the Holy Ghost*. This he did in the extraordinary gifts of the Spirit conferred upon the apostles, to which Christ himself applies these words of John. This he does in the graces and comforts of the Spirit given to them that ask him.

They who are baptized with the Holy Ghost are baptized as *with fire*. Is fire enlightening? So the Spirit is a Spirit of illumination. Is it warming? And do not their hearts burn within them? Is it consuming? And does not the Spirit of judgment, as a Spirit of burning, consume the dross of their corruption? Does fire make all it seizes like itself? And does it move upwards? So does the Spirit make the soul holy like itself, and its tendency is heavenward.

May 25

The Comforter

Christ here promises the Spirit: this great and unspeakable blessing
to them. It is promised that they shall have *another Comforter*. This is
the great New Testament promise, as that of the Messiah was of the
Old Testament; a promise adapted to the present distress of the
disciples, who were in sorrow, and needed a Comforter. Observe
here:

(1) the blessing promised: the word is used only here in these
discourses of Christ, and 1 John 2:1, where we translate it an
advocate. The office of the Spirit was to be Christ's advocate with
them and others, to plead his cause, and take care of his concerns,
on earth, and to be their advocate with their opposers.

While they had Christ with them he excited and exhorted them to
their duty; but now that he is going he leaves one with them that
shall do this as effectually, though silently.

(2) the giver of this blessing: *The Father* shall give him, *my Father*
and *your Father*; it includes both. The same that gave the Son to be
our Saviour will give his Spirit to be our Comforter, pursuant to the
same design.

(3) how this blessing is procured—by the intercession of the Lord
Jesus: *I will pray the Father*: the gift of the Spirit is a fruit of Christ's
mediation, purchased by his merit, and taken out by his
intercession.

(4) the continuance of this blessing: *That he may abide with you for
ever*. 'With you, as long as you live. You shall never know the want of
a Comforter, nor lament his departure, as you are now lamenting
mine.'

May 26

The Spirit of truth

John 14:17

This Comforter is the *Spirit of truth, whom you know,* v.17. The disciples might think it impossible to have a Comforter equivalent to him who is the Son of God: Christ says, 'You shall have the Spirit of God, who is equal in power and glory with the Son.'

The Comforter promised is the *Spirit of truth.* He will be true to you, and to his undertaking for you, which he will perform to the utmost. He will *teach you the truth,* will enlighten your minds with the knowledge of it, will strengthen and confirm your belief of it, and will increase your love to it.

He is one *whom the world cannot receive; but you know him. Therefore he abideth with you.* The disciples of Christ are here distinguished from the world, for they are chosen and called out of the world that lies in wickedness; they are the children and heirs of another world, not of this. It is the misery of those that are devoted to the world that they *cannot receive* the Spirit of truth.

The best knowledge of the Spirit of truth is that which is got by experience: *You know him, for he dwelleth with you.* Christ had dwelt with them, and by their acquaintance with him they could not but know *the Spirit of truth.* Those that have an experimental acquaintance with the Spirit have a comfortable assurance of his continuance: He *dwelleth with you, and shall be in you,* for the blessed Spirit does not shift his lodging. Their communion with him shall be intimate, and their union with him inseparable.

May 27

The teacher

John 14:26

Christ comforts his disciples with the encouragement that they should be under the tuition of his Spirit. They are to expect another teacher, and that Christ would find a way of speaking to them after his departure from them, v.26.

'The Father will send him *in my name*; that is, for my sake, at my special instance and request;' or, 'as my agent and representative.' He came in his Father's name, as his ambassador: the Spirit comes in his name, as resident in his absence, to carry on his undertaking, and to ripen things for his second coming. Hence he is called *the Spirit of Christ*; for he pleads his cause and does his work.

Note the two things he shall do. *He shall teach you all things*, as a Spirit of wisdom and revelation. Christ was a teacher to his disciples; if he left them now that they have made so little proficiency, what will become of them? Why, the Spirit shall teach them, he shall be their standing tutor. He shall teach them all things necessary for them either to learn themselves or to teach others. For those that would teach the things of God; this is the Spirit's work.

He shall bring all things to your remembrance, whatsoever I have said unto you. Many a good lesson Christ had taught them, which they had forgotten, and which would be sought for when they had occasion for it. Many things they did not retain the remembrance of, because they did not rightly understand the meaning of them. The Spirit shall not teach them a new gospel, but bring to their minds that which they had been taught, by leading them into the understanding of it. To all the saints the Spirit of grace is given to be a remembrancer, and to him by faith and prayer we should commit the keeping of what we hear and know.

May 28

The guide

John 16:13

The coming of the Spirit would be of unspeakable advantage to the disciples themselves. The Spirit has work to do, not only on the enemies of Christ, to convince and humble them, v.8–11, but upon his servants and agents, to instruct and comfort them; and therefore it was *expedient for them that he should go away*.

Christ assures them of sufficient assistance by the pouring out of the Spirit. They were now conscious to themselves of great dullness, and many mistakes; and what shall they do now their Master is leaving them? '*But when he, the Spirit of truth is come*, all will be well.'

Well indeed; for he shall undertake to guide the apostles, and glorify Christ.

The Spirit will take care that they do not miss their way: *He will guide you*, as the camp of Israel was guided through the wilderness by *the pillar of cloud and fire*. The Spirit guided their tongues in speaking, and their pens in writing, to secure them from mistakes. The Spirit is given us to be our guide, not only to show us the way, but to go along with us, by his continuing aids and influences.

He will guide them into all truth, as the skilful pilot guides the ship into the port it is bound for. To be led *into a truth* is more than barely to know it; it is to be intimately and experimentally acquainted with it; to be strongly affected with it; not only to have the notion of it in our heads, but the relish and savour and power of it in our hearts; it denotes a gradual discovery of truth shining more and more.

May 29

He shall glorify me

John 16:14–15

The Spirit undertakes to *glorify* Christ, v.14,15. Even the sending of the Spirit was the glorifying of Christ. God the Father glorified him in heaven, and the Spirit glorified him on earth. It was the honour of the Redeemer that the Spirit was both sent in his name and sent on his errand, to carry on and perfect his undertaking. All the gifts and graces of the Spirit, all the preaching and all the writing of the apostles, under the influence of the Spirit, the tongues, and miracles, were to glorify Christ.

The Spirit glorified Christ by leading his followers into *the truth as it is in Jesus*. Christ assures them that the Spirit would communicate the things of Christ to them: *He shall receive of mine, and shall show it unto you*. As in essence *he proceeded from the Son*, so in influence and operation he derives from him. *He shall take of that which is mine*. All that the Spirit shows us, that it applies to us, for our instruction and comfort, all that he gives us for our strength and quickening, and all that he secures and seals to us, all belonged to Christ, and was had and received from him. All was his, for he bought it, and paid dearly for it, and therefore he had reason to call it his own; his, for he first received it; it was given him as the head of the church, to be communicated by him to all his members.

In the Spirit, the things of God are communicated to us. Lest any should think that the receiving of this would not make them much the richer, he adds, *All things that the Father hath are mine.* Spiritual blessings in heavenly things are given by the Father to the Son for us, and the Son entrusts the Spirit to convey them to us.

May 30

The promise of the Father

Acts 1:4

Here we have the assurance Christ gave the disciples that their waiting was not in vain. *You shall be baptized with the Holy Ghost*; that is 'The Holy Ghost shall be poured out upon you more plentifully than ever.' They had already been breathed upon with the Holy Ghost (John 20:22), and they had found the benefit of it; but now they shall have larger measures of his gifts, graces, and comforts, and *be baptized with them*, in which there seems to be an allusion to those Old Testament promises of the pouring out of the Spirit.

This gift of the Holy Ghost he speaks of as *the promise of the Father, which they had heard of him.* and might therefore depend upon. The Spirit was given by promise, and it was at this time the great promise, as that of the Messiah was before, and that of eternal life is now. The Spirit of God is not given as the spirit of men is given us, and formed within us, by a course of nature, but by the word of God.

That the gift may be the more valuable, Christ thought the promise of the Spirit a legacy worth leaving to his church. It was *the promise of the Father*: of *Christ's* Father. Christ, as Mediator, had an eye to God as his Father, fathering his design, and owning it all along. Of *our* Father, who, if he give us *the adoption of sons*, will certainly give us *the Spirit of adoption*. He will give the Spirit, as the *Father of lights*, as *the Father of spirits*, and as *the Father of mercies*; it is *the promise of the Father*.

May 31

You shall be my witnesses

Christ here appoints the disciples to their work, and with authority assures them of an ability to go on with it, and of success in it.

Christ here tells them:

(1) that their work should be honourable and glorious: *You shall be witnesses unto me*. They shall proclaim him king, and declare those truths to the world by which his kingdom should be set up, and he would rule.

(2) that their power for this work should be sufficient. They had not strength of their own for it, nor wisdom nor courage enough. '*But you shall receive the power of the Holy Ghost coming upon you*'; you shall be animated and actuated by a better spirit than your own; you shall have power to preach the gospel.

(3) that their influence should be great and very extensive: '*You shall be witnesses* for Christ *in Jerusalem*; there you must begin, and many there will receive your testimony; and those that do not will be left inexcusable. Your light shall then shine throughout all Judaea, where before you have laboured in vain. Then you shall proceed *to Samaria*, though at your first mission you were forbidden to preach in *any of the cities of the Samaritans*. Your usefulness shall reach *to the uttermost part of the earth*, and you shall be a blessing to the whole world.'

June 1

The day of Pentecost

Acts 2:1

We have here an account of the descent of the Holy Ghost upon the disciples of Christ. Observe when and where this was done. This feast of Pentecost happened on *the first day of the week*, which was an additional honour put on that day, and a confirmation of it to be the Christian sabbath, *the day which the Lord hath made*, to be a standing memorial in his church of those two great blessings—the resurrection of Christ, and the pouring out of the Spirit, both on that day of the week. This serves not only to justify us in observing that day under the style and title of *the Lord's day*, but to direct us in the sanctifying of it to give God praise particularly for those two great blessings.

It was when they were all with one accord in one place. Here the disciples were in one place, and they were not as yet so many but that one place, and no large one, would hold them all. And here they were *with one accord*. We cannot forget how often, while their Master was with them, there were *strifes among them, who should be the greatest*; but now all these strifes were at an end, we hear no more of them. Let us be all of one accord, and, in spite of a variety of sentiments and interests, as no doubt there was among those disciples, let us agree to love one another; for, where *brethren dwell together in unity*, there it is that *the Lord commands his blessing*.

June 2

Tongues of fire

Acts 2:2–3

Observe here how the Holy Ghost came upon them. Here is an audible summons given them to awaken their expectations of something great, v.2. It is here said that it came *suddenly*, did not rise gradually, as common winds do, but was at the height immediately.

It was a *sound from heaven*. It was *a rushing mighty wind*; it was strong and violent, and came not only with a great noise, but with great force, as if it would bear down all before it. This was to signify the powerful influences and operations of the Spirit of God upon the minds of men, and thereby upon the world. *It filled* not only the room, but *all the house where they were sitting*.

Here is a visible sign of the gift they were to receive. They saw *cloven tongues, like as of fire*, v.3, and those cloven tongues, that is the Spirit (signified thereby), rested upon each of them. There was an appearance of something like flaming fire lighting on every one of them, which divided asunder, and so formed the resemblance of tongues.

There was an outward sign for the confirming of the faith of the disciples themselves, and for the convincing of others. The sign given was fire, that John Baptist's saying concerning Christ might be fulfilled, *He shall baptize you with the Holy Ghost and with fire*. This fire appeared in cloven tongues. The operations of the Spirit were many; that of speaking with diverse tongues was one, and was singled out to be the first indication of the gift of the Holy Ghost and to that this sign had a reference.

June 3

Filled with the Holy Spirit

Acts 2:4

They were all filled with the Holy Ghost, more plentifully and powerfully than the disciples were before. They were filled with the graces of the Spirit, and were more than ever under his sanctifying influences—were now holy, and heavenly, and spiritual, more weaned from this world and better acquainted with the other. They were more filled with the comforts of the Spirit, rejoiced more than ever in the love of Christ and the hope of heaven, and in it all their griefs and fears were swallowed up. They were also, for the proof of this, filled with the gifts of the Holy Ghost, which are especially meant here; they were endued with miraculous powers for the furtherance of the gospel.

It seems evident that not only the twelve apostles, but all the hundred and twenty disciples were *filled with the Holy Ghost* alike at this time—all the seventy disciples, who were apostolic men, and employed in the same work, and all the rest too that were to preach the gospel.

They began to speak with other tongues, besides their native language, though they had never learned any other. They spoke not matters of common conversation, but the word of God, and the praises of his name, *as the Spirit gave them utterance*.

Now this was a very great miracle; it was a miracle upon the mind (and so had most of the nature of a gospel miracle), for in the mind words are framed.

This was also a very proper and needful miracle. The disciples were commissioned to *preach the gospel to every creature*, to disciple *all nations*. But here is an insuperable difficulty at the threshold. How

[130]

shall they master the several languages so as to speak intelligibly to all nations? To prove that Christ could give authority to preach to the nations, he gives ability to preach to them in their own language.

June 4

True spirituality

Romans 8:9

You are not in the flesh, but in the Spirit. This expresses states and conditions of the soul vastly different. All the saints have flesh and spirit in them; but to be in the flesh and to be in the Spirit are contrary. It denotes our being overcome and subdued by one of these principles. As we say, a man is in love, that is, overcome by it.

Now the great question is whether we are in the flesh or in the Spirit; and how may we come to know it? Why, by enquiring whether the Spirit of God dwells in us. The Spirit visits many that are unregenerate with his motions, which they resist and quench; but in all that are sanctified he dwells; there he resides and rules. He is there as a man at his own house, where he is constant and welcome, and has the dominion.

If any man has not the Spirit of Christ, he is none of his. To be Christ's (that is, to be a Christian indeed, one of his children, his servants, his friends, in union with him) is a privilege and honour which many pretend to have no part nor lot in the matter. None are his but those that have his Spirit; that is are spirited as he was spirited—are meek, lowly, humble, peaceable, patient, and charitable as he was—and are actuated and guided by the Holy Spirit of God, as a sanctifier, teacher, and Comforter.

June 5

Life in the Spirit

Romans 8:11–13

The same Spirit that raises the soul now will raise the body shortly: *By his Spirit that dwelleth in you.* The bodies of the saints are the temples of the Holy Ghost. Hence the apostle infers how much it is our duty to walk not after the flesh, but after the Spirit, v.12,13. Let not our life be after the wills and motions of the flesh.

Two motives he mentions here:

(1) We are not debtors to the flesh, neither by relation, gratitude, nor any other bond of obligation. We owe no service to our carnal desires; we are indeed bound to clothe, and feed, and take care of the body, as a servant to the soul in the service of God, but no further. We are not debtors to it; the flesh never did us so much kindness as to oblige us to serve it.

(2) Consider the consequences, what will be at the end of the way. Here are life and death, blessing and cursing, set before us. *If you live after the flesh, you shall die*; that is, die eternally. It is the pleasing, and serving, and gratifying, of the flesh, that are the ruin of souls. Dying indeed is the soul's dying; the death of the saints is but a sleep.

But, on the other hand, *You shall live*, live and be happy to eternity; that is the true life: *If you through the Spirit mortify the deeds of the body,* subdue and keep under all fleshly lusts and affections, deny yourselves in the pleasing of the body, and this through the Spirit; we cannot do it without the Spirit working it in us, and the Spirit will not do it without our doing our endeavour.

June 6

Children of God

Romans 8:14–15

The *Spirit of adoption* is another privilege belonging to those that are in Christ Jesus. All that are Christ's are taken into the relation of children to God, v.14. They are *led by the Spirit of God* as a scholar in his learning is led by his tutor, as a traveller in his journey is led by his guide, as a soldier in his engagements is led by his captain; not driven as beasts, but led as rational creatures, drawn with the cords of a man and the bands of love. It is the undoubted character of all true believers that they are led by the Spirit of God. Having submitted themselves in believing to his guidance, they do in their obedience follow that guidance, and are sweetly led into all truth and all duty.

Observe their privilege: *They are the sons of God*, received into the number of God's children by adoption, owned and loved by him as his children.

Those that are sons of God have the Spirit to work in them the disposition of children. *You have not received the spirit of bondage again to fear*, v.15. Of that spirit of bondage which many of the saints themselves were under at their conversion, under the convictions of sin and wrath set home by the Spirit, as those in Acts 2:37, the jailer (Acts 16:30), and Paul (Acts 9:6). Then the Spirit himself was to the saints a spirit of bondage: 'But,' says the apostle, 'with you this is over.' Though a child of God may come under fear of bondage again, and may be questioning his sonship, yet the blessed Spirit is not again a spirit of bondage, for then he would witness an untruth.

June 7

The Spirit of adoption

Romans 8:15–16

But you *have received the Spirit of adoption*. It is God's prerogative, when he adopts, to give a spirit of adoption—the nature of children. The Spirit of adoption works in the children of God a filial love to God as a Father, a delight in him, and a dependence upon him, as a Father. A sanctified soul bears the image of God, as the child bears the image of the father.

Whereby we cry, Abba, Father. Praying is here called crying, which is not only an earnest, but a natural, expression of desire; children that cannot speak vent their desires by crying.

Abba, Father. This denotes an affectionate endearing importunity, and a believing stress laid upon the relation. Little children, begging of their parents, can say little but Father, Father, and that is rhetoric enough.

[133]

The Spirit witnesses to the relation of children, v.16. *Beareth witness with our spirit.* Many a man has the witness of his own spirit to the goodness of his state who has not the concurring testimony of the Spirit. Many speak peace to themselves to whom the God of heaven does not speak peace. But those that are sanctified have God's Spirit witnessing with their spirits, which is to be understood not as any immediate extraordinary revelation, but an ordinary work of the Spirit, in and by the means of comfort, speaking peace to the soul. This testimony is always agreeable to the written word, and is therefore always grounded upon sanctification; for the Spirit in the heart cannot contradict the Spirit in the word.

June 8

The fruit of the Spirit

Galatians 5:22–23

The apostle specifies the fruits of the Spirit, or the renewed nature, which as Christians we are concerned to bring forth, v.22,23. And here we may observe that as sin is called *the work of the flesh*, because the flesh, or corrupt nature, is the principle that moves and excites men to it, so grace is said to be *the fruit of the Spirit*, because it wholly proceeds from the Spirit, as the fruit does from the root.

He particularly recommends to us, *love*, to God especially, and to one another for his sake,—*joy*, which may be understood as cheerfulness in our conduct with our friends, or rather a constant delight in God,—*peace*, with God and conscience, or a peaceableness of temper and behaviour towards others,—*longsuffering*, patience to defer anger, and a contentedness to bear injuries,—*gentleness*, such a sweetness of temper, and especially towards our inferiors, as disposes us to be affable and courteous, and easy to be entreated when any have wronged us,—*goodness* or kindness, which shows itself in a readiness to do good to all as we have opportunity,—*faith*, fidelity, justice, and honesty, in what we profess and promise to others,—*meekness*, with which to govern our passions and resentments, so as not to be easily provoked, and, when we are so, to be soon pacified,—and *temperance*, in food and drink, and other enjoyments of life, so as not to be excessive and immoderate in the use of them.

June 9

Be filled with the Spirit

Ephesians 5:17-18

Here the apostle warns against the sin of drunkenness: *And be not drunk with wine*, v.18. This was a sin very frequent among the heathens; and particularly on occasion of the festivals of their gods, therefore the apostle adds, *wherein*, or in which drunkenness *is excess*. This may signify 'luxury' or 'dissoluteness'; and it is certain that drunkenness is no friend to chastity and purity of life, but it virtually contains all manner of extravagance, and transports men into gross sensuality and vile enormities.

Instead of being filled with wine, he exhorts them to *be filled with the Spirit*. Those who are full of drink are not likely to be full of the Spirit; and therefore this duty is opposed to the former sin. The meaning of the exhortation is that men should labour for a plentiful measure of graces of the Spirit, that would fill their souls with great joy, strength, and courage, which things sensual men expect their wine should inspire them with. We cannot be guilty of any excess in our endeavours after these: no, we ought not to be satisfied with a little of the Spirit, but to be aspiring after greater measures, so as to be filled with the Spirit.

Now by this means we shall come to *understand what the will of the Lord is*; for the Spirit of God is given as a Spirit of wisdom and of understanding.

June 10

Spiritual worship

Ephesians 5:19-20

Because those who are filled with the Spirit will express themselves in acts of devotion, therefore the apostle exhorts them *to sing unto the Lord*, v.19. The joy of Christians should express itself in songs of praise to their God. In these they should *speak to themselves* in their assemblies and meetings together, for mutual edification. By *psalms* may be meant David's Psalms, or such composures as were fitly sung with musical instruments. By *hymns* may be meant such others as were confined to matter of praise, as those of Zacharias, Simeon, etc. *Spiritual songs* may contain a greater variety of matter, doctrinal, prophetical, historical, etc.

God's people have reason to rejoice, and to sing for joy. They are to *sing and to make melody in their hearts*; not only with their voices, but with inward affection.

Thanksgiving is another duty that the apostle exhorts to, v.20. We are appointed to sing psalms, etc., for the expression of our thankfulness to God; but, though we are not always singing, we should be *always giving thanks*; that is, we should never lack a disposition for this duty, as we never lack matter for it.

We must continue it throughout the whole course of our lives; and we should give thanks *for all things*; not only for spiritual blessings enjoyed, and eternal ones expected, but for temporal mercies too; not only for our comforts, but also for our sanctified afflictions; not only for what immediately concerns ourselves, but for the instances of God's kindness and favour to others also. It is our duty in everything *to give thanks unto God and the Father.*

June 11

The Spirit of God

1 Corinthians 2:10–11

We here see by whom the wisdom of God is discovered to us: *God hath revealed them to us by his Spirit*, v.10. The apostles spoke by inspiration of the same Spirit, as he taught them, and gave them utterance. Here is a proof of the divine authority of the holy scriptures. Paul wrote what he taught: and what he taught was revealed of God by his Spirit, *that Spirit that searches all things, yea, the deep things of God, and knows the things of God, as the spirit of a man that is in him knows the things of a man*, v.11.

A double argument is drawn from these words in proof of the divinity of the Holy Ghost: omniscience is attributed to him: *He searches all things, even the deep things of God.* He has exact knowledge of all things, and enters into the very depths of God, penetrates into his most secret counsels. Now who can have such a thorough knowledge of God but God?

This allusion seems to imply that the Holy Spirit is as much in God as a man's mind is in himself. Now the mind of the man is plainly essential to him. He cannot be without his mind. Nor can God be without his Spirit. He is as much and as intimately one with God as the man's mind is with the man. The man knows his own mind because his mind is one with himself. The Spirit of God knows the things of God because he is one with God.

And as no man can come at the knowledge of what is in another man's mind till he communicates and reveals it, so neither can we know the secret counsels and purposes of God till they are made known to us by his Holy Spirit. We cannot know them at all till he has proposed them objectively in the external revelation; we cannot know or believe them to salvation till he enlightens the faculty, opens the eye of the mind, and gives us such a knowledge and faith of them.

June 12

The revelation of the Spirit

1 Corinthians 2:12–13

It was by the Holy Spirit that the apostles had received the wisdom of God in a mystery, which they spoke. '*Now we have received not the spirit of the world, but the Spirit which is of God, that we might know the things freely given to us of God* (v.12); not the spirit which is in the *wise men of the world* (v.6), nor in the *rulers of the world* (v.8), but the *Spirit which is of God*, or proceedeth from God. It is by his gracious illumination and influence that *we know the things freely given to us of God* unto salvation'—that is the great privileges of the gospel, which are the free gift of God, distributions of mere and rich grace.

Though these things are given to us, and the revelation of this gift is made to us, we cannot know them to any saving purpose till we have the Spirit. The apostles had the revelation of these things from the Spirit of God, and the saving impression of them from the same Spirit.

We see here in what manner this wisdom was taught or communicated: *Which things we speak, not in the words which man's wisdom teaches, but which the Holy Ghost teaches*, v.13. The apostles had received the wisdom they taught, not from the wise men of the world, not from their own enquiry nor invention, but from the Spirit of God. Nor did they put a human dress on it, but plainly declared the doctrine of Christ, in terms also taught them by the Holy Spirit. He not only gave them the knowledge of these things, but gave them utterance. Observe, the truths of God need no garnishing by human skill or eloquence, but look best in the words which the Holy Ghost teaches. The Spirit of God knows much better how to speak of the things of God than the best critics, orators, or philosophers.

June 13

Babes in Christ

1 Corinthians 3:1-2

Paul blames the Corinthians for their weakness and non-proficiency. Those who are sanctified are so only in part: there is still room for growth and increase both in grace and knowledge. Those who through divine grace are renewed to a spiritual life may yet in many things be defective. The apostle tells *them he could not speak to them as unto spiritual* men, *but as unto carnal* men, *as to babes in Christ,* v.1.

They were so far from forming their maxims and measures upon the ground of divine revelation, and entering into the spirit of the gospel, that it was but too evident they were much under the command of carnal and corrupt affections. They were still mere babes in Christ. They had received some of the first principles of Christianity, but had not grown up to maturity of understanding in them, or of faith and holiness; and yet it is plain, from several passages in this epistle, that the Corinthians were very proud of their wisdom and knowledge.

It is but too common for persons of very moderate knowledge and understanding to have a great measure of self-conceit. The apostle assigns their little proficiency in the knowledge of Christianity as a reason why he had communicated no more of the deep things of it to them. They could not bear such food, they needed to be fed with milk, not with meat.

It is natural for babes to grow up to men; and babes in Christ should endeavour to grow in stature, and become men in Christ. It was a reproach to the Corinthians that they had so long sat under the ministry of Paul and had made no more improvement in Christian knowledge. Christians are utterly to blame who do not endeavour to grow in grace and knowledge.

June 14

The blessing of God

1 Corinthians 3:3–7

The apostle blames the Corinthians for their carnality, and mentions their contention and discord about their ministers as evidence of it: *For you are yet carnal; for whereas there are among you envying, and strife, and divisions, are you not carnal, and walk as men?* v.3. They had mutual emulations, quarrels, and factions among them, upon the account of their ministers, *while one said, I am of Paul; and another, I am of Apollos*, v.4. These were proofs of their being carnal, that fleshly interests and affections too much swayed them. The apostle instructs them how to cure this inclination and rectify what was amiss among them. He reminds them that the ministers about whom they contended were but ministers: *Who then is Paul, and who is Apollos, but ministers by whom you believed? Even as the Lord gave to every man*, v.5. They are but ministers, mere instruments used by the God of all grace. We should take care not to deify ministers nor put them into the place of God.

Paul had planted and Apollos had watered, v.6. Both were useful, one for one purpose, the other for another. God makes use of variety of instruments, and fits them to their several uses and intentions.

The success of the ministry must be derived from the divine blessing: *Neither he that planteth is any thing, nor he that watereth, but God who giveth the increase*, v.7. Even apostolical ministers are nothing of themselves, can do nothing with efficacy and success unless God give the increase. The best qualified and most faithful ministers have a just sense of their own insufficiency, and are very desirous that God should have all the glory of their success.

June 15

Building on the firm foundation

1 Corinthians 3:11–12

Here the apostle informs us what foundation he had laid at the bottom of all the labours among them—*even Jesus Christ, the chief cornerstone.* Upon this foundation all the faithful ministers of Christ built. Upon this rock all Christians found their hopes. Those that build their hopes of heaven on any other foundation build upon the sand. *Other foundation can no man lay besides what is laid—even Jesus Christ.*

The doctrine of our Saviour and his mediation is the principal doctrine of Christianity. It lies at the bottom, and is the foundation, of all the rest. Leave out this, and you lay waste all our comforts, and leave no foundation for our hopes as sinners. But of those that hold the foundation and embrace the general doctrine of Christ's being the mediator between God and man, there are two sorts:

(1) Some build upon this foundation *gold, silver, and precious stones,* v.12, namely those who receive and propagate the pure truths of the gospel, who hold nothing but the truth as it is in Jesus, and preach nothing else. This is building well upon a good foundation, when ministers not only depend upon Christ as the great prophet of the church, and take him for their guide and infallible teacher, but receive and spread the doctrines he taught, in their purity, without any corrupt mixtures, without adding or diminishing.

(2) Others *build wood, hay, and stubble* on this foundation; that is though they adhere to the foundation, they depart from the mind of Christ in many particulars, substitute their own fancies and inventions in the room of his doctrines and institutions, and build upon the good foundation what will not abide the test when the day of trial shall come, and the fire must make it manifest, as wood, hay, and stubble, will not bear the trial by fire, but must be consumed in it.

June 16

The test of fire

1 Corinthians 3:13–15

There is a time coming when a discovery will be made of what men have built on this foundation: *Every man's work shall be made manifest*, shall be laid open to view, to his own view and that of others. Some may, in the simplicity of their hearts, build wood and stubble on the good foundation, and know not what they have been doing; but in the day of the Lord their own conduct shall appear to them in its proper light.

For the day shall declare it (that is, every man's work), *because it shall be revealed by fire; and the fire shall try every man's work, of what sort it is*, v.13. The day shall declare and make it manifest, the last day, the great day of trial.

There is a day coming that will distinguish one man from another, and one man's work from another's, as the fire distinguishes gold from dross, or metal that will bear the fire from other materials that will be consumed in it.

In that day some men's works will withstand the trial—will be found standard. It will appear that they not only held the foundation, but that they built regularly and well upon it—that they laid on proper materials, and in due form and order.

There are others *whose works shall be burnt*, v.15, whose corrupt opinions and doctrines or vain inventions and usages in the worship of God, shall be discovered, disowned, and rejected, in that day—shall be first manifested to be corrupt, and then disapproved of God and rejected. A person's weakness and corruption will be the lessening of his glory, though he may in the general have been an honest and an upright Christian. He shall be saved, *yet so as by fire*, saved out of the fire. He himself shall be snatched out of that flame which will consume his work.

June 17

The temple of the Holy Spirit

1 Corinthians 3:16–17

Know you not that you are the temple of God, and that the Spirit of God dwelleth in you? This may be understood as referring to the church of Corinth collectively, or of every single believer among them; Christian churches are temples of God. He dwells among them by his Holy Spirit. Every Christian is a living temple of the living God.

God dwelt in the Jewish temple, took possession of it, and resided in it, by that glorious cloud that was the token of his presence with that people. So Christ by his Spirit dwells in all true believers. The temple was devoted and consecrated to God, and set apart from every common to a holy use, to the immediate service of God. So all Christians are separated from common uses, and set apart for God and his service. They are sacred to him—a very good argument against all fleshly lusts, and all doctrines that give countenance to them.

If we are temples of God, we must do nothing that shall alienate ourselves from him, or corrupt and pollute ourselves, and thereby unfit ourselves for his use; and we must hearken to no doctrine nor teacher that would seduce us to any such practices.

Christians are holy by profession, and should be pure and clean both in heart and conversation. We should heartily abhor, and carefully avoid, what will defile God's temple and prostitute what ought to be sacred to him.

June 18

Gifts of the Spirit

1 Corinthians 12:4–8

The spiritual gifts, though proceeding from the same Spirit, are different. They have one author and origin, but are themselves of various kinds. A free cause may produce a variety of effects; and the same giver may bestow various gifts, v.4. *There are diversities of gifts,* such as revelations, tongues, prophecy, interpretations of tongues; *but the same Spirit*. There are *differences of administrations*, or different offices, and officers to discharge them, different ordinances and institutions (see v.28–30), but the same Lord, who appointed all, v.6. *There are diversities of operations*, or miraculous powers, v.10, *but it is the same God that worketh all in all*. There are various gifts, administrations, and operations, but all proceed from one God, one Lord, one Spirit; that is, from Father, Son, and Holy Ghost, the spring and origin of all spiritual blessings and bequests: all issue from the same fountain; all have the same author. However different they may be in themselves, in this they agree; all are from God.

And several of the kinds are here specified. Several persons had their several gifts, some one, some another, all from and by the same Spirit. To one was given the *word of wisdom*; that is, say some, a knowledge of the mysteries of the gospel, and ability to explain them, an exact understanding of the design, nature, and doctrines of the Christian religion. Others say an uttering of grave sentences, like Solomon's proverbs. Some confine this word of wisdom to the revelations made to and by the apostles.

To another the word of knowledge, by the same Spirit; that is, say the knowledge of mysteries wrapped up in the prophecies, types, and histories of the Old Testament: say others, a skill and readiness to give advice and counsel in perplexed cases.

June 19

Grace gifts

1 Corinthians 12:9–11

The apostle continues to show the variety of spiritual gifts with which the first ministers and churches were blessed: *To another faith, by the same Spirit*; that is, the faith of miracles, or a faith in the divine power and promise, whereby they were enabled to work miracles; or an extraordinary impulse from above, whereby they were enabled to trust God in any emergency, and go on in the way of their duty, and own and profess the truths of Christ, whatever was the difficulty or danger.

To another the gifts of healing, by the same Spirit; that is, healing the sick, either by laying on of hands, or anointing with oil, or with a bare word.

To another the working of miracles; the efficacies of powers, such as raising the dead, restoring the blind to sight, giving speech to the dumb, hearing to the deaf, and the use of limbs to the lame.

To another prophecy, that is, ability to foretell future events, which is the more usual sense of prophecy; or to explain scripture by a peculiar gift of the Spirit.

To another the discerning of Spirits, power to distinguish between true and false prophets, or to discern the real and internal qualifications of any person for an office, or to discover the inward workings of the mind by the Holy Ghost.

To another divers kinds of tongues or ability to speak languages by inspiration. To another *the interpretation of tongues*, or ability to render foreign languages readily and properly into their own.

All these worketh one and the same Spirit, dividing to every man as he will. It is according to the sovereign pleasure of the donor. What is more free than a gift? And shall not the Spirit of God do what he will with his own? It is not as men will, nor as they may think fit, but as the Spirit pleases. But though he distributes these gifts freely and uncontrollably, they are intended by him, not for private honour and advantage, but for public benefit, for the edification of the body, the church.

June 20

The body of Christ

1 Corinthians 12:12–13

The apostle here compares the church of Christ to a human body by telling us that one body may have many members, and that the many members of the same body make but one body, v.12: *As the body is one, and hath many members, and all the members of that one body, being many, are one body, so also is Christ*; that is, Christ mystical. Christ and his church making one body, as head and members, this body is made up of many parts or members, yet but one body; for all the members are *baptized into the same body, and made to drink of the same Spirit*, v.13.

Jews and Gentiles, bond and free, are upon a level in this: all are baptized into the same body, and made partakers of the same Spirit. Christians become members of this body by baptism: they are baptized into one body. The outward rite is of divine institution, significant of the new birth, called therefore *the washing of regeneration*. But it is by the Spirit, by the renewing of the Holy Ghost, that we are made members of Christ's body. It is the Spirit's operation, signified by the outward administration, that makes us members.

The outward administration is a means appointed of God for our participation in this great benefit; but it is baptism by the Spirit, it is internal renovation and drinking into one Spirit, partaking of his sanctifying influence from time to time, that makes us true members of Christ's body, and maintains our union with him. Being animated by one Spirit makes Christians one body.

All who have the Spirit of Christ, without difference, are the members of Christ, whether Jew or Gentile, bond or free; and none but such. And all the members of Christ make up one body; the members many, but the body one. They are one body, because they have one principle of life; all are quickened and animated by the same Spirit.

June 21

Many parts, yet one body

1 Corinthians 12:15–20

Every member of the body mystical cannot have the same place and office; but what then? Shall it then disown any relation to the body? Because it is not fixed in the same position, or favoured with the same gifts as others, shall it say, 'I do not belong to Christ'? No, the lowliest member of his body is as much a member as the noblest, and as truly regarded by him. All his members are dear to him.

There must be a distinction of members in the body: *Were the whole body an eye, where were the hearing? Were the whole hearing, where were the smelling?* v.17. *If all were one member, where were the body?* v.19. *They are many members*, and for that reason must have distinction among them, and yet *are but one body*, v.20. One member of a body is not a body; this is made up of many; and among these many there must be a distinction, difference of situation, shape, use, etc.

So it is in the body of Christ; its members must have different uses, and therefore have different powers, and be in different places, some having one gift, and others a different one. Variety in the members of the body contributes to the beauty of it. What a monster would a body be if it were all ear, or eye, or arm! So it is for the beauty and good appearance of the church that there should be diversity of gifts and offices in it.

The disposal of members in a natural body, and their situation, are as God pleases: *But now hath God set the members, every one of them, in the body, as it hath pleased him*, v.18. We may plainly perceive the divine wisdom in the distribution of the members; but it was made according to the counsel of his will; he distinguished and distributed them as he pleased. So is it also in the members of Christ's body: they are chosen to such positions and endued with such gifts as God pleases.

June 22

Diversity of gifts

1 Corinthians 12:21–22

All the members of the body are, in some respect, useful and necessary to each other: *The eye cannot say to the hand, I have no need of thee; nor the head to the feet, I have no need of you: no, those members of the body which seem to be more feeble are necessary* (v.21,22); God has so fitted and tempered them together that they are all necessary to one another, and to the whole body; there is no part redundant and unnecessary.

Every member serves some good purpose or other: it is useful to its fellow-members, and necessary to the good state of the whole body. Nor is there a member of the body of Christ but may and ought to be useful to his fellow-members, and at some times, and in some cases, is needful to them.

None should despise and envy another, seeing God has made the distinction between them as he pleased, yet so as to keep them all in some degree of mutual dependence, and make them valuable to each other, and concerned for each other, because of their mutual usefulness.

Those who excel in any gift cannot say that they have no need of those who in that gift are their inferiors, while perhaps, in other gifts, they exceed them. No, the lowest members of all have their use, and the highest cannot do well without them. The eye has need of the hand, and the head of the feet.

June 23

Live a new life

John 3:3

Birth is the beginning of life; to be *born again* is to begin anew, as those that have up to that time lived either much amiss or to little purpose. We must not think to patch up the old building, but begin from the foundation.

We must have a new nature, new principles, new affections, new aims. We must be born both 'again', and 'from above'. We must be born *anew*; by our first birth we are corrupt, shapen in sin and iniquity; we must therefore undergo a second birth; our souls must be fashioned and enlivened anew. We must be born *from above*; this new birth has its origin *from* heaven and its tendency *to* heaven.

Christ shows the indispensable necessity of the new birth: 'Except *a man* (anyone that partakes of the human nature, and consequently of its corruptions) *be born again, he cannot see the kingdom of God*, the kingdom of the Messiah begun in grace and perfected in glory.'

Unless we are *born from above*, we cannot *see* this. We cannot understand the nature of the kingdom of God. Such is the nature of things pertaining to the kingdom of God that the soul must be remodelled and moulded, the natural man must become a spiritual man, before he is capable of receiving and understanding them. And unless we are born from above, we cannot receive the comfort of the kingdom of God, cannot expect any benefit by Christ and his gospel, nor have any part or lot in the matter.

June 24

The new birth

John 3:5-7

The Lord Jesus explains to Nicodemus:

(1) the *author* of this blessed change, and who it is that works it. To be born again is to be *born of the Spirit*. The change is not brought about by any wisdom or power of our own, but by the power and influence of the blessed Spirit of grace.

(2) the *nature* of this change, and what it is which is brought about; it is *spirit*, v.6. Those that are regenerated are made spiritual, and refined from the dross and dregs of sensuality. The Pharisees placed their religion in external purity and external performances; and it would be a mighty change indeed with them, no less than a new birth, to become spiritual.

(3) the *necessity* of this change. Christ makes it necessary by his own word: *Marvel not that I said unto thee, You must be born again*, v.7. We are not to *marvel* at it; for when we consider the holiness of the God with whom we have to do, the great design of our redemption, the depravity of our nature, and the constitution of the happiness set before us, we shall not think it strange that so much stress is laid upon this as the one thing needful, that we must be born again.

June 25

Water and wind

John 3:5-8

The change of the new birth is illustrated by two comparisons.

The regenerating work of the Spirit is compared to *water*, v.5. To be born again is to be *born of water and of the Spirit*, that is, of the Spirit working like water. That which is primarily intended here is to show that the Spirit, in sanctifying a soul, cleanses and purifies it as water, takes away its filth, by which it was unfit for the kingdom of God. The Spirit also cools and refreshes the soul, as water does the hunted hart and the weary traveller.

[148]

It is compared to *wind: The wind bloweth where it listeth, so is every one that is born of the Spirit*, v.8. The same word signifies both the wind and the Spirit. This comparison is here used to show that the Spirit, in regeneration, works *arbitrarily*, and as a free agent. The Spirit dispenses his influences where, and when, on whom, and in what measure and degree, he pleases.

The Spirit also works *powerfully*, and with evident effects: *Thou hearest the sound thereof;* though its causes are hidden, its effects are manifest.

The Spirit works *mysteriously* and in secret, hidden ways: *Thou canst not tell whence it comes, nor whither it goes.* How it gathers and how it spends its strength is a riddle to us; so the manner and methods of the Spirit's working are a mystery.

June 26

Our weakness in prayer

Romans 8:26

The apostle here suggests the privileges to which true Christians are entitled: the help of the Spirit in prayer. While we are in this world, hoping and waiting for what we see not, we must be praying. Hope supposes desire, and that desire offered up to God in prayer.

Observe our weakness in prayer: *We know not what we should pray for as we ought.* As to the matter of our requests, we know not what to ask. We are not competent judges of our own condition. We are short-sighted, and very much biased in favour of the flesh, and apt to separate the end from the way. We are like foolish children that are ready to cry for fruit before it is ripe and fit for them.

As to the manner, we know not how to pray as we ought. It is not enough that we do that which is good, but we must do it well, seek in a due order; and here we are often at a loss—graces are weak, affections cold, thoughts wandering, and it is not always easy to find the heart to pray.

Observe the apostle speaks of this in the first person: *We know not.* He puts himself among the rest. Folly, weakness, and distraction in prayer are what all the saints are complaining of. If so great a saint as Paul knew not what to pray for, what little reason have we to go forth about that duty in our own strength!

[149]

June 27

The help of the Spirit

Romans 8:26

Here we have the assistance which the Spirit gives us in the duty of prayer. He *helps our infirmities*, especially our praying infirmities, which most easily beset us in that duty, against which the Spirit helps. The Spirit in the word helps; many rules and promises there are in the word for our help. The Spirit in the heart helps, dwelling in us, working in us, as a Spirit of grace and supplication, especially with respect to the infirmities we are under when we are in a suffering state, when our faith is most apt to fail; for this end the Holy Ghost was poured out.

Helpeth, heaves with us, over against us, helps as we help one that would lift up a burden, by lifting over against him at the other end—helps with us, that is, with us doing our endeavour, putting forth the strength we have. We must not sit still, and expect that the Spirit should do all; when the Spirit goes before us we must bestir ourselves. We cannot without God, and he will not without us.

What help? Why, the *Spirit itself makes intercession for us*, dictates our requests, expresses our petitions, draws up our plea for us. Christ intercedes for us in heaven, the Spirit intercedes for us in our hearts; so graciously has God provided for the encouragement of the praying remnant.

The Spirit, as an enlightening Spirit, teaches us what to pray for, as a sanctifying Spirit works and excites praying graces, as a comforting Spirit silences our fears, and helps us over all our discouragements. The Holy Spirit is the spring of all our desires and breathings towards God.

June 28

Ask, seek, knock

Matthew 7:7–8

We must not only *ask* but *seek*; we must second our prayers with our endeavours; we must, in the use of the appointed means, *seek* for that which we *ask* for, else we tempt God. God gives knowledge and grace to those that search the scriptures, and wait at wisdom's gates; and power against sin to those that avoid the occasions of it.

We must not only *ask*, but *knock*; we must come to God's door, must *ask* importunately: not only pray, but plead and wrestle with God; we must *seek* diligently; we must continue knocking; must persevere in prayer, and in the use of means; must endure to the end in the duty.

Here is a promise annexed: our labour in prayer, if indeed we do labour in it, shall not be in vain, where God finds a praying heart, he will be found a prayer-hearing God.

The promise is made, and made so as exactly to answer the precept, v.7. God will meet those that attend on him: *Ask, and it shall be given you*; not lent you, not sold you, but *given you*; and what is more free than gift? Whatever you pray for, according to the promise, whatever you ask, shall be given you, if God see it fit for you, and what would you have more? It is but ask and have; *Ye have not, because ye ask not*, or *ask* not aright: what is not worth asking, is not worth having, and then it is worth nothing.

Seek and *ye shall find*, and then you do not lose your labour; God is himself found of those that seek him, and if we find him we have enough. '*Knock, and it shall be opened*; the door of mercy and grace shall no longer be shut against you as enemies and intruders, but opened to you as friends and children. If the door be not opened at the first knock, continue in prayer.'

[151]

June 29

The path of prayer

John 14:13-14

Observe in what way the disciples were to keep up communion with
Christ, and derive power from him, when he was gone to the Father
—by prayer. Here is liberty: '*Ask* anything, anything that is good
and proper for you; anything, provided you know what you ask,
you may ask; you may ask for assistance in your work, for a mouth
and wisdom, for preservation out of the hands of your enemies, for
power to work miracles when there is occasion, for the success of the
ministry in the conversion of souls; ask to be informed, directed,
vindicated.'

Observe in what name they were to present their petitions: *Ask in
my name.* To ask in Christ's name is to plead his merit and
intercession, and to depend upon that plea. It is to aim at his glory
and to seek this as our highest end in all our prayers.

Observe what success they should have in their prayers: 'What
you ask, *that will I do*,' (v.13). And again (v.14), 'I will do it. You
may be sure I will: not only it shall be done, I will see it done, or
give orders for the doing of it, but *I will do it;*' for he has not only the
interest of an intercessor, but the power of a sovereign Prince, who
sits at the right hand of God, the hand of action, and has the going
of all in the kingdom of God.

Finally, note for what reason their prayers should speed so well:
That the Father may be glorified in the Son. This they ought to aim at,
and have their eye upon, in asking. In this all our desires and
prayers should meet as in their centre; to this they must all be
directed, that God in Christ may be honoured by our services and in
our salvation.

June 30

Wisdom from God

James 1:5–6

Prayer is a duty recommended to Christians who are suffering; and here the apostle shows what we ought more especially to pray for—wisdom: *If any lack wisdom, let him ask of God.* We should not pray so much for the removal of an affliction as for wisdom to make a right use of it. And who is there that does not want wisdom under any great trials or exercises to guide him in his judging of things, in the government of his own spirit and temper, and in the management of his affairs?

We have the greatest encouragement to do this: *he giveth to all men liberally, and upbraideth not.* Yes, it is expressly promised that *it shall be given*, v.5. Here is something in answer to every discouraging turn of the mind, when we go to God, under a sense of our own weakness and folly, to ask for wisdom. He to whom we are sent, we are sure, has it to give: and he is of a giving disposition, inclined to bestow this upon those who ask. Nor is there any fear of his favours being limited to some in this case, so as to exclude others, or any humble petitioning soul; for *he gives to all men.*

If you should say you want a great deal of wisdom, a small portion will not serve your turn, the apostle affirms, he *gives liberally*; and lest you should be afraid of going to him unseasonably, or being put to shame for your folly, it is added, *he upbraideth not.*

But there is one thing necessary to be observed in our asking, namely, that we do it with a believing, steady mind: *Let him ask in faith, nothing wavering*, v.6. The promise above is very sure, taking this proviso along with us; wisdom shall be given to those who ask it of God, provided they believe that God is able to make the simple wise, and is faithful to make good his word to those who apply to him.

July 1

The salt of the earth

Matthew 5:13

Ye are the salt of the earth. The doctrine of the gospel is as salt; it is penetrating, quick, and powerful; it reaches the heart. It is cleansing, it is relishing, and preserves from putrefaction.

See in this what the disciples are to be in themselves—seasoned with the gospel, with the salt of grace; thoughts and affections, words and actions, all seasoned with grace.

See what great blessings they are to the world. Mankind, lying in ignorance and wickedness, was a vast heap of unsavoury stuff, ready to putrefy; but Christ sent forth his disciples, by their lives and doctrines, to season it with knowledge and grace, and so to render it acceptable to God.

If they are not, they are as *salt* that has *lost its savour*. If you, who should season others, are yourselves unsavoury, void of spiritual life, relish, and vigour; if a Christian be so, especially if a minister be so, his condition is very sad; for:

(1) he is *irrecoverable*: *Wherewith shall it be salted?* Salt is a remedy for unsavoury meat, but there is no remedy for unsavoury salt. Christianity will give a man a relish; but if a man can take up and continue the profession of it, and yet remain flat and foolish, and graceless and insipid, no other doctrine, no others means, can be applied, to make him savoury. If Christianity does not do it, nothing will.

(2) he is *unprofitable*: *It is thenceforth good for nothing*; what use can it be put to, in which it will not do more hurt than good? As a man without reason, so is a Christian without grace.

(3) he is doomed to ruin and rejection; he shall be cast out—expelled from the church and the communion of the faithful, to which he is a blot and a burden; and he shall be *trodden under foot of men*.

July 2

The light of the world

Matthew 5:14–16

Christ's disciples are to be as the *light of the world*, they are intended
to illuminate and give light to others v.15, and therefore they shall
be set up as lights. Christ having lighted these candles, they shall not
be put under a bushel, not confined always, as they are now, to the
cities of Galilee, or the lost sheep of the house of Israel, but they
shall be sent into all the world.

The gospel is so strong a light and carried with it so much of its
own evidence, that, *like a city on a hill, it cannot be hid*, it cannot but
appear to be from God, to all those who do not wilfully shut their
eyes against it. It will *give light to all that are in the house*, to all that will
draw near to it, and come where it is.

See here how our light must shine—by doing such *good works* as
men *may see* and may approve of. We must do good works *that may be
seen* to the edification of others, but not *that they may be seen* to our own
ostentation; we are bid to pray in secret, and what lies between God
and our souls must be kept to ourselves; but that which is of itself
open and obvious to the sight of men, we must study to make
congruous to our profession and praiseworthy.

Observe for what end our light must shine—'that those who see
your good works may be brought, not to glorify you (which was the
thing the Pharisees aimed at, and it spoiled all their performances),
but to *glorify your Father which is in heaven.*' Note the glory of God is
the great thing we must aim at in everything we do in religion. In
this centre the lines of all our actions must meet. We must not only
endeavour to glorify God ourselves, but we must do all we can to
bring others to glorify him.

July 3

Keep them from the world

John 17:11–15

Christ prays for his disciples' preservation; to this end he commits them all to his Father's custody.

Keep them from the world. There were two ways of their being delivered from the world: by taking them out of it; and he does not pray that they might be so delivered: *I pray not that thou shouldest take them out of the world*; that is, 'I pray not that they may be speedily removed by death,' nor 'I pray not that they may be totally freed and exempted from the troubles of this world, and taken out of the toil and terror of it into some place of ease and safety, there to live undisturbed; this is not the preservation I desire for them.' Not that they may be kept from all conflict with the world, but that they may not be overcome by it.

It is more the honour of a Christian soldier by faith to *overcome the world* than by a monastical vow to retreat from it; and more for the honour of Christ to serve him in a city than to serve him in a cell.

Another way is by keeping them from the corruption that is in the world; and he prays they may be thus kept, v.11,15.

Holy Father, keep those whom thou hast given me. It is the unspeakable comfort of all believers that Christ himself has committed them to the care of God. Those cannot but be safe whom the almighty God keeps.

July 4

Keep them in thy name

John 17:11–15

Holy Father, v.11; observe the title he gives to him he prays to. He speaks to God as a *holy Father*. In committing ourselves and others to the divine care, we may take encouragement from the attribute of his holiness, for this is engaged for the preservation of his holy ones. If he is a Father, he will take care of his own children, will teach them and keep them; who else should?

[156]

He also speaks of them as those whom the Father had *given him*. What we receive as our Father's gifts, we may comfortably remit to our Father's care.

Keep them *through thine own name:* 'Keep them in the knowledge and fear of thy name; keep them in the profession and service of thy name, whatever it costs them. Keep them by thine own power, in thine own hand; keep them thyself, undertake for them, let them be thine own immediate care.'

Keep them from the evil, or out of the evil. 'Keep them from the evil one, the devil and all his instruments; that wicked one and all his children. Keep them from the evil thing, that is, sin; from everything that looks like it, or leads to it. Keep them from the evil of the world, and of their tribulation in it, so that it may have no sting in it, no malignity;' not that they might be kept from affliction, but kept through it, that the property of their afflictions might be so altered as that there might be no evil in them, nothing to do them any harm.

July 5

We walk by faith not by sight

2 Corinthians 5:6–8

The apostle deduces an inference for the comfort of believers in their present state and condition in this world, v.6–8. Here observe:

(1) what their present state or condition is: they *are absent from the Lord*, v.6; they are pilgrims and strangers in this world; they do but sojourn here in their earthly home, or in this tabernacle; and though God is with us here, by his Spirit and in his ordinances, yet we are not with him as we hope to be: we cannot see his face while we live: *For we walk by faith, not by sight*, v.7.

We have not the vision and fruition of God, as of an object that is present with us, and as we hope for hereafter, when we *shall see as we are seen*. Faith is for this world, and sight is reserved for the other world: and it is our duty, and will be our interest, to walk by faith, till we come to live by sight.

(2) how comfortable and courageous we ought to be in all the troubles of life, and in the hour of death: *Therefore we are*, or ought to be, *always confident*, v.6 and again v.8, *We are confident, and willing*

rather to be absent from the body. True Christians, if they duly considered the prospect faith gives them of another world, and the good reasons of their hope of blessedness after death, would be comforted under the troubles of life, and supported in the hour of death: they should take courage, when they are encountering the last enemy, and be willing rather to die than live, when it is the will of God that they should *put off this tabernacle*.

As those who are born from above long to be there, so it is but being absent from the body, and we shall very soon be present with the Lord—but to die, and be with Christ—but to close our eyes to all things in this world, and we shall open them in a world of glory. *Faith* will be turned into *sight*.

July 6

All have sinned

Romans 3:20–23

The apostle here argues the guiltiness of man, to prove that we cannot be justified by the works of the law. The argument is very plain: we can never be justified and saved by the law that we have broken. All are guilty, and therefore all have need of a righteousness wherein to appear before God. *For all have sinned*, v.23; all are sinners by nature, by practice, and *have come short of the glory of God*—have failed of that which is the chief end of man.

Man was placed at the head of the visible creation, actively to glorify that great Creator whom the inferior creatures could glorify only objectively; but man by sin comes short of this, and instead of glorifying God, dishonours him. It is a very melancholy consideration, to look upon the children of men, who were made to glorify God, and to think how few there are that do it.

Further to drive us from expecting justification by the law, the apostle ascribes this conviction to the law, v.20: *For by the law is the knowledge of sin*. That law which convicts and condemns us can never justify us.

The law is the straight rule, that which points out the right and the wrong; it is the proper use and intention of the law to open our wound, and therefore not likely to be the remedy. That which is searching does not heal. Those that would know sin must get the

[158]

knowledge of the law in its strictness, extent, and spiritual nature. If we compare our own hearts and lives with the rule, we shall discover where we have turned aside.

July 7

The righteousness of God

Romans 3:21–22

The apostle argues from God's glory to prove that justification must be expected only by faith in Christ's righteousness. There is no justification by the works of the law. Must guilty man then remain eternally under wrath? Is there no hope? Has the wound become incurable because of transgression? No, blessed God, it is not, v.21,22; there is another way laid open for us, *the righteousness of God without the law is manifested* now under the gospel. Justification may be obtained apart from the keeping of Moses' law.

Now concerning this righteousness of God, observe that it is manifested. The gospel-way of justification is a highway, a plain way, it is laid open for us.

It is *without the law*. Here he obviates the method of the Judaizing Christians, who would insist on joining Christ and Moses together.

Yet *it is witnessed by the law and the prophets*; that is, there were types, prophecies, and promises in the Old Testament that pointed at this.

It is by the *faith of Jesus Christ*, that faith which has Jesus Christ for its object—an anointed Saviour, so Jesus Christ signifies. It is by this that we become interested in that righteousness which God has ordained, and which Christ has brought in.

It is *to all, and upon all, those that believe*. In this expression he inculcates that which he had been often harping upon, that Jews and Gentiles, if they believe, stand upon the same level, and are alike welcome to God through Christ; *for there is no difference*.

July 8

The heart of the gospel

Romans 3:24-25

Justified freely by his grace. It is by his grace, by the gracious favour of God to us, without any merit in us so much as foreseen. And, to make it the more emphatic, he says it is *freely by his grace*, to show that it must be understood as grace in the most proper and genuine sense. It is *all through the redemption that is in Christ Jesus.* It comes freely to us, but Christ bought it, and paid dearly for it, which yet is so ordered as not to detract from the honour of free grace. Christ's purchase is no bar to the freeness of God's grace; for grace provided and accepted this vicarious satisfaction.

Whom God hath set forth to be a propitiation. . . . Jesus Christ is the great propitiation, or propitiatory sacrifice, typified by the *mercy-seat*, under the law. He is our throne of grace, in and through whom atonement is made for sin, and our persons and performances are accepted of God.

God hath set him forth to be so. God, the party offended, makes the first overtures towards a reconciliation; he fore-ordained him to this, in the counsels of his love from eternity, appointed, anointed him to it, qualified him for it, and has exhibited him to a guilty world as their propitiation.

It is *by faith in his blood* that we become interested in this propitiation. Christ is the propitiation; there is the healing plaster provided. Faith is the applying of this plaster to the wounded soul. And this faith in the business of justification has a special regard to *the blood of Christ*, as that which made the atonement; for such was the divine appointment that without blood there should be no remission, and no blood but his would do it effectually.

July 9

No condemnation

Romans 8:1

The apostle here describes one signal privilege of true Christians: *There is therefore now no condemnation to those that are in Christ Jesus*, v.1. It is the unspeakable privilege and comfort of all those that are in Christ Jesus that there is therefore now no condemnation to them. He does not say, 'There is no accusation against them,' for this there is; but the accusation is thrown out, and the indictment quashed. He does not say, 'There is nothing in them that deserves condemnation,' for this there is, and they see it, and own it, and mourn over it, and condemn themselves for it; but it shall not be their ruin. He does not say, 'There is no cross, no affliction to them or no displeasure in the affliction,' for this there may be; but *no condemnation*. They may be chastened of the Lord, but not condemned with the world.

Now this arises from their being in Christ Jesus; because of their union with him through faith they are thus secured. They are in Christ Jesus, as in their city of refuge, and so are protected from the avenger of blood. He is their Advocate and he rescues them. There is therefore no condemnation, because they are interested in the satisfaction that Christ by dying made to the law. In Christ, God does not only not condemn them, but is well pleased with them. It is the undoubted character of all those who are so in Christ Jesus as to be freed from condemnation that *they walk not after the flesh, but after the Spirit*.

July 10

The law of the Spirit

Romans 8:2–3

How do we come by these privileges—the privilege of justification, that *there is no condemnation to us*—the privilege of sanctification, that *we walk after the Spirit, and not after the flesh*, which is no less our privilege than it is our duty?

[161]

The law could not do it, v.3. It could neither justify nor sanctify, neither free us from the guilt nor from the power of sin, having not the promises either of pardon or grace. The law made nothing perfect: *It was weak*. Some attempt the law made towards these blessed ends, but, alas, it was weak!; it could not accomplish them: yet that weakness was not through any defect in the law, but *through the flesh*, through the corruption of human nature, by which we become incapable either of being justified or sanctified by the law. We had become unable to keep the law, and, in case of failure, the law, as a covenant of works, made no provision, and so left us as it found us.

The law of the Spirit of life in Christ Jesus does it, v.2. The covenant of grace made with us in Christ is a treasury of merit and grace, and from that we receive pardon and a new nature, *are freed from the law of sin and death*, that is, both from the guilt and power of sin—from the course of the law, and the dominion of the flesh. We are under another covenant, another master, another husband, under the *law of the Spirit*, the law that gives the Spirit, spiritual life to qualify us for eternal life.

July 11

God sent his own Son

Romans 8:3-4

The foundation of this freedom is laid in Christ's undertaking for us, of which he speaks v.3, *God sending his own Son*. When the law failed, God provided another method. Christ comes to do that which the law could not do. Observe:

(1) how Christ appeared: *In the likeness of sinful flesh*. Not sinful, for he was holy, harmless, and undefiled; but in the likeness of that flesh which was sinful. *And for sin*: God sent him *in the likeness of sinful flesh*, and as a sacrifice *for sin*.

(2) what was done by this appearance: Sin *was condemned*, that is, God did in this more than ever manifest his hatred of sin; and not only so, but for all that are Christ's both the damning and the domineering power of sin is broken and taken out of the way. Christ was made sin for us, and, being so made, when he was condemned, sin was condemned in the flesh of Christ, condemned in the human

nature: so was satisfaction made to divine justice, and way made for the salvation of the sinner.

(3) the happy effect of this upon us, v.4: *That the righteousness of the law might be fulfilled in us.* Both in our justification and in our sanctification, the righteousness of the law is fulfilled. A righteousness of satisfaction for the breach of the law is fulfilled by the imputation of Christ's complete and perfect righteousness, which answers the utmost demands of the law. A righteousness of obedience to the commands of the law is fulfilled in us, when by the Spirit the law of love is written upon the heart, and that love is the fulfilling of the law. Though the righteousness of the law is not fulfilled by us, yet, blessed be God, it is fulfilled in us; there is that to be found upon and in all true believers which answers the intention of the law.

July 12

God is for us

Romans 8:31

The apostle closes this excellent discourse on the privileges of believers in Romans 8 with a holy triumph. Having set forth the mystery of God's love to us in Christ, and the exceedingly great and precious privileges we enjoy by him, he concludes like an orator: *What shall we then say to these things?* He speaks as one amazed and swallowed up with the contemplation and admiration of it, wondering at the height and depth, and length and breadth, of the love of Christ, which passes knowledge. The more we know of other things the less we wonder at them; but the further we are led into an acquaintance with gospel mysteries the more we are affected with the admiration of them. If Paul was at a loss what to say to these things, it is no marvel if we are.

And what does he say? He here makes a challenge, throws down the gauntlet, as it were, dares all the enemies of the saints to do their worst: *If God be for us, who can be against us?* The ground of the challenge is God's being for us; in this he sums up all our privileges. This includes all, that *God is for us*; not only reconciled to us, and so not against us, but in covenant with us, and so engaged for us—all his attributes for us, his promises for us. All that he is, and has, and does, is for his people. He performs all things for them. He is for them, even when he seems to act against them.

And, if so, *who can be against us*, so as to prevail against us, so as to hinder our happiness? Be they ever so great and strong, ever so many, ever so mighty, ever so malicious, what can they do?

While God is for us, and we keep in his love, we may with a holy boldness defy all the powers of darkness. Let Satan do his worst, he is chained; let the world do its worst, it is conquered: principalities and powers are spoiled and disarmed, and triumphed over in the cross of Christ. Who then dares fight against us, while God himself is fighting for us?

July 13

God spared not his Son

Romans 8:32

Who can be against us, to strip us, to deprive us of our comforts? Who can cut off our streams, while we have a fountain to go to? Observe what God has done for us, on which our hopes are built: *He spared not his own Son*. When he was to undertake our salvation, the Father was willing to part with him, did not think him too precious a gift to bestow for the salvation of poor souls; now we may know that he loves us, in that he has not withheld his Son, his own Son, his only Son.

Thus did he *deliver him up for us all*, that is, for all the elect; for us all, not only for our good, but in our stead, as a sacrifice of atonement to be a propitiation for sin. When he had undertaken it, he did not spare him. Though he was his own Son, yet, being made sin for us, it pleased the Lord to bruise him.

Observe what we may therefore expect he will do: He will *with him freely give us all things*. It is implied that he will give us Christ, for other things are bestowed with him: not only with him given for us, but with him given to us. He that put himself to so much charge to make the purchase for us surely will not hesitate at making the application to us.

He will with them freely give us all things, all things that he sees to be needful and necessary for us, all good things, and more we should not desire.

How shall he not? Can it be imagined that he should do the greater and not do the less? That he should give so great a gift for us when we were enemies, and should deny us any good thing, now that through him we are friends and children?

July 14

God, the justifier

Romans 8:33–34

We have here an answer ready to all accusations and a security against all condemnations, v.33,34: *Who shall lay any thing?* Does the law accuse them? Do their own consciences accuse them? Is the devil, the accuser of the brethren, accusing them before our God day and night? This is enough to answer all those accusations, *It is God that justifieth.* He is the judge, the king, the party offended, and his judgment is according to truth, and sooner or later all the world will be brought to be of his mind; so that we may challenge all our accusers to come and put in their charge.

Who is he that condemneth? Though they cannot make good the charge, yet they will be ready to condemn; but we have a plea ready to move in arrest of judgment, a plea which cannot be overruled.

It is Christ that died. By the merit of his death he paid our debt; and the surety's payment is a good plea to an action of debt. It is Christ, an able all-sufficient Saviour.

Yea, rather, that has risen again. This is convincing evidence that divine justice was satisfied by the merit of his death. His resurrection was his acquittance, a release from debt, a legal discharge.

He is even at the right hand of God—further evidence that he has done his work, and a mighty encouragement to us in reference to all accusations, that we have a friend, such a friend at court.

At the right hand of God, which denotes that he is ready there—always at hand; and that he is ruling there—all power is given to him. Our friend is himself the judge.

He is there, not unconcerned about us, not forgetful of us, but *making intercession.* He is agent for us there, an Advocate for us, to answer all accusations, to put in our plea, and to prosecute it with effect, to appear for us and to present our petitions. And is not this abundant matter for comfort?

[165]

July 15

No separation from Christ's love

Romans 8:35-36

We have here from the apostle a daring challenge to all the enemies of the saints to separate them, if they could, from the love of Christ. *Who shall?* None shall. Observe here:

(1) the present calamities of Christ's beloved ones supposed—that they meet with *tribulation* on all hands, are in *distress*, know not which way to look for any help and relief in this world, are followed with *persecution* from an angry malicious world that always hated those whom Christ loved, pinched with *famine*, and starved with *nakedness*, when stripped of all creature-comforts, exposed to the greatest *perils*, the *sword* of the magistrate drawn against them. Can a case be supposed more black and dismal? It is illustrated, v.36, by a passage quoted from Psalm 44:22.

(2) the inability of all these things to separate us from the love of Christ. Shall they, can they, do it? No, by no means. All this will not cut the bond of love and friendship that is between Christ and true believers.

Christ does not, will not, love us the less for all this. All these troubles are very consistent with the strong and constant love of the Lord Jesus. They are neither cause nor evidence of the abatement of his love. When Paul was whipped, and beaten, and imprisoned, and stoned, did Christ love him the less? Were his favours discontinued? By no means, but the contrary. Whatever persecuting enemies may rob us of, they cannot rob us of the love of Christ, they cannot intercept his love-tokens, they cannot interrupt nor exclude his visits: and therefore, let them do their worst, they cannot make a true believer miserable.

July 16

More than conquerors

Romans 8:37

We are *conquerors*: though killed all the day long, yet conquerors. A strange way of conquering, but it was Christ's way; thus he triumphed over principalities and powers in his cross. It is a surer and a nobler way of conquest by faith and patience than by fire and sword. The enemies have sometimes confessed themselves baffled and overcome by the invincible courage and constancy of the martyrs, who thus overcame the most victorious princes by not loving their lives to the death.

We are *more than conquerors*. In our patiently bearing these trials we are not only conquerors, but more than conquerors, that is, triumphers. Those are more than conquerors that conquer. First, with little loss. It is no great loss to lose things which are not—a body that is of the earth, earthy. Secondly, with great gain. The spoils are exceedingly rich; glory, honour, and peace, and a crown of righteousness that fades not away.

It is only *through Christ that loved us*, the merit of his death taking the sting out of all these troubles, the Spirit of his grace strengthening us, and enabling us to bear them with holy courage and constancy, and coming in with special comforts and supports. Thus we are conquerors, not in our own strength, but in the grace that is in Christ Jesus. We are conquerors because of our interest in Christ's victory. He has overcome the world for us; so that we have nothing to do but to pursue the victory, and to divide the spoil, and so are more than conquerors.

July 17

The diligent Christian

2 Peter 1:10–11

The apostle proposes two particular advantages that will attend or follow on diligence in the work of a Christian: stability in grace and a triumphant entrance into glory. Here we may observe it is the duty of believers *to make their election sure*. It requires a great deal of diligence and labour to make sure our calling and election; there must be a very close examination of ourselves, a very narrow search and strict enquiry, whether we are thoroughly converted, our minds enlightened, our wills renewed, and our whole souls changed as to the bent and inclination thereof; and to come to a fixed certainty in this requires the utmost diligence, and cannot be attained and kept without divine assistance.

However great the labour is, do not think much of it, for great is the advantage you gain by it; for by this you will be kept from falling, and that at all times and seasons, even in those hours of temptation that shall be on the earth.

Those who are diligent in the work of religion shall have a triumphant entrance into glory; while of those few who get to heaven some are scarcely saved, with a great deal of difficulty, *even as by fire*. Those who are *growing in grace* and *abounding in the work of the Lord* shall have an *abundant* entrance into *the joy of their Lord*, even that everlasting kingdom where Christ reigns, and they shall *reign with him for ever and ever*.

July 18

A new heaven and a new earth

Revelation 21:1–3

We have here a general account of the happiness of the church of God in the future state, by which it seems most safe to understand the heavenly state. A new world now opens to our view, v.1: *I saw a new heaven and a new earth*; that is, a new universe. To make way for

[168]

the commencement of this new world, the old world, with all its troubles and commotions, *passed away*.

In this new world the apostle *saw the holy city, the new Jerusalem, coming down from heaven*, not locally, but as to its original: this new Jerusalem is the church of God in its new and perfect state, *prepared as a bride adorned for her husband*, beautified with all perfection of wisdom and holiness, suitable for the full fruition of the Lord Jesus Christ in glory.

The blessed presence of God with his people is here proclaimed and admired: *I heard a great voice out of heaven, saying, Behold, the tabernacle of God is with men*, v.3. The presence of God with his church is the glory of the church. It is matter of wonder that a holy God should ever dwell with any of the children of men.

The presence of God with his people in heaven will not be interrupted as it is on earth, but he will dwell with them continually. The covenant, interest, and relation, that there are now between God and his people, will be filled up and perfected in heaven. *They shall be his people*; their souls shall be assimilated to him, filled with all the love, honour, and delight in God which their relation to him requires, and this will constitute their perfect holiness: *He will be their God*: his immediate presence with them, his love fully manifested to them, and his glory put upon them, will be their perfect happiness.

July 19

No more sorrow

Revelation 21:4–6

This new and blessed state wil be free from all trouble and sorrow, for all the effects of former trouble shall be done away. They have been often before in tears, by reason of sin, affliction, and the calamities of the church; but now *all tears shall be wiped away*; no signs, no remembrance of former sorrows shall remain, any further than to make their present happiness the greater.

All the causes of future sorrow shall be for ever removed: *There shall be neither death nor pain*; and therefore *no sorrow nor crying*; these are things naturally attached to that state in which they were before, but now all *former things have passed away*.

The truth and certainty of this blessed state are ratified by the word and promise of God, and ordered to be committed to writing, as a matter of perpetual record, v.5,6.

Observe the certainty of the promised affirmed: *These words are faithful and true*; and it follows, *It is done*, is as sure as if it were done already.

He gives us his titles of honour as a pledge or surety of the full performance, even those titles of *Alpha and Omega, the beginning and the end.*

The desires of his people towards this blessed state furnish another evidence of the truth and certainty of it. They thirst after a state of sinless perfection and the uninterrupted enjoyment of God, and God has brought about in them these longing desires, which cannot be satisfied with anything else, and therefore would be the torment of the soul if they were disappointed; but it would be inconsistent with the goodness of God, and his love to his people, to create in them holy and heavenly desires, and then deny them their proper satisfaction; and therefore they may be assured that, when they have overcome their present difficulties, *he will give them of the fountain of the water of life freely.*

July 20

Into action!

1 Peter 1:13

Wherefore gird up the loins of your mind . . . , v.13. '*Wherefore*, since you are so honoured and distinguished, *Gird up the loins of your mind.* You have a journey to go, a race to run, warfare to accomplish, and a great work to do; as the traveller, the racer, the warrior, and the labourer, gather in and gird up their long and loose garments that they may be more ready, prompt, and expeditious in their business, so do you by your minds, your inner man, and affections seated there: *gird them*, gather them in, let them not hang loose and neglected about you; restrain their extravagances, and let the loins or strength and vigour of your minds be exerted in your duty; disengage yourselves from all that would hinder you, and go on resolutely in your obedience.'

Be sober, 'be vigilant against all your spiritual dangers and enemies, and be temperate and modest in eating, drinking, apparel, recreation, business, and in the whole of your behaviour. Be sober-minded also in opinion, as well as in practice, and humble in your judgment of yourselves.'

And hope to the end, for the grace that is to be brought to you at the revelation of Jesus Christ. Some refer this to the last judgment, as if the apostle directed their hope to the final revelation of Jesus Christ; but it seems more natural to take it, as it might be rendered, '*Hope perfectly*, or *thoroughly, for the grace that is brought to you* in or by *the revelation of Jesus Christ*; that is, by the gospel, which brings life and immortality to light.'

A Christian's work is not over as soon as he has got into a state of grace; he must still hope and strive for more grace. When he has entered the narrow gate, he must still walk in the narrow way, and gird up the loins of his mind for that purpose.

July 21

The way of holiness

1 Peter 1:14–15

As obedient children . . . , v.14. These words may be taken as a rule of holy living, which is both positive—'You ought to live *as obedient children*, as those whom God hath adopted into his family, and regenerated by his grace;' and negative—'You must *not fashion yourselves according to the former lusts, in your ignorance.*'

But as he who hath called you . . . , v.15,16. Here is a noble rule enforced by strong arguments: *Be you holy.* Who is sufficient for this? And yet it is required in strong terms, and enforced by reasons taken from the grace of God in calling us from his command, *it is written*, and from his example, *Be you holy, for I am holy.*

The grace of God in calling a sinner is a powerful engagement to holiness. It is a great favour to be called effectually by divine grace out of a state of sin and misery into the possession of all the blessings of the new covenant; and great favours are strong obligations; they enable as well as oblige us to be holy.

Complete holiness is the desire and duty of every Christian. We must be holy, and be so in all that we do; in all civil and religious affairs, in every condition, prosperous or reverse; towards all people, friends and enemies; in all our social intercourse and business still we shall be holy.

We must *be holy, as God is holy*: we must imitate him, though we can never equal him. He is perfectly, unchangeably, and eternally holy; and we should aspire after such a state.

July 22

We are not our own

1 Corinthians 6:19–20

Christians are *the temples of the Holy Ghost which is in them, and which they have of God*, v.19. He that is joined to Christ is one spirit. He is yielded up to him, is consecrated and set apart for his use, and is possessed, occupied, and inhabited by his Holy Spirit. This is the proper notion of a temple—a place where God dwells, and sacred to his use, by his own claim and his creature's surrender. Such temples real Christians are of the Holy Ghost.

The inference is plain: we are not our own. We are yielded up to God, and possessed by and for God; and this because of a purchase made of us: *You are bought with a price.* In short, our bodies were made for God, they were purchased for him. If we are Christians indeed they are yielded to him, and he inhabits and occupies them by his Spirit: so that our bodies are not our own, but his. And shall we desecrate his temple, defile it, prostitute it, and offer it up to the use and service of a harlot? Horrid sacrilege! This is robbing God in the worst sense. Note, the temple of the Holy Ghost must be kept holy. Our bodies must be kept as his whose they are, and fit for his use and residence.

We are under obligation *to glorify God both with our body and spirit, which are his*, v.20. He made both, he bought both, and therefore both belong to him and should be used and employed for him, and therefore should not be defiled, alienated from him, and prostituted by us. No, they must be kept as vessels fitted for our Master's use. We must look upon our whole selves as holy to the Lord, and must use our bodies as property which belongs to him and is sacred to his use and service.

Put off . . . , put on . . .

Ephesians 4:22–24

That you put off the old man. There must be sanctification, which consists of these two things:

(1) the old man must be *put off*. The corrupt nature is called a man, because, like the human body, it consists of several parts, mutually supporting and strengthening one another. It is said to be corrupt; for sin in the soul is the corruption of its faculties.

According to the deceitful lusts. Sinful inclinations and desires are deceitful lusts: they promise men happiness, but render them more miserable, and if not subdued and mortified betray them into destruction. These therefore must be put off as an old garment that we should be ashamed to be seen in: they must be subdued and mortified.

(2) the new man must be *put on*. It is not enough to shake off corrupt principles, but we must be actuated by gracious ones. We must embrace them, espouse them, and get them written on our hearts: it is not enough to cease to do evil, but we must learn to do well.

'*Be renewed in the spirit of your mind,* v.23; use the proper and prescribed means in order to have the mind, which is a spirit, renewed more and more.' *And that you put on the new man,* v.24. By the new man is meant the new nature, the new creature, which is actuated by a new principle, regenerating grace, enabling a man to lead a new life, that life of righteousness and holiness which Christianity requires. This new man *is created,* or produced out of confusion and emptiness, by God's almighty power, whose workmanship it is, truly excellent and beautiful. *After God,* in imitation of him, and in conformity to that grand model and pattern. *In righteousness* towards men *and in holiness* towards God.

The new lifestyle

Ephesians 4:25–27

The apostle proceeds to some particular things. Take heed of *lying*, and be ever careful to *speak the truth*, v.25. Lying is a part of the old man that must be put off; and that branch of the new man that must be put on in opposition to it is *speaking the truth* in all our converse with others.

The reason here given for veracity is, *We are members one of another*. Truth is a debt we owe to one another; and, if we love one another, we shall not deceive nor lie one to another. We belong to the same society or body, which falsehood or lying tends to dissolve; and therefore we should avoid it, and speak truth.

'Take heed of anger and ungoverned passions. *Be you angry*, and sin not,' v.26. *Be you angry*. This we are apt enough to be, God knows: but we find it difficult enough to observe the restriction, *and sin not*. 'If you have a just occasion to be angry at any time, see that it is without sin; and therefore take heed of excess in your anger.' 'If you have been provoked and have had your spirits greatly discomposed, and if you have bitterly resented any affront that has been offered, before night calm and quiet your spirits, be reconciled to the offender, and let all be well again: *Let not the sun go down upon your wrath*. If it burn into wrath and bitterness of spirit, see to it that you suppress it speedily.'

Though anger in itself is not sinful, yet there is the utmost danger of its becoming so if it is not carefully watched and speedily suppressed.

Neither give place to the devil, v.27. Those who persevere in sinful anger and in wrath let the devil into their hearts, and permit him to gain upon them, till he brings them to malice, mischievous intrigue, and the like.

July 25

Working and talking

Ephesians 4:28–29

We are here warned against the sin of stealing and advised to honest industry and to active kindness: *Let him that stole steal no more*, v.28. It is a caution against all manner of wrong-doing, by force or fraud. 'Let those of you who have been guilty of this enormity, be no longer guilty of it.' But we must not only take heed of the sin, but conscientiously abound in the opposite duty: not only not steal, *but rather let him labour, working with his hands the thing that is good*. Those who will not work expose themselves greatly to temptations to thievery. Men should therefore be diligent and industrious, not in any unlawful way, but in some honest calling: *Working the thing which is good*.

People ought to be industrious so that they may be capable of doing some good: *That he may have to give to him that needeth*. They must labour not only that they may live themselves, and live honestly, but they may distribute for supplying the wants of others.

We are here warned against corrupt talk or communication and directed to that which is useful and edifying, v.29. We must not only put off corrupt talk, but *put on that which is good to the use of edifying*. The great use of speech is to edify those with whom we converse: *that it may minister grace unto the hearers*; that it may be good for and acceptable to the hearers, in the way of information, counsel, pertinent reproof, or the like.

July 26

Do not grieve the Holy Spirit

Ephesians 4:30

In the midst of these exhortations and cautions the apostle inserts that general one, *And grieve not the Holy Spirit of God*, v.30. By looking to what precedes, and to what follows, we may see what it is that grieves the Spirit of God. In the previous verses it is intimated that all lewdness and filthiness, lying, and corrupt talk that stir up filthy appetites and lusts grieve the Spirit of God. In what follows it is intimated that those corrupt passions of bitterness, wrath, anger, clamour, evil speaking, and malice grieve this good Spirit.

By this we are not to understand that this blessed Being could properly be grieved or vexed as we are; but the design of the exhortation is that we should not act towards him in such a manner as is wont to be grievous and disquieting to our fellow-creatures: we must not do that which is contrary to his holy nature and his will; we must not refuse to hearken to his counsels, nor rebel against his government.

O provoke not the blessed Spirit of God to withdraw his presence and his gracious influences from you! It is a good reason why we should not grieve him that *by him we are sealed unto the day of redemption*. There is to be a day of redemption; the body is to be redeemed from the power of the grave at the resurrection-day, and then God's people will be delivered from all the effects of sin, as well as from all sin and misery, which they are not till rescued out of the grave: and then their full and complete happiness commences. All true believers are sealed to that day. God has distinguished them from others, having set his mark upon them; and he gives them the earnest assurance of a joyful and a glorious resurrection; and the Spirit of God is the seal.

July 27

Real kindness

Ephesians 4:31–32

Here is another caution against wrath and anger, with further advice to mutual love and kindly dispositions towards each other, v.31,32. By *bitterness, wrath, and anger* are meant violent inward resentment and displeasure against others: and, by *clamour*, big words, loud threatenings, and other kinds of intemperate speech, by which bitterness, wrath, and anger, vent themselves. *Evil speaking* signifies all railing, reviling, and reproachful speech. And by *malice* we are to understand that rooted anger which prompts men to design and to do mischief to others.

The contrary to all this follows: *Be you kind one to another*. This implies the principle of love in the heart, and the outward expression of it in affable, humble, and courteous behaviour. It becomes the disciples of Jesus to be kind to one another. *Tenderhearted*; that is merciful, and having a tender sense of the distresses and sufferings of others, so as to be quickly moved to compassion and pity. *Forgiving one another.* Occasions of difference will happen among Christ's disciples; and therefore they must be placable and ready to forgive, resembling God himself, who *for Christ's sake hath forgiven them*, and that more than they can forgive one another.

With God there is forgiveness; and he forgives sin for the sake of Jesus Christ, and on account of that atonement which he has made to divine justice. Further, those who are forgiven of God should be of a forgiving spirit, remembering that they pray, *Forgive us our trespasses, as we forgive those who trespass against us.*

July 28

True worship

John 4:23–24

Christ here describes the evangelical worship which alone God would accept and be well pleased with. Having shown that the place is unimportant he comes to show what is necessary and essential—that we worship God *in spirit and in truth*, v.23,24. The stress is not to be laid upon the place where we worship God, but upon the state of mind in which we worship him.

In gospel times the *true worshippers shall worship the Father in spirit and in truth.* As creatures, we worship the Father of all: as Christians, we worship *the Father of our Lord Jesus.* Now the change shall be:

(1) in the *nature* of the worship. Christians shall worship God, not in the ceremonial observances of the Mosaic institution, but in the spiritual observances, animated and invigorated with divine power and energy.

(2) in the *disposition* of the worshippers; and so the true worshippers are real Christians, distinguished from hypocrites; all should, and they will, worship God *in spirit and in truth.* It is spoken of (v.23) as their character, and (v.24) as their duty. We must depend upon *God's Spirit* for strength and assistance, laying our souls under his influences and operations; we must devote our own

[177]

spirits to, and employ them in, the service of God; we must worship him with fixedness of thought and a flame of affection, with *all that is within us*. *In truth*, that is, in sincerity. God requires not only the inward part of our worship, but *truth in the inward part*. We must mind the power more than the form, must aim at God's glory, and not to be *seen of men*; we are to *draw near with a true heart*.

July 29

Spiritual worship

John 4:23–24

Christ here intimates the reasons why God must be worshipped in spirit and truth:

(1) because in gospel times they, and they only, are accounted the true worshippers. The gospel erects a spiritual way of worship, so that professors of the gospel are not true in their profession, do not live up to gospel light and laws, if they do not worship God *in spirit and in truth*.

(2) because *the Father seeketh such worshippers of him*. This intimates that God is greatly well pleased with and graciously accepts such worship and such worshippers. God is in all ages gathering in to himself a generation of spiritual worshippers.

(3) because *God is a spirit*: for he is an infinite and eternal mind, and intelligent being, incorporeal, immaterial, invisible, and incorruptible. It is easier to say what God is not than what he is; a spirit *has not flesh and bones*. If God were not a spirit, he could not be perfect, nor infinite, nor eternal, nor independent, nor the Father of spirits.

The spirituality of the divine nature is a very good reason for the spirituality of divine worship. If we do not worship God, who is a spirit, in the spirit, we neither give him the glory due to his name, and so do not perform the act of worship, nor can we hope to obtain his favour and acceptance, and so we miss of the end of worship.

You are the Christ

Matthew 16:16

Christ enquires what the disciples' thoughts were concerning him: '*But who say ye that I am?*' v.15.

To the former question concerning the opinion others had of Christ, several of the disciples answered according as they had heard people talk, v.14; but to this Peter answers in the name of all the rest, they all consenting to it, and concurring in it.

Peter's answer is short, but it is full, and true, and to the purpose: *Thou art the Christ, the Son of the living God.* Here is a confession of the Christian faith, addressed to Christ, and so made an act of devotion. Here is a confession of the true God as the living God, in opposition to dumb and dead idols, and of *Jesus Christ, whom he hath sent.*

The people called him a *prophet*, but the disciples own him to be the *Christ*, the anointed One; the great Prophet, Priest, and King of the church; the true Messiah promised to the fathers, and depended on by them as he that shall come.

He called himself the *Son of Man*; but they owned him to be *the Son of the living God*. The people's notion of him was, that he was the ghost of a dead man, Elijah or Jeremiah; but they know and believe him to be *the Son of the living God*, who has life in himself, and has given to his Son to have life in himself, and to be the life of the world. Now can we with an assurance of faith subscribe to this confession? Let us then, with a fervency of affection and adoration, go to Christ, and tell him so; Lord Jesus, *thou art the Christ, the Son of the living God.*

July 31

Revelation from God

Matthew 16:17

Here we see Christ's approval of Peter's answer. Christ shows himself well pleased with Peter's confession, that it was so clear and explicit.

Blessed art thou, Simon Bar-jona. Christ reminds him of his origin, the lowliness of his parentage, and then makes him aware of his great happiness as a believer: *Blessed art thou.*

God must have the glory of Peter's confession: '*For flesh and blood have not revealed it to thee.* You have this neither by the invention of your own understanding and reason, nor by the instruction and information of others; this light sprang neither from nature nor from education, but from my Father who is in heaven.'

The Christian religion is a revealed religion, has its origin in heaven; it is a religion from above, given by inspiration of God, not the learning of philosophers, nor the politics of statesmen. Note too that saving faith is the gift of God, and, wherever it is, is brought about by him. *Therefore* thou art blessed, because *my Father has revealed it to thee.*

August 1

The foundation of the church

Matthew 16:18

It is here promised that Christ would build his church upon a rock. This body politic is incorporated by the style and title of Christ's church. It is not *Peter's* church, but *Christ's*.

The builder and maker of the church is Christ himself: *I will build it.* The foundation on which it is built is: *this rock.* Let the architect do his part ever so well, if the foundation is rotten, the building will not stand; let us therefore see what the foundation is. The church is built upon a *rock*; a firm, strong, and lasting foundation, which time will not waste, nor will it sink under the weight of the building.

Christ would not build his house upon the sand, for he knew that storms would arise.

It is built upon *this* rock; thou art *Peter*, which signifies 'a stone' or 'rock'; Christ gave him that name when he first called him and here he confirms it.

Some by this *rock* understand Peter himself as an apostle, the chief, though not the prince, of the twelve, senior among them, but not superior over them. The church is built upon the foundation of the apostles.

Others by this *rock* understand *Christ*; '*Thou art Peter*, thou hast the name of a 'stone', but *upon this rock*, pointing to himself, *I will build my church.*' Many scriptures speak of Christ as the only foundation of the church.

Others by this *rock* understand this confession which Peter made of Christ, 'Now,' said Christ, 'this is the great truth *upon which I will build my church.*'

August 2

The gates of hell

Matthew 16:18

Christ here promises to preserve and secure his church, when it is built: *The gates of hell shall not prevail against it*; neither against this truth, nor against the church which is built upon it.

This implies that the church has enemies that fight against it and endeavour to bring about its ruin and overthrow, here represented by *the gates of hell*, that is the city of hell.

The gates of hell are the powers and policies of the devil's kingdom, the dragon's head and horns, by which he *makes war with the Lamb*; all that comes out of hell-gates, as being hatched and contrived there. These fight against the church by opposing gospel truths, corrupting gospel ordinances, persecuting true ministers and true Christians; drawing or driving, persuading by craft or forcing by cruelty to that which is inconsistent with the purity of religion; this is the design of the gates of hell, to root out the name of Christianity.

This assures us that the enemies of the church shall not gain their point, shall not be superior. While the world stands, Christ will have a church in it, in which his truths and ordinances shall be owned and kept up, in spite of all the opposition of the powers of darkness. This gives no security to any particular church or church-governors that they shall never err, never apostatize or be destroyed; but that somewhere or other the Christian religion shall have a being, though not always in the same degree of purity and splendour. The church may be foiled in particular encounters, but in the main battle it shall come off *more than a conqueror*. Believers are *kept by the power of God through faith unto salvation*.

August 3

Life in the early church

Acts 2:42–47

In these verses we have the history of the early church:

They kept close to holy ordinances. They were diligent and constant in their attendance upon the preaching of the word: They *continued in the apostles' doctrine*. They kept up the communion of the saints. They continued *in fellowship*, v.42 and *continued daily with one accord in the temple*, v.46. They were much together. Worshipping God is to be our daily work. They were *with one accord*; not only no discord nor strife, but a great deal of holy love among them. They frequently joined in the ordinance of the Lord's supper. They continued *in the breaking of bread*. They broke bread from house to house. They continued *in prayers*. After the Spirit was poured out as well as before, they continued instant in prayer; for prayer will never be superseded till it comes to be swallowed up in everlasting praise. They abounded in thanksgiving; were continually *praising God*, v.47. This should have a part in every prayer, and not be crowded into a corner.

They were loving to one another and their joining together in holy ordinances very much endeared them to one another. They had frequent meetings for Christian converse, v.44: *All that believed were together*. They had *all things common*. There was such a readiness to help one another. They were very cheerful; they did *eat their meat with gladness and singleness of heart*. They raised a fund for charity, v.45: They *sold their possessions and goods*, and parted the money to their brethren, *as every man had need*. This was to destroy not property, but selfishness.

God owned them, and gave them signal tokens of his presence with them, v.43: *Many wonders and signs were done by the apostles.* But the Lord's giving them power to work miracles was not all he did for them; he *added to the church daily.*

The people were influenced by it, v.43: *Fear came upon every soul.* The souls of people were strangely influenced by their preaching and living.

August 4

Spiritual blessings

Ephesians 3:16–17

We come to Paul's devout and affectionate prayer to God for his beloved Ephesians. Observe what the apostle asks of God for his friends—spiritual blessings, which are the best blessings.

He asks for spiritual strength for the work and duty to which they were called, and in which they were employed: *That he would grant you, according to the riches of his grace, to be strengthened* . . . , v.16. The *inner man* is the heart or soul. To be *strengthened with might* is to be mightily strengthened, much more than they were at present; to be endued with a high degree of grace, and spiritual abilities for discharging duty, resisting temptations, enduring persecutions, etc.

The apostle prays that this may be *according to the riches of his glory*, or according to his glorious riches—answerable to that great abundance of grace, mercy, and power, which resides in God and is his glory: and this by his Spirit, who is the immediate worker of grace in the souls of God's people.

Observe from these things that strength from the Spirit of God in the inner man is the best and most desirable strength, strength in the soul, the strength of faith and other graces, strength to serve God and to do our duty, and to persevere in our Christian way with vigour and with cheerfulness.

The apostle also asks for the indwelling of Christ in their hearts, v.17. Christ is said to dwell in his people, as he is always present with them by his gracious influences and operations. It is a desirable thing to have Christ dwell in our hearts; and if the law of Christ is written there, and the love of Christ is shed abroad there, then Christ dwells there. Christ is an inhabitant in the soul of every true Christian.

[183]

Where his Spirit dwells, there he dwells; and he dwells in the heart *by faith*, by means of the continual exercise of faith upon him. Faith opens the door of the soul, to receive Christ; faith admits him and submits to him.

August 5

The love of Jesus Christ

Ephesians 3:17–18

Paul continues in prayer: *That you being rooted and grounded in love*, v.17, steadfastly fixed in your love to God, the Father of our Lord Jesus Christ, and to all the saints, the beloved of our Lord Jesus Christ. We should earnestly desire that good affections may be fixed in us, that we may be *rooted and grounded in love*.

He prays for their experimental acquaintance with the love of Jesus Christ. The more intimate acquaintance we have with Christ's love to us, the more our love will be drawn out to him, and to those who are his, for his sake: *That you may be able to comprehend with all saints*, v.18,19; that is, more clearly to understand, and firmly to believe, the wonderful love of Christ to his, which the saints do understand and believe in some measure, and shall understand more hereafter. We should desire to comprehend *with all saints*, to have so much knowledge as the saints are allowed to have in this world.

It is observable how magnificently the apostle speaks of the love of Christ. The dimensions of redeeming love are admirable: *The breadth, and length, and depth, and height*. By enumerating these dimensions the apostle designs to signify the exceeding greatness of the love of Christ, the unsearchable riches of his love. We should desire to comprehend this love: it is the character of all the saints that they do so; for they all have a satisfaction and a confidence in the love of Christ.

August 6

Filled with all the fulness of God

Ephesians 3:19-20

And to know the love of Christ which passeth knowledge, v.19. If it passeth knowledge, how can we know it? We must pray and endeavour to know something, and should still covet and strive to know more and more of it, though, after the best endeavours, none can fully comprehend it: in its full extent it surpasses knowledge. Though the love of Christ may be better perceived and known by Christians than it generally is, yet it cannot be fully understood on this side of heaven.

He prays that they may be *filled with all the fulness of God*. It is a high expression: we should not dare to use it if we did not find it in the scriptures. It is like those other expressions, of being *partakers of a divine nature*, and of being *perfect as our Father in heaven is perfect*. We are not to understand it as his fulness as God in himself, but as his fulness as a God in covenant with us, as a God to his people: such a fulness as God is ready to bestow, who is willing to fill them all to the utmost of their capacity, and that with all those gifts and graces which he sees they need.

Those who receive grace for grace from Christ's fulness may be said to be *filled with the fulness of God*, according to their capacity, all of which is to secure their arriving at the highest degree of the knowledge and enjoyment of God, and an entire conformity to him.

The apostle closes the chapter with a doxology, v.20,21. It is proper to conclude our prayers with praise. Take notice how he describes God, and how he ascribes glory to him. He describes him as a God that *is able to do exceedingly abundantly above all that we ask or think*. There is an inexhaustible fulness of grace and mercy in God, which the prayers of all the saints can never draw dry. Whatever we may ask, or think to ask, still God is still able to do more, abundantly more, exceedingly abundantly more.

August 7

Glory in the church

Ephesians 3:20–21

In our requests to God, we should encourage our faith by a consideration of his all sufficiency and almighty power. *According to the power which worketh in us.* It is as if the apostle had said, we have already had a proof of this power of God, in what he has worked in us and done for us, having quickened us by his grace, and converted us to himself. The power that still works for the saints is according to that power that has worked in them.

Wherever God gives of his fulness he gives experience of his power. Having thus described God, he ascribes glory to him. When we come to ask for grace from God, we ought to give glory to God. *Unto him be glory in the church by Christ Jesus.* In ascribing glory to God, we ascribe all excellence and perfection to him, glory being the effulgence and result of them all.

The seat of God's praises is in the church. That little rent of praise which God receives from this world is from the church, a sacred society constituted for the glory of God, every particular member of which, both Jew and Gentile, concurs in this work of praising God.

The Mediator of these praises is *Jesus Christ.* All God's gifts come from him to us through the hand of Christ; and all our praises pass from us to him through the same hand.

And God should and will be praised thus *throughout all ages, world without end*; for he will ever have a church to praise him, and he will ever have his tribute of praise from his church. *Amen.* So be it; and so it will certainly be.

August 8

The unity of the Spirit

Ephesians 4:3–4

The unity of the Spirit, v.3. The seat of Christian unity is in the heart or spirit: it does not lie in one set of thoughts, nor in one form and mode of worship, but in one heart and one soul. This unity of heart and affection may be said to be of the Spirit of God; it is brought about by him, and is one of the fruits of the Spirit.

This we should endeavour to keep. *Endeavouring* is a gospel word. We must do our utmost. If others will quarrel with us, we must take all possible care not to quarrel with them. If others will despise and hate us, we must not despise and hate them. *In the bond of peace.* Peace is a bond, as it unites persons, and makes them live friendly one with another. A peaceable disposition and conduct bind Christians together, whereas discord and quarrelling disband and disunite their hearts and affections.

Consider how many unities there are that are the joy and glory of our Christian profession. There should be one heart; for *there is one body, and one Spirit*, v.4. Two hearts in one body would be monstrous. If there is but one body, all that belong to that body should have one heart. The church is one mystical body of Christ, and all Christians make up but one body, incorporated by one charter, that of the gospel, animated by one Spirit, the same Holy Spirit who by his gifts and graces quickens, enlivens, and governs the body. If we belong to Christ, we are all actuated by one and the same Spirit, and therefore should be one.

August 9

Unity and diversity

Ephesians 4:4–7

Even as you are called in one hope of your calling. All Christians are called to the same hope of eternal life. There is one Christ that they all hope in, and one heaven that they are all hoping for; and therefore they should be of one heart.

[187]

One Lord, v.5, that is, Christ, the head of the church, to whom, by God's appointment, all Christians are immediately subject. *One faith*, that is, the gospel containing the doctrine of the Christian faith: or, it is the same grace of faith (faith in Christ) by which all Christians are saved. *One baptism*, by which we profess our faith, being baptized in the name of the Father, Son, and Holy Ghost; and so the same sacramental covenant, whereby we engage ourselves to the Lord Christ.

One God and Father of all, v.6. One God, who owns all the true members of the church for his children; for he is the Father of all such by special relation, as he is the Father of all men by creation: and he *is above all*, by his essence, and with respect to the glorious perfection of his nature, and as he has dominion over all creatures and especially over his church, *and through all*, by his providence upholding and governing them: *and in you all*, in all believers, in whom he dwells as in his holy temple, by his Spirit and special grace.

Consider the variety of gifts that Christ has bestowed among Christians: *But unto every one of us is given grace according to the measure of the gift of Christ*. Unto every one of us Christians is given grace, some gift of grace, in some kind or degree or other, for the mutual help of one another. All the ministers and all the members of Christ owe all the gifts and graces that they have to him; and this is a good reason why we should love one another, *because to every one of us is given grace*.

August 10

Gifts for the church

Ephesians 4:11–13

The gifts of Christ—apostles, prophets, and evangelists, and pastors and teachers—were intended for the good of his church, and in order to advance his kingdom and interest among men. All are *for the perfecting of the saints*, v.12; that is to bring into an orderly spiritual state and frame those who had been as it were dislocated and disjointed by sin, and then to strengthen, confirm, and advance them so that each, in his proper place and function, might contribute to the good of the whole.

For the work of the ministry, that is, that they might dispense the doctrines of the gospel, and successfully discharge the several parts of their ministerial function.

For the edifying of the body of Christ; that is, to build up the church, which is Christ's mystical body, by an increase of their graces, and an addition of new members.

All are designed to prepare us for heaven: *Till we all come . . .*, v.13. The gifts and offices (some of them) which have been spoken of are to continue in the church till the saints be perfected, which will not be *till they all come in the unity of the faith* (till all true believers meet together, by means of the same precious faith) *and of the knowledge of the Son of God*, by which we are to understand, not a bare speculative knowledge, or the acknowledging of Christ to be the Son of God and the great Mediator, but such as is attended with appropriation and affection, with all due honour, trust, and obedience.

August 11

The way of maturity

Ephesians 4:14–15

The apostle shows in these verses what was God's design in his sacred institutions, and what effect they ought to have upon us. *That we henceforth be no more children . . .*, v.14; that is, that we may be no longer children in knowledge, weak in the faith, and inconstant in our judgments, easily yielding to every temptation. Children are easily imposed upon. We must take care of this, and of being *tossed to and fro*, like ships without ballast, *and carried about*, like clouds in the air, with such doctrines as have no truth nor solidity in them, but nevertheless spread themselves far and wide, and are therefore compared to wind. *By the sleight of men*; this is a metaphor taken from gamesters, and signifies the mischievous subtlety of seducers: *and cunning craftiness*, by which is meant their skilfulness in finding ways to seduce and deceive.

The best method we can take to fortify ourselves against deceivers is to study the sacred oracles and to pray for the illumination and grace of the Spirit of Christ, that we may know the truth as it is in Jesus, and be established in it.

We should *speak the truth in love*, v.15, or follow the truth in love or be sincere in love to our fellow-Christians. While we adhere to the doctrine of Christ, which is the truth, we should live in love one with another. Love is an excellent thing; but we must be careful to preserve truth together with it. Truth is an excellent thing; yet it is requisite that we speak it in love, and not in contention. These two should go together—truth and peace.

August 12

Growing up in love

Ephesians 4:15–16

We are to *grow up into Christ in all things*, into Christ, so as to be more deeply rooted in him. In all things; in knowledge, love, faith, and all the parts of the new man. We should grow up towards maturity, which is opposed to being children.

We should be assisting and helpful one to another, as members of the same body, v.16. Here the apostle makes a comparison between the natural body and Christ's mystical body, that body of which Christ is the head.

From who, says he—that is, from Christ their head—*the whole body* of Christians, *fitly joined together and compacted*—being orderly and firmly united among themselves, every one in his proper place—*by that which every joint supplies*—by the assistance which every one of the parts gives to the whole, or by the Spirit, faith, love, sacraments, and so on, which serve to unite Christians to Christ their head, and to one another as fellow-members—*according to the effectual working in the measure of every part*—that is, according to the effectual working of every member in communicating to others of what it has received—*makes increase of the body*, such an increase as is suitable for the body.

Unto the edifying of itself in love. Mutual love among Christians is a great friend to spiritual growth: it is in love that the body edifies itself.

Living stones

1 Peter 2:4-5

The apostle here gives us a description of Jesus Christ as a living stone, to denote his invincible strength and everlasting duration, and to teach his servants that he is their protection and security, and the foundation on which they are built. He is the living stone, having eternal life in himself, and being the prince of life to all his people. The reputation and respect he has with God and man are very different. He is disallowed of men, reprobated or rejected by his own country-men the Jews, and by the generality of mankind; but chosen of God, separated and foreordained to be the foundation of the church, and precious, a most honourable, choice, worthy person in himself, in the esteem of God, and in the judgment of all who believe in him.

Having described Christ as the foundation, the apostle goes on to speak of the superstructure, the materials built upon him: *You also, as living stones, are built up*, v.5. Christ the foundation, is a living stone. Christians are lively stones, and these make a spiritual house, and they are a holy priesthood; and, though they have no bloody sacrifices of beasts to offer, yet they have much better and more acceptable, and they have an altar too on which to present their offerings; for they offer *spiritual sacrifices, acceptable to God by Jesus Christ*.

All sincere Christians have in them a principle of spiritual life communicated to them from Christ their head: therefore, as he is called a living stone, so they are called lively, or living stones; not dead in trespasses and sins, but alive to God by regeneration and the working of the divine Spirit.

The apostle speaks here of the generality of Christians, and tells them they are a holy priesthood; they are all select persons, sacred to God, of service to others, well endowed with heavenly gifts and graces, and well employed. The spiritual sacrifices which Christians are to offer are their bodies, souls, affections, prayers, praises, alms, and other duties.

The people of God

1 Peter 2:9-10

Those who receive Christ are highly privileged, v.9. They are *a chosen generation, a royal priesthood* . . .

All true Christians *are a chosen generation*; they all make one family, a sort and species of people distinct from the common world, of another spirit, principle, and practice, which they could never be if they were not chosen in Christ to be such, and sanctified by his Spirit.

All the true servants of Christ are a royal priesthood. They are royal in their relation to God and Christ, in their power with God, and over themselves and all their spiritual enemies; they are princely in the improvements and the excellency of their own spirits, and in their hopes and expectations; they are a royal priesthood, separated from sin and sinners, consecrated to God, and giving to God spiritual services and offerings, acceptable to God through Jesus Christ.

All Christians, wherever they are compose one holy nation. They are one nation, collected under one head, agreeing in the same manners and customs, and governed by the same laws; and they are a holy nation, because they are consecrated and devoted to God, renewed and sanctified by his Holy Spirit.

To make this people content and thankful for the great mercies and dignities brought to them by the gospel, the apostle advises them to compare their former and their present state. Time was when they were not a people, nor had they obtained mercy, but they were solemnly disclaimed and divorced; but now they are taken in again to be the people of God and have obtained mercy.

The calling of Christ

Matthew 10:1

Here we are told who they were that Christ ordained to be his apostles or ambassadors; they were *his disciples*, v.1. He had called them some time before to be disciples, his immediate followers and constant attendants, and he then told them that they should be made fishers of men, which promise he now performed.

All this while Christ had kept these twelve in a state of preparation. All this while he had been fitting them for this great work. Those whom Christ intends for, and calls to, any work, he first prepares and qualifies in some measure for it.

Observe what the commission was that he gave them: *He called them to him*, v.1. He had called them to come *after* him before; now he calls them to come *to* him, admits them to a greater familiarity, and will not have them to keep at such a distance as they had up to that time observed.

He *gave them power*, authority in his name, to command men to obedience, and for the confirmation of that authority, to command devils too into a subjection. All rightful authority is derived from Jesus Christ. All power is given to him without limitation, and the subordinate powers that be are ordained of him. It is an undeniable proof of the fulness of power which Christ used as Mediator that he could impart his power to those he employed and enable them to work the same miracles that he wrought in his name.

He gave them power over *unclean spirits*, and over *all manner of sickness*. The design of the gospel was to conquer the devil and to cure the world. These preachers were sent out destitute of all external advantages to recommend them; they had no wealth, learning, nor titles of honour, and they made a very mean figure; it was therefore requisite that they should have some extraordinary power to advance them above the scribes.

Little children

Mark 10:13–16

Here we have little children brought to Christ, v.13. Their parents, or whoever they were that had the nursing of them, brought them to him, that he should *touch them*, in token of his commanding and conferring a blessing on them. They believed that Christ's blessing would do their souls good; and therefore to him they brought them, that he might touch them, knowing that he could reach their hearts, when nothing their parents could say to them or do for them, would reach them.

Notice the discouragement which the disciples gave to the bringing of children to Christ: *They rebuked them that brought them*, v.13; as if they had been sure that they knew their Master's mind in this matter, whereas he had cautioned them not to despise the little ones.

Observe the encouragement Christ gave to it. *When he saw it, he was much displeased*, v.14. 'What do you mean? Will you hinder me from doing good, from doing good to the rising generation, to the lambs of the flock?' He ordered that they should be *brought to him*, and nothing said or done to hinder them.

There must be something of the temper and disposition of little children found in all that Christ will own and bless. We must *receive the kingdom of God as little children*, v.15; that is, we must stand to Christ and his grace as little children do to their parents, nurses, and teachers. We must be inquisitive, as children, must learn as children (that is the learning age), and in learning must believe. He received the children, and gave them what was desired, v.16: *He took them up in his arms*, in token of his affectionate concern for them; *put his hands upon them*, as was desired, and *blessed them*. See how he outdid the desires of these parents; they begged he would touch them, but he did more.

Who is the greatest?

Matthew 18:1–3

As there never was a greater pattern of humility, so there never was a greater preacher of it than Christ; he took all occasions to command it and to commend it to his disciples. The occasion of this discourse concerning humility was an unbecoming contest among the disciples for precedency; they *came to him, saying, Who is the greatest in the kingdom of heaven?*

Christ here teaches them to be humble:

(1) by a sign, v.2: *He called a little child to him, and set him in the midst of them.* Christ often taught by signs, as the prophets of old. Humility is a lesson so hardly learnt, that we have need by all ways and means to be taught it.

(2) by a sermon upon this sign; in which he shows them and us the necessity of humility, v.3. His preface is solemn, and commands both attention and assent: *Verily I say unto you, except ye be converted, and become as little children, ye shall not enter into the kingdom of heaven.* Observe what it is that he requires and insists upon: 'You must be converted, you must be of another mind, and in another frame and temper, must have other thoughts, both of yourselves and of the kingdom of heaven, before you are fit for a place in it. The pride, ambition, and affectation of honour and dominion which appear in you, must be repented of, mortified, and reformed, and you must come to yourselves.'

True humility

Matthew 18:3

You must *become as little children.* Converting grace makes us like little children, not foolish as children, nor fickle nor playful. As children we must be careful for nothing, but leave it to our heavenly Father to care for us; we must be harmless, inoffensive, void of malice, governable, under command and (which is here chiefly intended) we must be humble as little children, who do not stand upon the punctilios of honour. As children are little in body and low in stature, so we must be little and low in spirit, and in our thoughts of ourselves. This is a temper which leads to other good dispositions; the age of childhood is the learning age.

Observe what stress he lays upon this. Without this, *you shall not enter into the kingdom of heaven*. The disciples, when they put that question (v.1), thought themselves sure of the kingdom of heaven; but Christ awakens them to be jealous of themselves. Our Lord designs here to show the great danger of pride and ambition; whatever profession men make, if they allow themselves this sin, they will be rejected both from God's tabernacle and from his holy hill. Pride threw the angels that sinned out of heaven, and will keep us out, if we are not converted from it.

August 19

What is love?

1 Corinthians 13:4

The apostle gives us in these verses some of the properties and effects of love (*charity*), both to describe and commend it, that we may know whether we have this grace, and that if we have it not, we may not rest till we have obtained it. It is an excellent grace, and has a world of good properties belonging to it.

It is *long suffering*. It can endure evil, injury, and provocation, without being filled with resentment, indignation, or revenge. It makes the mind firm, gives it power over the angry passions, and furnishes it with a persevering patience.

It is *kind*. It is benign, bountiful; courteous and obliging. The heart is large, ready to show favours and to do good, seeking to be useful; and not only seizes on opportunities of doing good, but searching for them.

Love suppresses envy: it *envieth not*; it is not grieved at the good of others; neither at their gifts nor their good qualities, honours, nor estates. If we love our neighbour we shall be so far from envying his welfare, or being displeased with it, that we shall share in it and rejoice at it.

Love subdues pride and boastfulness: *It vaunteth not itself, is not puffed up*, is not bloated with self-conceit, does not swell upon its acquisitions, nor arrogate to itself that honour, power, or respect, which does not belong to it. It is not insolent, apt to despise others, or trample on them, or treat them with contempt and scorn. Those who are animated with a principle of true brotherly love will in honour give preference to one another.

August 20

What love does not do

1 Corinthians 13:5

Love is careful not to pass the bounds of decency; *it behaveth not unseemly*; it does nothing indecorous, nothing that in the common account of men is base or vile. It does nothing out of place or time; but behaves towards all men as becomes their rank and ours, with reverence and respect to superiors, with kindness and condescension to inferiors, with courtesy and goodwill towards all men.

Love is an utter enemy to selfishness: *Seeketh not its own*, does not inordinately desire nor seek its own praise, honour, profit, or pleasure. Indeed self-love, in some degree, is natural to all men; it enters into their very constitution. But love never seeks its own to the hurt of others or with the neglect of others. It often neglects its own for the sake of others; prefers their welfare, satisfaction, and advantage to its own; and it ever prefers the welfare of the public, of the community, whether civil or ecclesiastical, to its private advantage. It would not advance, nor aggrandize, nor enrich, nor gratify itself, at the cost and damage of the public.

It tempers and restrains the passions: it *is not easily provoked*. It corrects a sharpness of temper, sweetens and softens the mind, so that it does not suddenly conceive, nor long continue, a vehement passion. Love will never be angry without a cause, and will endeavour to confine the passions within proper limits, that they may not exceed the measure that is just, either in degree or duration.

True love

1 Corinthians 13:5-6

Love *thinks no evil*. It cherishes no malice, nor gives way to revenge: so some understand it. It is not soon, nor long, angry; it is never mischievous, nor inclined to revenge; it does not suspect evil of others, it does not reason out evil, charge guilt upon them by inference and innuendo, when nothing of this sort appears open. True love is not apt to be jealous and suspicious; it will hide faults that appear, and draw a veil over them, instead of hunting and raking out those that lie covered and concealed.

The matter of love's joy and pleasure is here suggested: *It rejoiceth not in iniquity*. It takes no pleasure in doing injury or hurt to any. It thinks not evil of anyone, without very clear proof. It wishes ill to none, much less will it hurt or wrong any, and least of all make this the matter of its delight, rejoice in doing harm and mischief. Nor will it rejoice at the faults and failings of others, and triumph over them, either out of pride or ill-will, because it will set off its own excellences or gratify its spite. The sins of others are rather the grief of a charitable spirit than its sport or delight; they will touch it to the quick, and stir all its compassion, but can give it no entertainment.

It rejoiceth in the truth, is glad of the success of the gospel, commonly called *the truth*, by way of emphasis, in the New Testament; and rejoices to see men moulded into an evangelical temper by it, and made good. It takes no pleasure in their sins, but is highly delighted to see them do well, to approve themselves men of probity and integrity.

August 22

All things

1 Corinthians 13:7

Love beareth all things, it endureth all things; love covers all things. It will draw a veil over them, as far as it can consistently with duty. It is not for blazing nor publishing the faults of a brother, till duty manifestly demands it.

It beareth all things, will pass by and put up with injuries, without indulging anger or cherishing revenge, will be patient upon provocation, and long patient. It holds firm, though it is much shocked and borne hard upon; sustains all manner of injury and ill usage, and bears up under it, such as curses, disobedience, slanders, prison, exile, bonds, torments, and death itself, for the sake of the injurious, and of others; and perseveres in this firmness. What a fortitude and firmness fervent love will give the mind!

Love believes and hopes well of others: *Believeth all things; hopeth all things.* Wisdom may dwell with love, and love is cautious. But it is apt to believe well of all, to entertain a good opinion of them when there is no appearance to the contrary; no, to believe well when there may be some dark appearances, if the evidence of ill is not clear.

All love is full of candour, apt to make the best of everything, and put on it the best face and appearance. It will judge well, and believe well, as far as it can with any reason, and will rather stretch its faith beyond appearance for the support of a kind opinion; but it will go into a bad one with the utmost reluctance, and fence against it as much as it fairly and honestly can. And when, in spite of inclination, it cannot believe well of others, it will yet hope well, and continue to hope as long as there is any ground for it.

The greatest is love

1 Corinthians 13:13

To sum up the excellences of love, the apostle prefers it not only to gifts, but to other graces, to faith and hope, v.13: *And now abide faith, hope, and charity; but the greatest of these is charity*. True grace is much more excellent than any spiritual gifts whatever. And faith, hope, and love, are the three principal graces, of which love is the chief, being the end to which the other two are but means. This is the divine nature, the soul's felicity, or its satisfying rest in God, and holy delight in all his saints.

Love is everlasting work, when faith and hope shall be no more. Faith fixes on the divine revelation, and assents to that: hope fastens on future felicity, and waits for that: and in heaven faith will be swallowed up in vision, and hope in fruition. There is no room to believe and hope, when we see and enjoy. But love fastens on the divine perfections themselves, and the divine image on the creatures, and our mutual relation both to God and them. These will all shine forth in the most glorious splendours in another world, and there will love be made perfect; there we shall perfectly love God, because he will appear amiable for ever, and our hearts will kindle at the sight, and glow with perpetual devotion. And there shall we perfectly love one another, when all the saints meet there, when none but saints are there, and saints made perfect.

O blessed state! How much surpassing the best below! O amiable and excellent grace of love! How much does it exceed the most valuable gift, when it outshines every grace, and is the everlasting consummation of them! When faith and hope are at an end, true love will burn for ever with the brightest flame.

Order in the church

Acts 14:23

They ordained them elders, or presbyters, *in every church*. Now at this second visit to Lystra, Iconium, and Antioch, Paul and Barnabas settled the churches in some order, formed them into religious societies under the guidance of a settled ministry, and settled that distinction between those that are taught in the word and those that teach.

Every church had its governors or presidents, whose office it was to pray with the members of the church, and to preach to them in their solemn assemblies, to administer all gospel ordinances to them, and to take the oversight of them.

Those governors were then elders, that had in their qualification the wisdom and gravity of seniors, and had in their commission the authority and command of seniors: not to make new laws (this is the prerogative of the Prince, the great Lawgiver—the government of the church in an absolute monarchy, and the legislative power entirely in Christ), but to see to the observance and execution of the laws Christ has made; and so far they are to be obeyed and submitted to.

These elders were *ordained* to them, to the disciples, to their service, for their good. Those that are in the faith have need to be built up in it, and have need of the elders' help in it—the pastors and teachers. Even when persons are brought to believe, and that sincerely, yet ministers' care concerning them is not over; there is need of watching over them still, instructing and admonishing them still; there is still that lacking in their faith which needs to be perfected.

August 25

Encouragement and incentive

Hebrews 10:25

We have here the means prescribed for preventing our apostasy, and promoting our fidelity and perseverance. The writer to the Hebrews mentions several:

(1) that we should *consider one another to provoke love and to good works.* Christians ought to have a tender consideration and concern for one another; they should affectionately consider what their several wants, weaknesses, and temptations are; and they should do this, not to reproach one another, to provoke one another not to anger, but to love and good works, calling upon themselves and one another to love God and Christ more, to love duty and holiness more, to love their brethren in Christ more, and to do all the good offices of Christian affection both to the bodies and the souls of each other.

(2) that we should *not forsake the assembling of ourselves together,* v.25. It is the will of Christ that his disciples should assemble together, sometimes more privately for meeting and prayer, and in public for hearing and joining in all the ordinances of gospel worship.

(3) to *exhort one another,* to exhort ourselves and each other, to warn ourselves and one another of the sin and danger of backsliding, to put ourselves and our fellow-Christians in mind of our duty of our failures and corruptions, to watch over one another, and be jealous of ourselves and one another with a godly jealousy. This, managed with a true gospel spirit, would be the best and most cordial friendship.

(4) that we should observe the approaching of times of trial, and so be quickened to greater diligence: *So much the more, as you see the day approaching.* Christians ought to observe the signs of the times, such as God has foretold.

I know thy works

Revelation 2:2–3

Here we have the commendation Christ gave the church at Ephesus:

(1) for their diligence in duty: *I know thy works, and thy labour*, v.2. This may more immediately relate to the ministry of this church, which had been laborious and diligent. Dignity calls for duty. *For my name's sake thou hast laboured, and hast not fainted*, v.3. Christ keeps an account of every day's work, and every hour's work, his servants do for him, and their labour shall not be in vain in the Lord.

(2) for their patience in suffering: *Thy labour and thy patience*, v.2. It is not enough that we be diligent, but we must be patient and endure hardness as good soldiers of Christ. Ministers must have and exercise great patience, and no Christian can be without it. There must be patience to endure the injuries of men and the rebukes of Providence. We shall meet with such difficulties in our way and work as require patience to go on and finish well.

(3) for their zeal against what was evil: *Thou canst not bear those that are evil*, v.2. It harmonizes very well with Christian patience not to give exemption from sin, much less allow it; though we must show all meekness to men, yet we must show a just zeal against their sins. Their zeal was the more to be commended because it was according to knowledge, a discreet zeal upon a previous trial made of the pretences, practices, and tenets of evil men: *Thou hast tried them which say they are apostles and are not, and hast found them liars.* Some had risen up in this church that pretended to be not ordinary ministers, but apostles; and their pretensions had been examined but found to be vain and false.

August 27

Where is your devotion?

Revelation 2:4–5

We have here the rebuke given to the church of Ephesus: *Nevertheless, I have somewhat against thee*, v.4. The sin that Christ charged this church with was their decay and declension in holy love and zeal: *Thou hast left thy first love*; not left and forsaken the object of it, but lost the fervent degree of it that at first appeared.

The first affections of men towards Christ, holiness and heaven are usually lively and warm. These lively affections will abate and cool if great care is not taken, and diligence used, to preserve them in constant exercise.

Observe the advice and counsel given from Christ: *Remember therefore from whence thou hast fallen, and repent* . . . Those that have lost their first love must compare their present with their former state, and consider how much better it was with them then than now.

They must repent. They must be inwardly grieved and ashamed for their sinful declension; they must humbly confess it in the sight of God and judge and condemn themselves for it.

They must return and do their first works. They must as it were begin again, go back step by step, till they come to the place where they took the first false step; they must endeavour to revive and recover their first zeal, tenderness, and seriousness, and must pray as earnestly, and watch as diligently, as they did when they first set out in the ways of God.

August 28

Lukewarmness at Laodicea

Revelation 3:15–16

We now come to the last and worst of all the seven Asian churches, here is nothing commended. Here is the heavy charge drawn up against this church, ministers, and people, by one who knew them better than they knew themselves: *Thou art neither cold nor hot*, but worse than either; *I would thou wert cold or hot*, v.15. Lukewarmness or indifference in religion is the worst temper in the world. If religion is a real thing, it is the most excellent thing, and therefore we should be in good earnest in it; if it is not a real thing, it is the vilest imposture, and we should be earnest against it. If religion is worth anything, it is worth everything; an indifference here is inexcusable. Here is no room for neutrality. An open enemy shall have fairer quarter than a perfidious neuter; and there is more hope of a heathen than of such. Christ expects that men should declare themselves in earnest either for him or against him.

A severe punishment is threatened: *I will spue thee out of my mouth.* As lukewarm water turns the stomach, and provokes vomiting, lukewarm professors turn the heart of Christ against them. He is sick of them, and cannot long bear them. They shall be rejected, and finally rejected; for far be it from the holy Jesus to return to that which has been thus rejected.

August 29

Rich, yet poor

Revelation 3:17

We have one cause of this indifference and inconsistency in religion assigned, and that is self-conceitedness or self-delusion. The church at Laodicea thought they were very well already. Notice the high thoughts they had of themselves: *Thou sayest, I am rich, and increased with goods, and have need of nothing*, rich, and growing richer, and increased to such a degree as to be above all want or possibility of wanting. Perhaps they were well provided for as to their bodies, and this made them overlook the necessities of their souls. Or they thought themselves well furnished in their souls: they had learning, and they took it for religion; they had gifts, and they took them for grace; they had knowledge, and they took it for true wisdom; they had ordinances, and they took up with them instead of the God of ordinances. How careful should we be not to cheat our own souls!

Now notice the low thoughts that Christ had of them; they were *wretched, and miserable, and poor, and blind, and naked.* They were poor, really poor, when they said and thought they were rich; they had no provision for their souls to live upon; their souls were starving in the midst of their abundance; they were vastly in debt to the justice of God, and had nothing to pay off the least part of the debt.

They were *blind*; they could not see their state, nor their way, nor their danger; they could not see into themselves. They were *naked*, without clothing and without house and harbour for their souls. They were without clothing, had neither the garment of justification nor that of sanctification. Their righteousnesses were but filthy rags; they were rags, and would not cover them, filthy rags, and would defile them.

August 30

Behold, I stand at the door

Revelation 3:19-20

Here is great and gracious encouragement to this sinful people to take the admonition and advice well that Christ had given them, v.18-20. He tells them it was given them in true and tender affection: Whom *I love, I rebuke and chasten.*

If they would comply with his admonitions, he was ready to make them good to their souls: *Behold, I stand at the door and knock . . . ,* v.20. Here observe Christ is graciously pleased by his word and Spirit to come to the door of the heart of sinners; he draws near to them in a way of mercy, ready to make them a kind visit. He finds this door shut against him; the heart of man is by nature shut up against Christ by ignorance, unbelief, sinful prejudices. When he finds the heart shut, he does not immediately withdraw, but he waits to be gracious, even till his head be filled with dew.

Christ uses all proper means to awaken sinners, and to cause them to open to him: he calls by his word, he knocks by the impulses of his Spirit upon their conscience. Those who open to him shall enjoy his presence, to their great comfort and advantage. He will sup with them; he will accept of what is good in them. If what he finds would make but a poor feast, what he brings will make up the deficiency: he will give fresh supplies of grace and comfort, and so stir up fresh acts of faith, love, and delight; and in all this Christ and his repenting people will enjoy pleasant communion with each other. What careless obstinate sinners lose by refusing to open the door of the heart to Christ!

Beholding Christ's glory

Matthew 17:2

Observe the manner of Christ's transfiguration, v.2: *He was transfigured before them.* The substance of his body remained the same, but the appearance of it was greatly altered; he was not turned into a spirit, but his body, which had appeared in weakness and dishonour, now appeared in power and glory. Christ was both God and man; but, in the days of his flesh, he took on him the form of a servant. He drew a veil over the glory of his Godhead; but now, in his transfiguration, he put by that veil, appeared in the form of God, and gave his disciples a glimpse of his glory, which could not but change his form.

Now his transfiguration appeared in two things:

His face did shine as the sun. The face is the principal part of the body, by which we are known; therefore such a brightness was put on Christ's face, that face which afterwards he hid not from shame and spitting. It shone as the sun when he goes forth in his strength, so clear, so bright; for he is the Sun of righteousness, the Light of the world. The face of Moses shone but as the moon, with a borrowed reflected light, but Christ's shone as the sun, with an innate inherent light, which was the more perceptibly glorious, because it suddenly broke out, as it were, from behind a black cloud.

His raiment was white as the light. All his body was altered, as his face was; so that beams of light, darting from every part through his clothes, made them white and glittering. The shining of the face of Moses was so weak, that it could easily be concealed by a thin veil; but such was the glory of Christ's body, that his clothes were enlightened by it.

September 1

The cloud of God's presence

Matthew 17:5

Observe here the glorious testimony which God the Father gave to our Lord Jesus, in which he received from him honour and glory, when *there came this voice from the excellent glory*. This was like proclaiming the titles of honour or the royal style of a prince, when, at his coronation, he appears in his robes of state; and be it known, to the comfort of mankind, the royal style of Christ is taken from his mediation.

Now concerning this testimony from heaven to Christ, observe how it came, and in what manner it was introduced. There was a cloud. We find often in the Old Testament that a cloud was the visible token of God's presence; he came down upon mount Sinai in a cloud, and so to Moses. It was a bright cloud. Under the law it was commonly a thick and dark cloud that God made the token of his presence; he came down upon mount Sinai in a thick cloud. But *we are now come, not to the mount that was covered with blackness and darkness*, but to the mount that is crowned with a bright cloud.

It overshadowed them. This cloud was intended to break the force of that great light which otherwise would have overcome the disciples, and have been intolerable; it was like the veil which Moses put upon his face when it shone. God, in manifesting himself to his people, considers their frame.

September 2

This is my Son

Matthew 17:5

There came a voice out of the cloud, and it was the voice of God. Here was no thunder, or lightning, or voice of a trumpet, as there was when the law was given by Moses, but only a voice, a still small voice, and that not ushered in with a strong wind or an earthquake, or fire, as when God spake to Elijah. This voice *came from the excellent glory*.

Here we have the great gospel mystery revealed: *This is my beloved Son, in whom I am well pleased.* This was the very same that was spoken from heaven at his baptism and it was the best news that ever came from heaven to earth since man sinned. Moses and Elijah were great men, and favourites of heaven, yet they were but servants, but Christ is *a Son.*

This repetition of the same voice that came from heaven at his baptism was no vain repetition; but, like the doubling of Pharaoh's dream, was to show the thing was established. It was spoken at his baptism, because then he was entering upon his temptation, and his public ministry; and now it was repeated, because he was entering upon his sufferings, which are to be dated from this time.

Here we also have the great gospel duty required, and it is the condition of our benefit by Christ: *Hear ye him.* God is well pleased with none in Christ but those that hear him. It is not enough to give him the hearing (what will that avail us?) but we must hear him and believe him, as the great Prophet and teacher; hear him, and be ruled by him, as the great Prince and Lawgiver; hear him, and heed him.

Fear and encouragement

Matthew 17:5-7

Christ now appeared in glory; and the more we see of Christ's glory, the more cause we shall see to hearken to him, v.5; but the disciples were gazing on that glory of his which they say; they are therefore bid not to look at him, but to hear him.

Moses and Elijah were now with him; the law and the prophets. The disciples were ready to equal them with Christ, when they must have tabernacles for them as well as for him. They had been talking with Christ, and probably the disciples were very desirous to know what they said, and to hear something more from them. No, said God, *hear him*, and that is enough; him, and not Moses and Elijah.

Observe the fright which the disciples were put into by this voice, and the encouragement Christ gave them.

The disciples *fell on their faces, and were sore afraid.* The greatness of the light and the surprise of it might have a natural influence upon them to dispirit them. But that was not all, ever since man sinned, and heard God's voice in the garden, extraordinary appearances of God have ever been terrible to man, who, knowing he has no reason to expect any good, has been afraid to hear anything immediately from God.

Christ graciously raised them up with abundance of tenderness. The glories and advancement of our Lord Jesus do not at all lessen his regard to, and concern for, his people that are surrounded by infirmity. Now, in his exalted state, he has a compassion for, and condescends to, the lowliest true believer. Observe what he did: *he came, and touched them.* His approaches banished their fears. Observe what he said: *Arise and be not afraid.* It is Christ by his word, and the power of his grace going along with it, that raises up good men from their dejections, and silences their fears; and none but Christ can do it.

September 4

Down from the mountain

Matthew 17:8-9

Here we have the disappearing of the vision, v.8: they *lifted up their eyes,* and *saw no man, save Jesus only.* Moses and Elijah were gone, the rays of Christ's glory were laid aside, or veiled again. They hoped this would have been the day of Christ's entrance into his kingdom, and his public appearance in that external splendour which they dreamed of; but see how they are disappointed. Note, it is not wisdom to raise our expectation high in this world, for the most valuable of our glories and joys here are vanishing, even those of near communion with God are so, not a continual feast, but a running banquet. If sometimes we are favoured with special manifestations of divine grace, glimpses and pledges of future glory, yet they are withdrawn presently; two heavens are too much for those to expect that never deserve one.

Now *they saw no man, save Jesus only.* Note, Christ will tarry with us when Moses and Elijah are gone.

They came down from the mountain. We must come down from the holy mountains, where we have communion with God, and pleasure in that communion, and of which we are saying, *It is good to be here;*

even there we have no continuing city. Blessed be God, there is a mountain of glory and joy before us, from which we shall never come down. But observe when the disciples came down, Jesus came with them. When we return to the world again after an ordinance, it must be our care to take Christ with us, and then it may be our comfort that he is with us.

As they came down, they talked of Christ. When we are returning from holy ordinances, it is good to entertain ourselves and one another with discourse suitable to the work we have been about. That communication which is good to the use of edifying is then in a special manner seasonable.

September 5

The vision of heaven

Revelation 4:1–3

We have here an account of a second vision with which the apostle John was favoured. Those who improve the discoveries they have had of God already are prepared thereby for more, and may expect them. The vision begins with the strange sights that the apostle saw, and they were such as these: He saw *a throne set in heaven*, the seat of honour, authority, and judgment. Heaven is the throne of God; there he resides in glory, and from there he gives laws to the church and to the whole world, and all earthly thrones are under the jurisdiction of this throne that is set in heaven.

He saw a glorious one upon the throne. This throne was not empty; there was one who filled it, and that was God, who is here described by those things that are most pleasant and precious in our world: *His countenance was like a jasper and a sardine* (sardius) *stone*; he is not described by any human features, so as to be represented by an image, but only by his transcendent brightness. The jasper is a transparent stone, which offers to the eye a variety of the most vivid colours, signifying the glorious perfections of God; the sardius stone is red, signifying the justice of God, that essential attribute of which he never divests himself in favour of any, but gloriously exerts it in the government of the world, and especially of the church, through our Lord Jesus Christ. This attribute is displayed in pardoning as well as in punishing, in saving as well as in destroying sinners.

[211]

He saw a *rainbow about the throne, like unto an emerald,* v.3. The rainbow was the seal and token of the covenant of providence that God made with Noah and his posterity with him, and is a fit emblem of that covenant of promise that God has made with Christ as the head of the church, and all his people in him, which covenant is as the waters of Noah unto God, an everlasting covenant, ordered in all things and sure.

September 6

Around his throne

Revelation 4:4–8

The apostle John saw twenty-four seats round about the throne, not empty, but filled with twenty-four *elders,* representing, very probably, the whole church of God, both in the Old Testament and in the New Testament state; not the ministers of the church, but rather the representatives of the people. Their sitting denotes their honour, rest, and satisfaction; their sitting about the throne signifies their relation to God, their nearness to him, the sight and enjoyment they have of him, and their continual regard to him.

They are clothed in white raiment, the righteousness of the saints, both imputed and inherent; *they had on their heads crowns of gold,* signifying the honour and authority given them of God, and the glory they have with him.

He perceived lightnings and voices proceeding out of the throne; that is, the awful declarations that God makes to his church of his sovereign will and pleasure. Thus he gave forth the law on Sinai; and the gospel has not less glory and authority than the law though it is of a more spiritual nature. He saw *seven lamps of fire burning before the throne,* which are explained to be the *seven Spirits of God,* v.5, the various gifts, graces, and operations of the Spirit of God in the churches of Christ; these are all dispensed according to the will and pleasure of him who sits upon the throne.

He saw *before the throne a sea of glass, like unto crystal.* As in the temple there was a great vessel of brass filled with water, in which the priests were to wash when they went to minister before the Lord, so in the gospel church the sea or laver for purification is the blood of the Lord Jesus Christ, who cleanses from all sin, even from sanctuary-sins.

He saw four animals, living creatures, between the throne and the circle of the elders, standing between God and the people; these seem to signify the ministers of the gospel. The elders sit and are ministered unto; these stand and minister: they rest not night nor day.

September 7

Songs of adoration

Revelation 4:8–10

Observe the songs that the apostle John heard. He heard the song of the four living creatures, of the ministers of the church. They adore one God, and one only, the *Lord God Almighty*, unchangeable and everlasting. They adore three holies in this one God, the Holy Father, the Holy Son, and the Holy Spirit; and these are one infinitely holy and eternal Being, who sits upon the throne, and lives for ever and ever.

He heard the adorations of the twenty-four *elders*, that is, of the Christian people represented by them; the ministers led, and the people followed, in the praises of God, v.10,11.

The object of their worship is the same as that the ministers adored: *Him that sat on the throne*, the eternal ever-living God. The true church of God has one and the same object of worship.

They *fell down before him that sat on the throne*; they discovered the most profound humility, reverence, and godly fear. They *cast their crowns before the throne*; they gave God the glory of the holiness with which he had crowned their souls on earth and the honour and happiness with which he crowns them in heaven. They owe all their graces and all their glories to him, and acknowledge that his crown is infinitely more glorious than theirs, and that it is their glory to be glorifying God.

Universal praise

Revelation 4:11

Notice the elders' words of adoration: they said, *Thou art worthy, O Lord, to receive glory, and honour, and power*, v.11. They do not say, 'We give thee glory, and honour, and power'; for what can any creature pretend to give unto God? But they say, *Thou art worthy to receive glory*. In this they tacitly acknowledge that God is exalted far above all blessing and praise. He was worthy to receive glory, but they were not worthy to praise, nor able to do it according to his infinite excellence.

We have the ground and reason of their adoration, which is threefold:

(1) He is the Creator of all things, the first cause; and none but the Creator of all things should be adored; no made thing can be the object of religious worship.

(2) He is the preserver of all things, and his preservation is a continual creation; they are created still by the sustaining power of God. All beings but God are dependent upon the will and power of God, and no dependent being must be set up as an object of religious worship. It is the part of the best dependent beings to be worshippers, not to be worshipped.

(3) He is the final cause of all things: *For thy pleasure they are and were created*. It was his will and pleasure to create all things; he was not put upon it by the will of another; there is no such thing as a subordinate creator that acts under and by the will and power of another. As God made all things at his pleasure, so he made them for his pleasure, to deal with them as he pleases and to glorify himself by them one way or other.

Our Father's care

Matthew 10:29,31

Christ comforts and encourages his disciples that the providence of God is a special manner conversant about the saints, in their suffering. It is good to have recourse to our first principles, and particularly to the doctrine of God's universal providence, extending itself to all the creatures, and all their actions, even the smallest and most minute.

See here, the general extent of providence to all the creatures, even the least, and least considerable, to the *sparrows*, v.29. These little animals are of so small account, that one of them is not valued; there must go two to be worth *a farthing* and yet they are not shut out of the divine care: *One of them shall not fall to the ground without your Father*: They do not light on the ground for food, to pick up a grain of corn, but *your* heavenly *Father*, by his providence, laid it ready for them. Now he that feeds the sparrows will not starve the saints.

This God, who has such an eye to the sparrows, because they are his creatures, much more will have an eye to you, who are his children. If a sparrow dies not *without your Father*, surely a man does not,—a Christian,—a minister,—my friend, my child. Therefore be not afraid of death, for your enemies have no power against you, but what is given them from above.

Fear ye not, therefore, v.31. There is enough in the doctrine of God's providence to silence all the fears of God's people: *Ye are of more value than many sparrows*. All men are so, for the other creatures were made for man, and *put under his feet*; much more the disciples of Jesus Christ, who are the excellent ones of the earth, however despised as if not worth one sparrow.

September 10

The providence of God

Matthew 10:30

Observe here the particular notice which providence takes of the disciples of Christ, especially in their sufferings, v.30: *But the very hairs of your head are all numbered.* This is a proverbial expression, denoting the account which God takes and keeps of all the affairs of his people, even those that are most minute, and least regarded. This is not to be made a matter of. curious enquiry, but of encouragement to live in a continual dependence upon God's providential care, which extends itself to all occurrences, yet without disparagement to the infinite glory, or disturbance to the infinite rest, of the eternal Mind.

If God numbers their hairs, much more does he number their heads, and take care of their lives, their comforts, their souls. It intimates that God takes more care of them than they do of themselves. They who are solicitous to number their money, and goods, and cattle, yet were never careful to number their hairs, which fall and are lost, and they never miss them: but God *numbers the hairs of* his people, and *not a hair of their head shall perish*; not the least hurt shall be done them, but upon a valuable consideration: so precious to God are his saints and their lives and deaths!

September 11

God is faithful

1 Corinthians 10:13

The apostle gives a word of comfort, v.13. Though it is displeasing to God for us to presume, it is not pleasing to him for us to despair.

We live indeed in a tempting world, where we are surrounded by snares. Every place, condition, relation, employment, and enjoyment, abounds with them; yet what comfort may we fetch from such a passage! '*No temptation hath yet taken you, but such as is common to man*, what is human; that is, such as you may expect from men of such principles and power; or else such as is common to mankind in the present state; or else such as the spirit and resolution of mere men may bear you through.'

God is faithful. Though Satan is a deceiver, God is true. Men may be false, and the world may be false; but God is faithful, and our strength and security are in him. He keeps his covenant and will never disappoint the filial hope and trust of his children.

God is wise as well as faithful, and will proportion our burden to our strength. *He will not suffer us to be tempted above what we are able.* He knows what we can bear, and what we can bear up against; and he will, in his wise providence, either proportion our temptations to our strength or make us able to grapple with them. He will take care that we are not overcome, if we rely upon him, and resolve to approve ourselves faithful to him.

We need not perplex ourselves with the difficulties in our way when God will take care that they shall not be too great for us to encounter, especially when he will make them to turn out well. *He will make a way to escape*, either the trial itself, or at least the harm or injury of it. There is no valley so dark but he can find a way through it, no affliction so grievous but he can prevent, or remove, or enable us to support it, and in the end overrule it to our advantage.

September 12

Cast all your cares on him

1 Peter 5:7

The apostle, knowing that these Christians were already under very hard circumstances, rightly supposes that what he had foretold of greater hardships yet coming might excite in them an abundance of care and fear about the event of these difficulties.

Foreseeing this anxious care would be a heavy burden, and a sore temptation, he gives them the best advice and supports it with a strong argument.

His advice is to *cast all their care upon God*. 'Throw your cares, which are so cutting and distracting, which wound your souls and pierce your hearts, upon the wise and gracious providence of God; trust in him with a firm composed mind, *for he careth for you*. He is willing to release you of your care, and take the care of you upon

[217]

himself. He will either avert what you fear, or support you under it. He will order all events to you so as shall convince you of his paternal love and tenderness towards you; and all shall be so ordered that no hurt, but good, shall come unto you.'

The best of Christians are apt to labour under the burden of anxious and excessive care; the apostle calls it, *all your care*, intimating that the cares of Christians are various and of more sorts than one: personal cares, family cares, cares for the present, cares for the future, cares for themselves, others, and the church.

The best remedy against immoderate care is to *cast our care upon God*, and resign every event to his wise and gracious determination.

September 13

Conviction of sin

John 16:9

See what the Spirit shall convince the world of. He shall convince *of sin* (v.9), *because they believe not on me*. The Spirit is sent to convince sinners of sin, not barely to tell them of it; in conviction there is more than this; it is to prove it upon them, and force them to own it. The Spirit convinces of the fact of sin, that we have done so and so; of the fault of sin, that we have done ill in doing so; of the folly of sin, that we have acted against right reason, and our true interest; of the filth of sin, that by it we are become odious to God; of the fountain of sin, the corrupt nature; and, lastly, of the fruit of sin, that its end is death. The Spirit demonstrates the depravity and degeneracy of the whole world, that all the world is guilty before God.

The Spirit, in conviction, fastens especially upon the sin of unbelief, their not believing in Christ. There is a world of people that believe not in Jesus Christ, and they are not aware that it is their sin. Natural conscience tells them that murder and theft are sin; but it is a supernatural work of the Spirit to convince them that it is a sin to suspend their belief of the gospel, and to reject the salvation offered by it.

Natural religion, after it has given us its best discoveries and directions, lays and leaves us under this further obligation, that whatever divine revelation shall be made to us at any time, with sufficient evidence to prove it divine, we accept it, and submit to it.

September 14

The Spirit and righteousness

John 16:10

The Spirit shall convince the world *of righteousness, because I go to my Father, and you see me no more,* v.10. We may understand this as Christ's personal righteousness. He shall convince the world that Jesus of Nazareth was Christ the righteous one. His enemies put him under the worst of characters, and multitudes were not or would not be convinced but that he was a bad man, which strengthened their prejudices against his doctrine; but his is *justified by the Spirit,* he is proved to be a *righteous man,* and not a deceiver.

Now by what medium or argument will the Spirit convince men of the sincerity of the Lord Jesus? His *going to the Father* would be a full conviction of it. The coming of the Spirit, according to the promise, was a proof of Christ's exaltation to God's right hand, and this was a demonstration of his righteousness; for the holy God would never set a deceiver at his right hand.

We may also understand this as Christ's righteousness communicated to us for our justification and salvation; that everlasting righteousness which Messiah was to bring in. The Spirit shall convince men of this righteousness. Having by conviction of sin shown them their need of a righteousness, lest this should drive them to despair, he will show them where it is to be had, and how they may, upon their believing, be acquitted from guilt, and accepted as righteous in God's sight.

Christ's ascension is the great argument proper to convince men of this righteousness: *I go to the Father, and,* as an evidence of my welcome with him, *you shall see me no more.*

The Spirit and judgment

John 16:11

The Spirit shall convince the world *of judgment, because the prince of this world is judged,* v.11. The devil, *the prince of this world*, was judged, was discovered to be a great deceiver and destroyer, and as such judgment was entered against him, and execution in part done. He was cast out of the Gentile world when his oracles were silenced and his altars deserted, cast out of the bodies of many in Christ's name, which miraculous power continued long in the church; he was cast out of the souls of people by the grace of God working with the gospel of Christ; he *fell as lightning from heaven.*

This is a good argument with which the Spirit convinces the world of judgment. By *the judgment of the prince of this world*, it appears that Christ is stronger than Satan, and can disarm and dispossess him, and set up his throne upon the ruins of his.

Further, he shall show that Christ's errand into the world was to set things to right in it, and to introduce times of reformation and regeneration; and he proves it by this, that *the prince of this world*, the great master of misrule, is judged and expelled. All will be well when his power is broken who made all the mischief.

The Spirit shall also convince the world that *all judgment is committed to him*, and that he is the Lord of all, which is evident by this, that he has judged the prince of this world, has broken the serpent's head, *destroyed him that had the power of death, and spoiled principalities*; if Satan be thus subdued by Christ, we may be sure no other power can stand before him.

Finally, this points to the final day of judgment: all the obstinate enemies of Christ's gospel and kingdom shall certainly be reckoned with at last, for the devil, their ringleader, is judged.

Fishers of men

Matthew 4:19

Follow me, and I will make you fishers of men. The disciples had followed Christ before, as ordinary disciples, but so they might follow Christ, and follow their calling too; therefore they were called to a more close and constant attendance, and must leave their calling. Even they who have been called to follow Christ, have need to be called to follow on, and to follow nearer, especially when they are designed for the work of the ministry.

Observe what Christ intended them for: *I will make you fishers of men*; this alludes to their former calling. Let them not be proud of the new honour designed them, they are still but fishers; let them not be afraid of the new work cut out for them, for they have been used to fishing, and fishers they are still. It was usual with Christ to speak of spiritual and heavenly things under such allusions, and in such expressions, as took rise from common things that offered themselves to his view.

I will make you fishers of men. It is Jesus Christ that qualifies men for this work, calls them to it, authorizes them in it, and gives them success in it; gives them commission to fish for souls, and wisdom to win them.

Observe what they must do in order to do this: *Follow me.* They must separate themselves to a diligent attendance on him, and set themselves to a humble imitation of him; must follow him as their leader. Those whom Christ employs in any service for him, must first be fitted and qualified for it. Those who would preach Christ, must first learn Christ, and learn of him. How can we expect to bring others to the knowledge of Christ, if we do not know him well ourselves?

Instant obedience

Matthew 4:20‑22

Observe here the success of Christ's call. Peter and Andrew *straightway left their nets*, v.20; and James and John *immediately left the ship and their father* v.22; *and they all followed him*. Those who would follow Christ aright, must *leave all* to follow him. Every Christian must leave all in affection, sit loose to all, must *hate father and mother*—must love them less than Christ, must be ready to part with his interest in them rather than with his interest in Jesus Christ; but those who are devoted to the work of the ministry are, in a special manner, concerned to disentangle themselves from all the affairs of this life, that they may give themselves wholly to that work which requires the whole man.

This instance of the power of the Lord Jesus gives us good encouragement to depend upon the sufficiency of his grace. How strong and effectual is his word! *He speaks and it is done*.

This instance of the pliableness of the disciples gives us a good example of obedience to the command of Christ. It is the good property of all Christ's faithful servants to come when they are called, and to follow their Master wherever he leads them. They objected not to their present employments, their engagements to their families, the difficulties of the service they were called to, or their own unfitness for it; but, being called, they obeyed, and, like Abraham, *went out not knowing whither they went*, but knowing very well whom they followed. James and John *left their father*: it is not said what became of him; their mother Salome was a constant follower of Christ; no doubt, their father Zebedee was a believer, but the call to follow Christ fastened on the young ones. Youth is the learning age, and the labouring age.

What shall we do?

Acts 2:37

In these verses we find the word of God the means of beginning and carrying on a good work of grace in the hearts of many.

The hearers of the gospel were startled, and convinced, and put upon a serious enquiry, v.37. *When they heard they were pricked to the heart* or *in the heart*, and, under a deep concern and perplexity, applied themselves to the preachers with this question, *What shall we do?* It was very strange that such impressions should be made upon such hard hearts all of a sudden.

It put them in pain: *They were pricked in their hearts*. These were pricked to the heart with indignation at themselves for having been accessory to the death of Christ. Sinners, when their eyes are opened, cannot but be pricked to the heart for sin, cannot but experience an inward uneasiness; this is having the *heart rent, a broken and contrite heart*. Those that are truly sorry for their sins and are ashamed of them, afraid of the consequences of them, are *pricked to the heart*.

What shall we do? They speak as men at a stand, that did not know what to do; in a perfect surprise: 'Is that Jesus whom we have crucified both Lord and Christ? Then what will become of us who crucified him? We are all undone!' Note, there is no way of being happy but by seeing ourselves miserable. When we find ourselves in danger of being lost for ever, there is hope of our being made for ever, and not till then. Those that are convinced of sin would gladly know the way to peace and pardon.

Repent and be baptized

Acts 2:38–39

Peter and the other apostles direct the people in short to what they must do, v.38,39. Sinners convinced must be encouraged; though their case is sad, it is not desperate; there is hope for them.

He here shows them the course they must take. *Repent*; this is a plank after shipwreck. This was the same duty that John the Baptist and Christ had preached, and it is still insisted on: 'Repent, change your mind, change your way.' *Be baptized every one of you in the name of Jesus Christ*; that is, 'firmly believe the doctrine of Christ, and make an open solemn profession of this, and renounce your infidelity.'

They must be baptized *in the name of Jesus Christ*. Believe in the name of Jesus, that he is the Christ, the Messiah promised to the fathers. They must be baptized *in his name* for the *remission of sins*. This is pressed upon each particular person: *Every one of you.* 'Even those of you that have been the greatest sinners, if they repent and believe, are welcome to be baptized. There is grace enough in Christ for everyone of you, be you ever so many, and grace suited to the case of everyone.'

Peter gives them encouragement to take this course: 'You shall *receive the gift of the Holy Ghost* as well as we.' All that receive the remission of sins *receive the gift of the Holy Ghost*.

'Your children shall still have an interest in the covenant, for the promise of the remission of sins, and the gift of the Holy Ghost, is *to you and to your children*,' v.39. Now it is proper for an Israelite to ask, 'What must be done with my children? Must they be thrown out, or taken in with me?' 'Taken in,' says Peter 'by all means; for the promise is as much to you and to your children now as ever it was.'

'Though the promise is still extended to your children, yet it is not confined to you and them, but the benefit of it is designed for *all that are afar off.*' To this generality the following limitation must refer, *even as many of them*, as many particular persons in each nation, *as the Lord our God shall call*. God can make his call to reach those that are ever so far off.

September 20

The way of salvation

Romans 10:9–10

What is the word of faith? We have the tenor of it, v.9,10. What is promised to us? *Thou shalt be saved.* It is salvation that the gospel exhibits and tenders which Christ is the author of, a Saviour to the uttermost.

Upon what terms? Two things are required as conditions of salvation:

(1) *Confessing the Lord Jesus*—openly professing relation to him and dependence on him, standing by him in all weathers. Our Lord Jesus lays a great stress upon this confessing of him before men; see Matthew 10:32,33.

(2) *Believing in the heart that God raised him from the dead.* The profession of faith with the mouth, if there is not the power of it in the heart, is but a mockery; especially concerning his resurrection, which is the fundamental article of the Christian faith.

This is further illustrated, v.10, and the order inverted, because there must first be faith in the heart before there can be an acceptable confession with the mouth. It is *with the heart that man believeth*, which implies more than an assent of the understanding, and takes in the consent of the will. This is unto *righteousness*. There is the righteousness of justification and the righteousness of sanctification. Faith is to both.

It is with *the mouth that confession is made*—confession to God in prayer and praise, confession to men by owning the ways of God before others. And this is said to be *unto salvation*, because it is the performance of the condition of that promise. So that we have here a brief summary of the terms of salvation, that we must give up, to God, our souls and our bodies—our souls in believing with the heart, and our bodies in confessing with the mouth.

Justified by faith

Romans 5:1-2

It is sin that breeds the quarrel between us and God, creating an enmity; the holy righteous God cannot be at peace with a sinner while he continues under the guilt of sin. Justification takes away the guilt, and so makes way for peace. By faith we lay hold of God's arm and his strength, and so are at peace. There is more in this peace than barely a cessation of enmity, there is friendship and loving-kindness, for God is either the worst enemy or the best friend. And surely a man needs no more to make him happy than to have God as friend! This is *through our Lord Jesus Christ*—through him as the great peacemaker, *the Mediator between God and man.*

Observe the saints' happy state: a state of grace, God's loving-kindness to us and our conformity to God; he that has God's love and God's likeness is in a state of grace. Now into this grace we have access—we are brought into it. We are led into it as blind, or lame, or weak people are led,—are introduced as pardoned offenders,—are introduced by some favourite at court to kiss the king's hand, as strangers, that are to have audience, are conducted.

Wherein we stand. The phrase denotes progress; while we stand, we are going. We must not lie down as if we had already attained, but stand as those that are pressing forward, stand as servants attending on Christ as master.

Besides the happiness in hand, there is a happiness in hope, *the glory of God*, the glory which God will put upon the saints in heaven, glory which will consist in the vision and fruition of God. Those, and those only, that have access by faith into the grace of God now may hope for the glory of God hereafter. There is no good hope of glory but what is founded in grace; grace is glory begun, the earnest and assurance of glory.

Glory in suffering

Romans 5:3–4

What a growing, increasing happiness the happiness of the saints is: *Not only so*. One would think such peace, such grace, such glory, and such a joy in hope of it, were more than such poor undeserving creatures as we are could pretend to; and yet it is *not only so*: there are more instances of our happiness—*we glory in tribulations also*, especially tribulations for righteousness' sake, which seemed the greatest objection against the saints' happiness, whereas really their happiness did not only harmonize with, but take rise from, those tribulations.

How do we come to glory in tribulations? Why, because tribulations, by a chain of causes, greatly befriend hope, which he shows in the method of its influence.

Tribulation worketh patience, not in and of itself, but the powerful grace of God working in and with the tribulation. Tribulation in itself worketh impatience; but, as it is sanctified to the saints, it worketh patience.

Patience, experience, v.4. It works an experience of God, and the songs he gives in the night; the patient sufferers have the greatest experience of the divine consolations, which abound as afflictions abound. It is by tribulation that we make an experiment of our own sincerity, and therefore such tribulations are called trials.

Experience, hope, v.4. He who, being thus tried, comes forth as gold, will be encouraged to hope. This experiment, or approbation, is not so much the ground, as the evidence, of our hope, and a special friend to it.

September 23

The love of God in our hearts

Romans 5:5

This *hope maketh not ashamed*; that is, it is a hope that will not deceive us. Nothing confounds more than disappointment. Everlasting shame and confusion will be caused by the perishing of the expectation of the wicked, *but the hope of the righteous shall be gladness*. It is in a good cause, for a good Master, and in good hope; and therefore we are not ashamed.

Because the love of God is shed abroad. This hope will not disappoint us, because it is sealed with the Holy Spirit as a Spirit of love. It is the gracious work of the blessed Spirit to shed abroad the love of God in the hearts of all the saints. *The love of God*, that is, the sense of God's love to us, drawing out love in us to him again. Or, the great effects of his love: special grace and the pleasant sense of it.

It is shed abroad, as sweet ointment, perfuming the soul, as rain watering it and making it fruitful. The ground of all our comfort and holiness, and perseverance in both, is laid in the *shedding abroad of the love of God in our hearts*. A sense of God's love to us will make us not ashamed, either of our hope in him or our sufferings for him.

September 24

Amazing grace!

Ephesians 2:4–9

Here the apostle gives his account of the glorious change that was accomplished in them by converting grace, where observe, by whom, and in what manner, it was brought about and effected:

(1) Negatively: *Not of yourselves*, v.8. Our faith, our conversion, and our eternal salvation, are not the mere product of any natural abilities, nor of any merit of our own: *Not of works, lest any man should boast*, v.9. These things are not brought to pass by any thing done by us, and therefore all boasting is excluded; he who glories must not glory in himself, but in the Lord.

[228]

(2) Positively: *But God, who is rich in mercy* . . . , v.4. God himself is the author of this great and happy change, and his great love is the spring and original cause of it; hence he resolved to show mercy. Love is his inclination to do us good considered simply as creatures; mercy respects us as apostate and as miserable creatures.

God's eternal love or goodwill towards his creatures is the fountain from which all his mercies condescend to reach us; and that love of God is great love, and that mercy of his is rich mercy, inexpressibly great and inexhaustibly *rich*.

By grace are you saved through faith—it is the gift of God, v.5,8. Every converted sinner is a saved sinner. Such are delivered from sin and wrath; they are brought into a state of salvation, and have a right given them by grace to eternal happiness. The grace that saves them is the free undeserved goodness and favour of God; and he saved them, not *by the works of the law*, but through faith in Christ Jesus, by means of which they come to partake of the great blessings of the gospel; and both that faith and that salvation on which it has so great an influence are the gift of God.

September 25

Seated with Christ

Ephesians 2:5–6

We who were dead are quickened, v.5, we are saved from the death of sin and have a principle of spiritual life implanted in us. Grace in the soul is a new life in the soul. As death locks up the senses, seals up all the powers and faculties, so does a state of sin as to anything that is good. Grace unlocks and opens all, and enlarges the soul.

A regenerate sinner becomes a living soul: he lives a life of sanctification, being born of God; and he lives in the sense of the law, being delivered from the guilt of sin by pardoning and justifying grace. *He hath quickened us together with Christ.* Our spiritual life results from our union with Christ; it is in him that we live: *Because I live, you shall live also.*

We who were buried are raised up, v.6. What remains yet to be done is here spoken of as though it were already past, though indeed we are raised up in virtue of our union with him whom God has raised from the dead. When he raised Christ from the dead, he did in effect raise up all believers together with him, he being their common head; and when he placed him at his right hand in heavenly places, he advanced and glorified them in and with him, their raised and exalted head and forerunner.

And made us sit together in heavenly places in Christ Jesus. This may be understood in another sense. Sinners roll themselves in the dust; sanctified souls sit in heavenly places, are raised above the world; the world is as nothing to them, compared with what it has been, and compared with what the other world is. Saints are not only Christ's freemen, but they are assessors with him; by the assistance of his grace they have ascended with him above this world to converse with another, and they live in the constant expectation of it. They are not only servants to the best of masters in the best work, but they are exalted to reign with him.

September 26

God's workmanship

Ephesians 2:7–10

Observe what is the great design and aim of God in producing and effecting this change:

(1) with respect to others: *That in the ages to come he might show . . . ,* v.7, that he might give a specimen and proof of his great goodness and mercy, for the encouragement of sinners in future time. What may we not hope for from such grace and kindness, from riches of grace, and from exceeding riches of grace, to which this change is owing? *Through Christ Jesus,* v.7, by and through whom God conveys all his favour and blessings to us.

(2) with respect to the regenerated sinners themselves: *For we are his workmanship, created in Christ Jesus unto good works,* v.10. It appears that all is of grace, because all our spiritual advantages are from God. *We are his workmanship*; he means in respect of the new creation; not only as men, but as saints. The new man is a new creature; and God is its Creator.

In Christ Jesus, that is, on account of what he has done and suffered, and by the influence and operation of his blessed Spirit.

Unto good works. The apostle having before ascribed this change to divine grace in exclusion of works, lest he should seem by this to discourage good works, he here observes that though the change is to be ascribed to nothing of that nature (*for we are the workmanship of God*), yet God, in his new creation, has designed and prepared us for good works: *Created unto good works*, with a design that we should be fruitful in them.

Which God hath before ordained, that is, decreed and appointed. Or, the words may be read, *To which God hath before prepared us*, that is, by blessing us with the knowledge of his will, and with the assistance of his Holy Spirit; and by producing such a change in us. *That we should walk in them*, or glorify God by exemplary behaviour and by our perseverance in holiness.

September 27

Believing and rejecting

John 3:36

He that believeth on the Son, hath life, v.36. If God has put this honour upon the Son, we must by faith give honour to him. As God offers and conveys good things to us by the testimony of Jesus Christ, so we receive and partake of those favours by *believing* the testimony. We have here the sum of that gospel which is to be preached to every creature.

Here is, first, the blessed state of all true Christians: *He that believes on the Son hath everlasting life*. It is the character of every true Christian that he believes on the *Son of God*; not only believes him, that what he said is true, but believes *on* him and confides in him.

The benefit of true Christianity is no less than *everlasting life*; this is what Christ came to purchase for us and confer upon us; it can be no less than the happiness of an immortal soul in an immortal God. True believers even now, have everlasting life; not only they shall have it hereafter, but they have it now.

Secondly, the wretched and miserable condition of unbelievers: *He that believeth not the Son* is undone. The word includes both incredulity and disobedience. They cannot be happy in this world, nor that to come: *He shall not see life*, that life which Christ came to bestow. They cannot but be miserable: *The wrath of God abides upon* an unbeliever.

September 28

The love of God

Titus 3:4–5

We have here the prime author of our salvation—God the Father,
therefore termed here *God our Saviour*. The Father begins, the Son
manages, and the Holy Spirit works and perfects all. God (namely,
the Father) is a Saviour by Christ, through the Spirit. *God so loved the
world that he gave his only begotten Son, that whoever believes in him should
not perish, but have everlasting life.*

Observe the spring and rise of our salvation—the divine *kindness
and love* of God to man. By grace we are saved from first to last. This
is the ground and motive. God's pity and mercy to man in misery
were the first wheel, or rather the Spirit in the wheels, that sets and
keeps them all in motion. God is not, cannot be, moved by anything
out of himself. The occasion is in man, namely, his misery and
wretchedness. Sin bringing that misery, wrath might have issued
out rather than compassion; but God, knowing how to adjust all
with his own honour and perfections, would pity and save rather
than destroy. He delights in mercy. *Where sin abounded, grace did much
more abound.* Let us acknowledge this, and give him the glory of it,
not turning it to wantonness, but to thankfulness and obedience.

Here is the means or instrumental cause—the shining out of this
love and grace of God in the gospel, after it *appeared*, that is, in the
word. The appearing of love and grace has, through the Spirit,
great virtue to soften and change and turn to God, and so in *the
power of God to salvation to every one that believeth.*

September 29

So great a salvation!

Titus 3:5

*Not by works of righteousness which we have done, but according to his mercy,
he saved us.* Works must be in the saved but not among the causes of
his salvation; they are the way to the kingdom, not the meriting

[232]

price of it. Faith and all saving graces are God's free gift and his work; the beginning, increase, and perfection of them in glory, all are from him.

We see here the formal cause of salvation, regeneration or spiritual renewing, as it is here called. A new prevailing principle of grace and holiness is brought about, which makes the man a new man, having new thoughts, desires, and affections. *He saved us.* What is so begun, as sure to be perfected in time, is expressed as if it already were so. We must be initially saved now, by regeneration, if on good ground we would expect complete salvation in heaven. The change then will be but in degree, not in kind. Grace is glory begun, as glory is but grace in its perfection.

Here is the outward sign and seal of salvation, called therefore *the washing of regeneration.* The work itself is inward and spiritual; but it is outwardly signified and sealed in the ordinance of baptism. Baptism saves figuratively and sacramentally, where it is rightly used. Slight not this outward sign and seal, yet rest not in the outward washing. The covenant sealed in baptism binds to duties, as well as conveys benefits and privileges; if the former are not minded, in vain are the latter expected.

In the plan of our salvation, the applying and effecting part is especially attributed to the Holy Spirit (*the renewing of the Holy Ghost*). We are said to be born of the Spirit, to be quickened and sanctified by the Spirit, to be led and guided, strengthened and helped, by the Spirit. Earnestly therefore is he to be sought, and greatly to be heeded by us, that we quench not his holy motions. As we act towards him, so may we expect he will to us; if we slight, resist, and oppose his workings, he will slacken them; if we continue to vex him, he will retire.

September 30

Hallelujah! What a Saviour!

Titus 3:6-7

The manner of God's communicating the Spirit in his gifts and graces is not with a scanty and niggardly hand, but most freely and plentifully: *Which he shed on us abundantly.* More of the Spirit in its gifts and graces is poured out under the gospel than was under the law. A measure of the Spirit the church has had in all ages, but more since the coming of Christ, than before. There was then great abundance of common gifts of illumination, outward calling and profession, and general faith, and of more special gifts of sanctification too, such as faith, and hope, and love. Let us get a share in these. What will it signify if much be shed forth and we remain dry? The procuring cause of all is Christ: *Through Jesus Christ our Saviour.* All come through him, and through him as Saviour. Let us praise God for him above all; let us go to the Father by him.

Observe the ends why we are brought into this new spiritual condition, justification, heirship, and hope of eternal life: *That being justified by his grace, we should be made heirs according to the hope of eternal life.* Justification is the free remission of a sinner, and accepting him as righteous through the righteousness of Christ received by faith. This God does freely as to us, yet through the intervention of Christ's sacrifice and righteousness, laid hold on by faith.

It is by grace, as the spring and rise, though *through the redemption that is in Christ*, and by faith applying that redemption.

Being justified by his grace, we should be made heirs. Our justification is by the grace of God, and our justification by that grace is necessary in order to our being made *heirs of eternal life.* Eternal life is set before us in the promise. The Spirit works faith in us and hope of that life, and so are we made heirs of it; faith and hope bring it near, and fill with joy in the well-grounded expectation of it.

October 1

Jesus, our example

Philippians 2:5–8

Let this mind be in you which was also in Christ Jesus, v.5. Christians must be of Christ's mind. We must bear a resemblance to his life, if we would have the benefit of his death. He was eminently humble, and this is what we are to learn of him. If we were lowly-minded, we should be like-minded; and, if we were like Christ, we should be lowly-minded. Walk in the same spirit with the Lord Jesus, who humbled himself to sufferings and death for us.

Here are the two natures of Christ:

(1) his divine nature: *Who being in the form of God*, v.6, partaking of

the divine nature, as the eternal Son of God. *He thought it no robbery to be equal with God*; did not think himself guilty of any invasion of what did not belong to him. It is the highest degree of robbery for any mere man or mere creature to pretend to be equal with God.

(2) his human nature: *He was made in the likeness of men*, and *found in fashion as a man*. He was really and truly man. And he voluntarily assumed human nature; it was his own act. He emptied himself, divested himself of the honours and glories of the upper world, and of his former appearance, to clothe himself with the rags of human nature.

October 2

The exalted servant

Philippians 2:7–11

Here is Christ's humiliation: The *form of a servant*. He was not only God's servant, but he came to minister to men, and was among them as one who serves. One would think that the Lord Jesus, if he would be a man, should have been a prince. But quite the contrary: *He took upon him the form of a servant*. His whole life was a life of humiliation. The lowest step of his humiliation was his dying the death of the cross. *He became obedient to death, even the death of the cross.* He not only suffered, but was voluntarily obedient. There is an emphasis laid upon the manner of his dying, which had in it all the circumstances possible which are humbling: *Even the death of the cross*, a cursed, shameful death—full of pain—and the death of a malefactor and a slave, not of a freeman—exposed as a public spectacle.

Here is Christ's exaltation: *Wherefore God also hath highly exalted him.* Because he humbled himself, God exalted him; and he *highly exalted him*. He exalted his whole person, the human nature as well as the divine.

He had a name above every name. Every knee must bow to him. The whole creation must be in subjection to him: *at the name of Jesus* all should pay a solemn homage. *Every tongue should confess that Jesus Christ is Lord.* The kingdom of Christ reaches to heaven and earth, and to all the creatures in each, and to the dead as well as the living. *To the glory of God the Father.* Whatever respect is paid to Christ redounds to the honour of the Father.

October 3

Work out your salvation

Philippians 2:12–13

The apostle exhorts the Philippians to diligence and seriousness in the Christian way: *Work out your own salvation.* It concerns us above all things to secure the welfare of our souls: whatever becomes of other things, let us take care of our best interests. It is our own salvation. It is not for us to judge other people; we have enough to do to look to ourselves.

We are required to *work out our salvation.* The word signifies 'working thoroughly' and taking 'true pains'. We must not only work at our salvation, by doing something now and then about it; but we must work out our salvation, by doing all that is to be done, and persevering in it to the end. We cannot attain salvation without the utmost care and diligence. *With fear and trembling*, that is, with great care and circumspection. Fear is a great guard and preservative from evil.

The apostle urges this from the consideration of their readiness always to obey the gospel: '*As you have always obeyed, not as in my presence only, but now much more in my absence*,' v.12. They were not merely awed by the apostle's presence, but did it even much more in his absence. 'And because *it is God who worketh in you*, you are to work out your salvation. Work, for he worketh.' God is ready to concur with his grace, and assist our faithful endeavours. The operations of God's grace in us are so far from excusing, that they are intended to quicken our endeavours. 'And work out our salvation *with fear and trembling*, for *he worketh in you*. Work with fear, for he works of his *good pleasure*.'

To will and to do. It is the grace of God which inclines the will to that which is good; and then enables us to perform it. *Of his good pleasure.* As we cannot act without God's grace, so we cannot pretend to deserve it. God's goodwill to us is the cause of his good work in us.

October 4

Rejoice always!

Philippians 4:4–5

The apostle here exhorts to holy joy and delight in God: *Rejoice in the Lord always, and again I say, Rejoice*, v.4. All our joy must terminate in God; and our thoughts of God must be delightful thoughts. It is our duty and privilege to rejoice in God, and to rejoice in him always; at all times, in all conditions; even when we suffer for him, or are afflicted by him. We must not think the worse of him or of his ways for the hardships we meet with in his service. There is enough in God to furnish us with joy in the worst circumstances on earth.

Joy in God is a duty of great consequence in the Christian life; and Christians need to be again and again called to it.

We are here exhorted to candour and gentleness, and good temper towards our brethren: *Let your moderation be known to all men*, v.5. The word *moderation* here signifies a good disposition towards other men. Some understand it as the patient bearing of afflictions, or the sober enjoyment of worldly good; and so it well agrees with the following verse. The reason is, *the Lord is at hand*.

October 5

The promise of peace

Philippians 4:6–7

Here is caution against disquieting perplexing care, v.6: *Be careful for nothing*: the same expression as that of Matthew 6:25, *Take no thought for your life*; that is, avoid anxious care and distracting thought in the wants and difficulties of life. It is the duty and interest of Christians to live without care. There is a care of diligence which is our duty, and consists in a wise forecast and due concern; but there is a care of diffidence and distrust which is our sin and folly.

As a sovereign antidote against perplexing care the apostle recommends to us constant prayer: *In every thing by prayer and supplication, with thanksgiving, let your requests be made known to God*. We must not only keep up stated times for prayer, but we must pray upon every particular emergency: *In every thing by prayer*. When anything burdens our spirits, we must ease our minds by prayer; when our affairs are perplexed or distressed, we must seek direction and support. We must also join thanksgiving with our prayers and supplications. We must not only seek supplies of good, but own receipts of mercy.

Prayer is the offering up of our desires to God, or making them known to him: *Let your requests be made known to God*. Not that God needs to be told either our wants or desires, but he will know them from us.

The effect of this will be the *peace of God keeping our hearts*, v.7. The *peace of God*, that is, the comfortable sense of our reconciliation to God and interest in his favour, and the hope of the heavenly blessedness, and enjoyment of God hereafter, *which passeth all understanding*, is a greater good than can be sufficiently valued or duly expressed. This peace will *keep our hearts and minds through Christ Jesus*; it will keep us from sinning under our troubles, and from sinking under them; keep us calm and sedate, without discomposure of passion, and with inward satisfaction.

October 6

Right thinking
Philippians 4:8–9

We are here exhorted to get and keep a good name, a name for good things with God and good men: *Whatsoever things are true and honest*, v.8, a regard to truth in our words and engagements, and to decency and becomingness in our behaviour, suitable to our circumstances and condition of life.

Whatsoever things are *just and pure*, agreeable to the rules of justice and righteousness in all our dealings with men, and without the impurity or mixture of sin.

Whatsoever things are *lovely and of good report*, that is amiable; that will render us beloved, and make us well spoken of, as well as well thought of, by others.

If there is any virtue, if there is any praise—anything really virtuous of any kind and worthy of commendation. The apostle would have the

Christians learn anything which was good of their non-Christian neighbours: '*If there be any virtue, think of these things,* imitate them in what is truly excellent among them, and let not them outdo you in any instance of goodness.' We should not be ashamed to learn any good thing of bad men, or those who have not our advantages.

In these things he proposes himself to them for an example, v.9: *Those things which you have learned, and received, and heard, and seen in me, do.* Observe, Paul's doctrine and life were consistent. What they saw in him was the same thing as what they heard from him. He could propose himself as well as his doctrine to their imitation. It gives a great force to what we say to others when we can appeal to what they have seen in us. And this is the way to have the *God of peace with us*—to keep close to our duty to him.

October 7

The secret of contentment

Philippians 4:11–13

Not that I speak in respect of want, v.11. Paul was content with the little he had, and that satisfied him; he depended upon the providence of God to provide for him from day to day, and that satisfied him: so that he did not speak in respect of want in any way.

For I have learned, in whatsoever state I am, therewith to be content. We have here an account of Paul's learning, not that which he got at the feet of Gamaliel, but that which he got at the feet of Christ. He had learnt to be content; and that was the lesson he had as much need to learn as most men, considering the hardships and sufferings with which he was exercised. He was often in bonds, imprisonments, and necessities; but in all he had learnt to be content, that is, to bring his mind to his condition, and made the best of it.

I know both how to be abased and I know how to abound, v.12. To accommodate ourselves to an afflicted condition—to know how to be abased, how to be hungry, how to suffer want, so as not to be overcome by the temptations of it, either to lose our comfort in God or distrust his providence, or to take any indirect course for our own supply.

To a prosperous condition—to know how to abound, how to be full, so as not to be proud, or secure, or luxurious. And this is as hard a lesson as the other; for the temptations of fulness and prosperity are not less than those of affliction and want.

But how must we learn it? *I can do all things through Christ who strengthens me*, v.13. We have need of strength from Christ, to enable us to perform not only those duties which are purely Christian, but even those which are the fruit of moral virtue. We need his strength to teach us to be content in every condition.

October 8

Christ will come again

Acts 1:10–11

The disciples, when Christ had gone out of their sight, still continued *looking up steadfastly to heaven*, v.10. Perhaps they hoped that Christ would come back to them again, so much did they still dote upon his bodily presence, though he had told them that *it was expedient for them that he should go away*. Perhaps they expected to see some change in the visible heavens now upon Christ's ascension. Christ had told them that hereafter they should *see heaven opened*, and why should not they expect it now?

Two angels appeared to them. To show how much Christ had at heart the concerns of his church on earth, he sent back to his disciples two of those that came to meet him, who appear as *two men in white apparel*. Now we are told what the angels said to them, to check their curiosity: *You men of Galilee, why stand you gazing up into heaven?* What would you see? You have seen all that you were called together to see, and why do you look any further? *Why stand you gazing?* Christ's disciples should never stand at a gaze, because they have a sure rule to go by.

What the angels said to them served to confirm their faith concerning Christ's second coming. Their Master had often told them of this. '*This same Jesus*, who came once in disgrace to be judged, will come again in glory to judge. He *shall come in like manner*. He is gone away in a *cloud*. You have now lost sight of him in the clouds; and *whither he is gone you cannot follow him now*, but shall then.' When we stand gazing and trifling, the consideration of our Master's second coming should quicken and awaken us; and, when we stand gazing and trembling, the consideration of it should comfort and encourage us.

October 9

The Christian's hope
1 Thessalonians 4:13–14

The apostle comforts the Thessalonians who mourned for the death of their relations and friends that died in the Lord. His design is to dissuade them from excessive grief. All grief for the death of friends is far from being unlawful; we may weep for our own loss, though it may be their gain. Yet we must not be immoderate in our sorrows.

This looks as if we had not hope, v.13. It is to act too much like the Gentiles, who had no hope of a better life after this. This hope is more than enough to balance all our griefs.

This is an effect of ignorance concerning those who are dead, v.13. There are some things which we cannot but be ignorant of concerning those that are asleep. Yet there are some things concerning those especially who die in the Lord that we need not to be ignorant of. They will be sufficient to allay our sorrow concerning them.

They sleep in Jesus: they *are asleep*, v.13. They have retired out of this troublesome world, to rest from all their labours and sorrows, and they *sleep in Jesus*, v.14. They are not lost, nor are they losers, but great gainers by death, and their removal out of this world is into a better.

They shall be raised up from the dead, and awakened out of their sleep for *God will bring them with him*, v.14. They then are with God, and are better where they are than when they were here; and when God comes he will bring them with him. The doctrine of the resurrection and the second coming of Christ is a great antidote against the fear of death and inordinate sorrow for the death of our Christian friends; and this doctrine we have a full assurance of, because *we believe that Jesus died and rose again*, v.14.

October 10

Christ's second coming

1 Thessalonians 4:15–18

The state and condition of those who have died in the Lord shall be glorious and happy at the second coming of Christ. This the apostle informs the Thessalonians of *by the word of the Lord*, v.15. The Lord Jesus will come down from heaven in all the pomp and power of the upper world, v.16: *The Lord himself shall descend from heaven with a shout.*

He will descend from heaven into this our air, v.17. The appearance will be with pomp and power, *with a shout—with the voice of the archangel.* The glorious appearance of this great Redeemer and Judge will be proclaimed and ushered in by the *trump of God.*

The dead shall be raised: *The dead in Christ shall rise first,* v.16. Those who shall then *be found alive shall not prevent* (precede) *those that are asleep,* v.15.

Those that shall be found alive will then be changed. They shall be *caught up together with them in the clouds, to meet the Lord in the air,* v.17. Those who are raised, and so changed, shall meet together in the clouds, and there meet with their Lord. Here is the bliss of the saints at that day: they shall *be ever with the Lord,* v.17.

The principal happiness of heaven is this, *to be with the Lord,* to see him, live with him, and enjoy him, for ever. This should comfort the saints upon the death of their friends. We and they with all the saints shall meet our Lord, and be with him for ever, no more to be separated either from him or from one another for ever. And the apostle would have us *comfort one another with these words,* v.18.

October 11

Continuing our work

2 Thessalonians 3:11

There were among the Thessalonians some *idle persons and busybodies*, v.11. It does not appear that they were gluttons or drunkards, but idle, and therefore disorderly people. It is not enough for any to say they do no hurt; for it is required of all persons that they do good in the places and relations in which providence has placed them.

It is probable that these people had a notion concerning the near approach of the coming of Christ, which served them as a pretence to leave off the work of their callings, and live in idleness. It is a great error, or abuse of religion, to make it a cloak for idleness or any other sin. If we were sure that the day of judgment were ever so near, we must nevertheless do the work of the day in its day, that when our Lord comes he may find us so doing.

The servant who rightly waits for the coming of his Lord must be working as his Lord has commanded, that all may be ready when he comes. Industry in our particular callings as men is a duty required of us by our general calling as Christians.

There were busybodies among them: and it should seem, by the connection, that the same persons who were idle were busybodies also. This may seem to be a contradiction; but so it is, that most commonly those persons who have no business of their own to do, or who neglect it, busy themselves in other men's matters. If we are idle, the devil and a corrupt heart will soon find us something to do.

October 12

Heart-burning on the Emmaus road

Luke 24:32

Here is the reflection which the two disciples on the way to Emmaus made on the influence which Christ's discourse had upon them, v.32: *They said one to another, Did not our hearts burn within us?* 'I am sure mine did,' said one, 'And so did mine,' said the other, 'I never was so affected with any discourse in all my life.' Thus do they not so much compare *notes* as compare *hearts*, in the review of the sermon Christ had preached to them. They found the preaching powerful, even when they did not know the preacher. It made things very plain and clear to them; and, what was more, brought a *divine heat* with a *divine light* into their souls, such as put their hearts into a glow, and kindled a holy fire of pious and devout affections in them.

Now this they take notice of, for the confirming of their belief, that it was indeed, as at last they saw, *Jesus himself* that had been talking with them all along. 'What fools were we, that we were not sooner aware who it was! For none but he, no word but his, could *make our hearts burn within us* as they did; it must be he that has the key of the heart; it could be no other.'

See here what preaching is likely to do good—such as Christ's was, plain preaching, and that which is familiar to our capacity—*he talked with us by the way*; and scriptural preaching—*he opened to us the scriptures*, the scriptures relating to himself. Ministers should show people their religion in their Bibles, and that they preach no other doctrine to them than what is there; they must show that they make that the fountain of their knowledge and the foundation of their faith.

Observe, too, what hearing is likely to do good—that which makes the heart burn; when we are much affected with the things of God, especially with the love of Christ in dying for us, and so have our hearts drawn out in love to him, and drawn up in holy desires and devotions, then our hearts *burn within us*.

October 13

The foundation of the scriptures

2 Timothy 3:14–15

Paul directs Timothy to what he had learnt out of the holy scriptures v.14,15: *Continue thou in the things which thou hast learned*. It is not enough to learn that which is good, but we must continue in it, and persevere in it to the end.

What we have learnt we must labour to be more and more assured of, that, being grounded in the truth, we may be guarded against error, for certainty in religion is of great importance and advantage.

'*Knowing* that thou hast had good teachers. *Consider of whom thou hast learned them*; not of evil men and seducers, but good men, who had themselves experienced the power of the truths they taught thee, and been ready to suffer for them, and thereby would give the fullest evidence of their belief of these truths. Knowing especially the firm foundation upon which thou hast built, namely, that of the scripture, v.15: *That from a child thou hast known the holy scriptures.*'

It is a great happiness to know the holy scriptures from our childhood; the age of children is the learning age; and those who would get true learning must get it out of the scriptures.

The scriptures we are to know are the *holy* scriptures; they come from the holy God, were delivered by holy men, contain holy precepts, treat holy things, and were designed to make us holy and to lead us in the way of holiness to happiness; being called the *holy scriptures*, they are by this distinguished from profane writings of all sorts, and from those that only treat of morality, common justice, and honesty, but do not meddle with holiness.

If we would know the holy scriptures, we must read and *search them daily*, as the noble Bereans did. They must not lie by us neglected, and seldom or never looked into.

October 14

The power of God's word

2 Timothy 3:15–17

Here observe what is the excellency of the scripture. It is *given by inspiration of God*, v.16, and therefore is his word. It is a divine revelation, which we may depend upon as infallibly true.

Observe what use it will be of to us. *It is able to make us wise to salvation*; that is, it is a sure guide in our way to eternal life. Those are wise indeed who are wise to salvation. The scriptures are able to make us truly wise, wise for our souls and another world. 'To make thee wise to salvation *through faith*.' The scriptures will make us wise to salvation, if they are mixed with faith.

It is *profitable* to us for all the purposes of the Christian life, *for doctrine, for reproof, for correction, for instruction in righteousness*. It answers all the ends of divine revelation. It instructs us in that which is true, reproves us for that which is amiss, directs us in that which is good.

That the man of God may be perfect, v.17. The Christian, the minister, is the man of God. That which finishes a man of God in this world is the scripture. By it we are *thoroughly furnished for every good work*. There is that in the scripture which suits every case. Whatever duty we have to do, whatever service is required from us, we may find enough in the scriptures to furnish us for it.

O that we may love our Bibles more, and keep closer to them than ever!

October 15

True consecration

Romans 12:1

We see here the apostle's exhortations concerning our duty to God. We see what is godliness. It is to surrender ourselves to God.

The *body* must be presented to him, v.1. The exhortation is here introduced with great emotion: *I beseech you, brethren*. Though he was a great apostle, yet he calls the lowliest Christians *brethren*, a term of affection and concern. He uses entreaty; this is the gospel way.

The duty pressed—to present our *bodies a living sacrifice. Your bodies*—your whole selves. Our bodies and spirits are intended. Sacrifice is here taken for whatever is by God's own appointment dedicated to himself. Christ, who was once offered to bear the sins of many, is the only sacrifice of atonement; but our persons and performances, tendered to God through Christ, are as sacrifices of acknowledgment to the honour of God. Presenting them denotes a voluntary act. It must be a free-will offering.

The presenting of the body to God implies not only the avoiding of the sins that are committed with or against the body, but the using of the body as a servant of the soul in the service of God. It is to yield the members of our bodies as instruments of righteousness. There must be that real holiness which consists in an entire rectitude of heart and life, our bodies must not be made the instruments of sin and uncleanness, but set apart for God, and put to holy uses. It is the soul that is the proper subject of holiness; but a sanctified soul communicates a holiness to the body. That is holy which is according to the will of God; when the bodily actions are so, the body is holy.

October 16

Our response to God's mercy

Romans 12:1

The apostle gives three arguments to support the duty he has explained:

(1) Consider the mercies of God: *I beseech you therefore by the mercies of God.* This is an argument most sweetly cogent. There is the mercy that is in God and the mercy that is from God—mercy in the spring and mercy in the streams: both are included here. God is a merciful God, therefore let us present our bodies to him; he will be sure to use them kindly. We receive from him every day the fruits of his mercy, particularly mercy to our bodies: he made them, he maintains them, he bought them.

The greatest mercy of all is that Christ made not his body only, but his soul, an offering for sin. Let us render ourselves as an acknowledgment of all these favours—all we are, all we have, all we can do; and, after all, it is but very poor returns, and yet, because it is what we have.

(2) It is *acceptable to God.* These living sacrifices are acceptable to God. If the presenting of ourselves will but please him, we may easily conclude that we cannot bestow ourselves better.

(3) It is our *reasonable service.* There is an act of reason in it; for it is the soul that presents the body. Our God must be served in the spirit and with the understanding. God does not impose upon us anything hard or unreasonable, but that which is altogether agreeable to the principles of right reason. That is a reasonable service which we are able and ready to give a reason for.

October 17

The renewing of our minds

Romans 12:2

Be you transformed by the renewing of your mind. Conversion and
sanctification are the renewing of the mind, a change not of the
substance, but of the qualities of the soul. The man is not what he
was—*old things are passed away, all things are become new.* The renewing
of the mind is the renewing of the whole man; the progress of
sanctification, dying to sin more and more and living to
righteousness more and more, is the carrying on of this renewing
work. This is called the *transforming* of us.

Not that we can work such a change ourselves: we could as soon
make a new world as make a new heart by any power of our own; it
is God's work. Use the means which God has appointed and
ordained for it. It is God that turns us, and then we are turned. Lay
your souls under the changing transforming influences of the
blessed Spirit.

Observe what is the great enemy to this renewing; and that is,
conformity to this world: *Be not conformed to this world.* All the
disciples and followers of the Lord Jesus must be non-conformists to
this world. *Do not fashion yourselves* according to the world. We must
not conform to the things of the world. We must not conform to the
men of the world, we must not follow a multitude to do evil. True
Christianity consists much in a sober singularity. Yet we must take
heed of the extreme of affected rudeness and moroseness, which
some run into.

October 18

Knowing God's will

Romans 12:2

Observe what is the great effect of this renewing, which we must
labour after: *That you may prove what is that good, and acceptable, and
perfect will of God.* By the will of God here we are to understand his

revealed will concerning our duty, what the Lord our God requires of us. This is the will of God in general, even our sanctification, that will which we pray may be done by us as it is done by the angels; especially his will as it is revealed in the New Testament.

The will of God is *good, and acceptable, and perfect*. It is good; it is exactly consonant to the eternal reason of good and evil. It is acceptable, it is pleasing to God; that and that only is so which is prescribed by him. The only way to attain his favour as the end is to conform to his will as the rule. It is perfect, to which nothing can be added. The revealed will of God is a sufficient rule of faith and practice, containing all things which tend to the perfection of the man of God, to furnish us thoroughly to every good work.

It concerns Christians to *prove* what is that will of God which is good, and acceptable, and perfect; that is to know it with judgment and approbation, to know it experimentally, to know the excellence of the will of God by the experience of a conformity to it. It is to approve *things that are excellent*; it is to try things that differ, in doubtful cases readily to apprehend what the will of God is and to close in with it.

Those are best able to prove what is the good, and acceptable, and perfect will of God who are transformed by the renewing of their mind. A living principle of grace is in the soul, as far as it prevails, an unbiased judgment concerning the things of God.

October 19

Right living

Romans 13:7−8

We are here taught a lesson of justice and love. *Render therefore to all their dues*. What we have we have as stewards; others have an interest in it, and must have their dues. Render to all their dues; and that readily and cheerfully, not tarrying till you are by law compelled to it.

Due taxes: *Tribute to whom tribute is due, custom to whom custom*. The apostle wrote this to the Romans, who, as they were rich, so they were drained by taxes and impositions, to the just and honest payment of which they are here pressed by the apostle. Our Lord was born when his mother went to be taxed; and he enjoined the payment of tribute to Caesar. Many, who in other things seem to be just, yet make no conscience of this, but pass it off with a false ill-favoured maxim, that it is no sin to cheat the king.

Due respect: *Fear to whom fear, honour to whom honour.* This sums up the duty which we owe to all that are over us in the Lord. Where there is not this respect in the heart to our superiors, no other duty will be paid aright.

Due payment of debts, v.8: '*Owe no man anything*; do not continue in anyone's debt, while you are able to pay it.' Many that are very aware of the trouble think little of the sin of being in debt.

Owe no man anything. 'Whatever you owe, it is eminently summed up in this debt of love. But to *love one another*, this is a debt that must be always in the paying and yet always owing.' Love is a debt. If love is sincere, it is accepted as the *fulfilling of the law*.

October 20

Beholding the glory of the Lord
2 Corinthians 3:17–18

The apostle writes here about the privilege and advantage of those who enjoy the gospel above those who lived under the law. The condition of those who enjoy and believe the gospel is much more happy. For they have liberty: *Where the Spirit of the Lord is*, and where he works, as he does under the gospel dispensation, *there is liberty*, v.17, freedom from the yoke of the ceremonial law, and from the servitude of corruption; liberty of access to God, and freedom of speech in prayer. The heart is set at liberty, and enlarged, to run the ways of God's commandments.

They have *light*; for with *open face we behold the glory of the Lord*, v.18. The Israelites saw the glory of God in a cloud, which was dark and dreadful; but Christians see the glory of the Lord as in a glass, more clearly and comfortably. It was the special privilege of Moses for God to converse with him face to face, in a friendly manner; but now all true Christians see him more clearly with open face. He shows them his glory.

This light and liberty *are transforming*; we are changed into *the same image, from glory to glory*, v.18, from one degree of glorious grace unto another, till grace here is consummated in glory for ever. How

[250]

much therefore should Christians prize and improve these privileges! We should not rest contented without an experimental knowledge of the transforming power of the gospel, by the operation of the Spirit, bringing us into a conformity to the temper and tendency of the glorious gospel of our Lord and Saviour Jesus Christ.

October 21

Sovereign Lord

Acts 4:24–28

Here we have the address by the apostles and their friends to God. *When they heard they lifted up their voice to God with one accord*, v.24. One in the name of the rest *lifted up his voice to God* and the rest joined with him, with one mind (so the word signifies); their hearts went along with him, and so, though but one spoke, they all prayed. Observe:

(1) their adoration of God as the Creator of the world, v.24. They said, '*O Lord, thou art God, our Master and sovereign Ruler*' (so the word signifies), 'thou are the God *who has made heaven, and earth, and the sea.*' It is very proper to begin our prayers, as well as our creed, with the acknowledgment of this, that God is the *Father almighty, Maker of heaven and earth, and of all things visible and invisible.*

(2) their reconciling themselves to the present dispensations of providence, by reflecting upon the Old Testament, v.25,26. It was foretold, Psalm 2:1, that the heathen would rage at Christ and his kingdom; that the people would imagine all the things that could be against it; that the kings of the earth, particularly, would stand up in opposition to the kingdom of Christ; and that the rulers would gather together against God and Christ.

(3) their representation of the present accomplishment of those predictions. What was foretold we see fulfilled, v.27,28. It is *of a truth* that Herod and Pilate, the two Roman governors with the *people of Israel*, were *gathered together against thy holy child Jesus whom thou hast anointed. God's hand and his counsel determined it.* His hand and his counsel always agree: *for whatsoever the Lord pleased that did he.*

October 22

Asking for boldness

Acts 4:29–30

Observe the prayer made by the apostles and their friends. They pray:

(1) that God would take cognizance of the malice of their enemies: *Now, Lord, behold their threatenings*, v.29. They do not dictate to God what he shall do, but refer themselves to him.

(2) that God, by his grace, would keep up their spirits, and animate them to go on cheerfully with their work: *Grant unto thy servants that with all boldness they may speak thy word.* In threatening times our care should not be so much that troubles may be prevented as that we may be enabled to go on with cheerfulness and resolution in our work and duty, whatever troubles we may meet with. Their prayer is not, '*Lord, behold their threatenings*, and frighten them, and stop their mouths, and fill their faces with shame'; but '*Behold their threatenings*, and animate us, open our mouths and fill our hearts with courage.'

(3) that God would still give them power to work miracles for the confirmation of the doctrine they preached: *Lord, grant us boldness, by stretching forth thy hand to heal.* Nothing emboldens faithful ministers more in their work than the tokens of God's presence with them, and a divine power going along with them. They pray *that signs and wonders might be done by the name of the holy child Jesus*, which would be convincing to the people, and confounding to the enemies. Christ had promised them a power to work miracles, for the proof of their commission; yet they must pray for the continuance of it. It is the honour of Christ that they aim at in this request, that the wonders might be done by the name of Jesus, and his name shall have all the glory.

October 23

God's encouragement

Acts 4:31

Here we have the gracious answer God gave to this address, not in word, but in power. God gave them a sign of the acceptance of their prayers, v.31: *When they had prayed* and when they had concluded the work of the *day, the place was shaken where they were assembled together*; there was *a strong mighty wind*, such as that when the Spirit was poured out upon them, *which shook the house*, which was now their house of prayer. This shaking of the place was designed to strike an awe upon them, to awaken and raise their expectations, and to give them a perceptible token that God was with them of a truth.

God gave them greater degrees of his Spirit, which was what they prayed for. Their prayer, without doubt, was accepted, for it was answered: *They were all filled with the Holy Ghost*, more than ever; by which they were not only encouraged, but enabled to *speak the word of God with boldness*, and not to be afraid of the proud and haughty looks of men. The Holy Ghost taught them not only *what* to speak, but *how* to speak. Those that were endued habitually with the powers of the Holy Ghost still had occasion for fresh supplies of the Spirit, according to the various occurrences of their service.

We have here an instance of the performance of that promise, *that God will give the Holy Spirit to those that ask him* (Luke 11:13), for it was in answer to prayer that *they were filled with the Holy Ghost*: and we have also an example of the improvement of that gift, which is required of all on whom it is bestowed; have it and use it, use it and have more of it.

October 24

No reason to be afraid

2 Timothy 1:7

The great hindrance of usefulness in the increase of our gifts is slavish fear. Paul therefore warns Timothy against this: *God hath not given us the spirit of fear*, v.7. It was through base fear that the evil servant buried his talent, and did not trade with it, Matthew 25:25. Now God has therefore armed us against the spirit of fear, by often bidding us fear not. 'Fear not the face of man; fear not the dangers you may meet with in the way of your duty.' God has delivered us from the spirit of fear, and has given us the spirit *of power, and of love, and of a sound mind.*

The spirit of *power*, or of courage and resolution to encounter difficulties and dangers;—the spirit of *love* to God, which will carry us through the opposition we may meet with; the spirit of love to God will set us above the fear of man, and all the hurt that man can do us;—and the spirit of *a sound mind*, or quietness of mind, a peaceable enjoyment of ourselves, for we are often discouraged in our way and work by the creations of our own fancy and imagination, which a sober, solid, thinking mind would obviate, and would easily answer.

The spirit God gives to his ministers is not a fearful, but a courageous spirit; it is a spirit of power, for they speak in his name who has all power, both in heaven and earth; and it is a spirit of love, for love to God and the souls of men must inflame ministers in all their service; and it is a spirit of a sound mind, for they speak the words of truth and soberness.

October 25

No reason to be ashamed

2 Timothy 1:8

Paul exhorts Timothy to count upon afflictions, and get ready for them: '*Be not thou therefore ashamed of the testimony of our Lord, nor of me his prisoner.* Be not thou ashamed of the gospel, of the testimony thou hast borne to it.'

The gospel of Christ is what none of us have reason to be ashamed of. We must not be ashamed of those who are suffering for the gospel of Christ. Timothy must not be ashamed of Paul, though he was now in bonds. As he must not himself be afraid of suffering, so he must not be afraid of owning those who were sufferers for the cause of Christ.

The gospel is the testimony of our Lord; in and by this he bears testimony of himself to us, and by professing our adherence to it we bear testimony of him and for him.

We have no reason to be ashamed either of the testimony of our

Lord or of his prisoners; if we are ashamed of either now, Christ will be ashamed of us hereafter. *'But be thou partaker of the afflictions of the gospel, according to the power of God,* that is, expect afflictions for the gospel's sake, prepare for them, count upon them, be willing to take thy lot with the suffering saints in this world.' Or, as it may be read, *Do thou suffer with the gospel;* 'not only sympathize with those who suffer for it, but be ready to suffer with them and suffer like them.' We are likely to bear afflictions well, when we draw forth strength and power from God to enable us to bear them.

October 26

The Lord of the harvest

Matthew 9:37

The harvest truly is plenteous, but the labourers are few. There was a great deal of work to be done, and a great deal of good likely to be done, but there lacked hands to do it. It was an encouragement that *the harvest* was so *plenteous.* It was not strange that there were multitudes that needed instruction, but it was what does not often happen, that they who needed it, desired it.

It is a blessed thing to see people in love with good preaching. The valleys are then covered over with corn, and there are hopes it may be well gathered in. A harvest-day should be a busy day. It was a pity when it was so that *the labourers* should be so *few*; that the corn should shed and spoil, and rot upon the ground for want of reapers; loiterers many, but labourers very few.

Observe what the disciples' duty was: *Pray ye therefore the Lord of the harvest.* When things look discouraging, we should pray more and then we should complain and fear less. God is *the Lord of the harvest.* It is for him and to him, and to his service and honour that the harvest is gathered in.

Ministers are and should be labourers in God's harvest; the ministry is a work and must be attended to accordingly; it is harvest-work, which is needful work; work that requires everything to be done in its season, and diligence to do it thoroughly; but it is pleasant work; they reap in joy, and the joy of the preachers of the gospel is likened to the joy of the harvest.

All that love Christ and souls, should show it by their earnest

[255]

prayers to God, especially when *the harvest is plenteous, that he would send forth* more skilful, faithful, wise, and industrious *labourers into his harvest.*

October 27

The last judgment

Matthew 25:31

We have here a description of the process of the last judgment in the great day. Observe here the placing of the judge upon the judgment-seat, v.31: *When the Son of man shall come.* There is a judgment to come, in which every man shall be sentenced according to what he did in this world of trial and probation.

The administration of the judgment of the great day is committed to the Son of man. Here, as elsewhere, when the last judgment is spoken of, Christ is called *the Son of man,* because he is to judge the sons of men.

Christ's appearing to judge the world will be splendid and glorious. Christ will come to the judgment-seat in real glory; and all the world shall see what the saints only do now believe—that he is the brightness of his Father's glory. His first coming was under a black cloud of obscurity; his second will be in a bright cloud of glory.

When Christ comes in his glory to judge the world, he will bring all his holy angels with him. This glorious person will have a glorious retinue, his holy myriads. He will then sit upon the throne of his glory. He is *now* set down with the Father upon his throne; and it is a throne of grace, to which we may come boldly; but *then* he will sit upon the throne of glory, the throne of judgment.

The great separation

Matthew 25:32–33

Observe here the appearing of all the children of men before him, v.32: *Before him shall be gathered all nations.* The judgment of the great day will be a general judgment. All must be summoned before Christ's tribunal; all nations, all those nations of men that are made of one blood, to dwell on all the face of the earth.

The distinction will then be made: *He shall separate them one from another*, as the tares and wheat are separated at the harvest, the good fish and the bad at the shore, the corn and chaff in the floor. Wicked and godly here dwell together and are not certainly distinguishable one from another; but in that day they will be separated, and parted for ever. They cannot separate themselves one from another in this world, nor can anyone else separate them; but the Lord knows them that are his, and he can separate them.

This is compared to a shepherd's dividing between the sheep and the goats. Jesus Christ is the great shepherd; he now feeds his flock like a shepherd, and will shortly distinguish between those that are his, and those that are not. The godly are like sheep—innocent, mild, patient, useful: the wicked are like goats, a baser kind of animal, unsavoury and unruly.

The sheep and goats are here feeding all day in the same sheltered pasture, but will be at night in different folds. Being thus divided, he will set the *sheep on his right hand*, and the *goats on his left*, v.33. Christ puts honour upon the godly. All other divisions and subdivisions will then be abolished; but the great distinction of men into saints and sinners, sanctified and unsanctified, will remain for ever.

Welcome home

Matthew 25:34

Here we have the process of the judgment concerning each of these. Observe here the glory conferred upon the godly, v.34: *The king shall say unto them.* He that was the shepherd is here the King. Where the word of this King is, there is power. Here are two things in this sentence:

(1) The acknowledging of the saints to be the blessed of the Lord: *Come, ye blessed of my Father.* He pronounces them *blessed*; and his saying they are blessed, makes them so. *Blessed of his Father*: reproached and cursed by the world, but blessed of God.

He calls them to *come*: this come is, in effect, 'Welcome, ten thousand welcomes, to the blessings of my Father; come to me, come to be for ever with me.'

(2) The admission of the saints into the blessedness and kingdom of the Father: *Inherit the kingdom prepared for you.* The happiness they shall own is very rich. It is a *kingdom*; which is reckoned the most valuable possession on earth, and includes the greatest wealth and honour. It is a kingdom *prepared*: the happiness must be great, for it is the product of the divine counsels. It is prepared *for them.* This speaks of their property and interest in it. It is prepared on purpose for them; not only for such as you, but for you, you by name. It is prepared *from the foundation of the world.* This happiness was designed for the saints, and they for it, before time began, from all eternity.

The tenure by which the saints shall hold and possess the kingdom is very good, they shall come and *inherit it.* It is God that makes heirs, heirs of heaven. We come to an inheritance by virtue of our sonship, our adoption: *if children, then heirs.*

October 30

Faith and works

Matthew 25:35–36

For I was an hungered, and ye gave me meat . . . We cannot infer from this
that any good works of ours merit the happiness of heaven; but it is
plain that Jesus Christ will judge the world by the same rule by which
he governs it, and therefore will reward those that have been obedient
to that law. This happiness will be adjudged to obedient believers,
upon the promise of God purchased by Jesus Christ. It is the purchase
and promise that give the title, the obedience is only the qualification
of the person designed.

The good works here mentioned are such as we call 'works of
charity to the poor', and it teaches us this in general, that faith
working by love is all in all in Christianity: *Show me thy faith by thy
works.* The good works here described imply three things, which must
be found in all that are saved:

(1) self-denial, and contempt of the world; reckoning the things of
the world no further good things, than as we are enabled to do good
with them.

(2) love to our brethren; which is the second great commandment.
We must give proof of this love by our readiness to do good, and to
share with others; good wishes are but mockeries without good works.

(3) a believing regard to Jesus Christ. That which is here rewarded
is the relieving of the poor for Christ's sake, out of love to him. Those
good works shall then be accepted which are done in the name of the
Lord Jesus.

October 31

Jesus knows

Matthew 25:37–40

I was an hungered and ye gave me meat . . . This reason is questioned by
the righteous, v.37–39. Not as if they were loth to inherit the
kingdom, or were ashamed of their good deeds. Christ has a mighty

regard to works of love, and is especially pleased with acts of kindness done to his people for his sake. They speak of the humble admiration which glorified saints will be filled with, to find such poor and worthless services, as theirs are, so highly celebrated, and richly rewarded: *Lord, when saw we thee an hungered, and fed thee?*

Gracious souls are apt to think lowly of their own good deeds; especially as unworthy to be compared with the glory that shall be revealed. Saints in heaven will wonder what brought them there, and that God should so regard them and their services. 'When saw we thee an hungered? We have seen the poor in distress many a time; but when saw we *thee?*' Christ is more among us than we think he is.

This reason is explained by the Judge himself, v.40: *Inasmuch as ye have done it to these my brethren*, to the least, to one of the least of them, *ye have done it unto me.* The good works of the saints, when they are produced in the great day shall all be remembered; and not the least overlooked, no not a cup of cold water. They shall be interpreted most to their advantage. As Christ makes the best of their infirmities, so he makes the most of their services.

November 1

Faith without works is dead

James 2:21–26

We are here taught that a justifying faith cannot be without works from two examples.

The first instance is that of Abraham, v.21. By what Abraham did, it appeared that he truly believed. The faith of Abraham was a working faith, v.22. Abraham believed God, *and it was imputed unto him for righteousness*, v.23, and thus he became the *friend of God.* You see then, v.24, how that *by works a man is justified, and not by faith only*; not by believing without obeying, but by having such a faith as is productive of good works. Those who would have Abraham's blessings must be careful to copy his faith: to boast of being Abraham's seed will not avail at all. Those works which evidence true faith must be such as God himself commands, and not the mere fruits of our own imagination and devising.

The second example is Rahab, v.25. The former instance was of one renowned for his faith all his life long. This is of one noted for sin. The strongest faith will not do, nor the lowliest be allowed to go without works. That which proved her faith sincere was, that, at the risk of her own life, she *received the messengers, and sent them out another way*. Where great sins are pardoned, there must be great acts of self-denial. Her former acquaintance must be discarded, her former course of life entirely abandoned, and she must give signal proof and evidence of this.

The apostle draws this conclusion: *As the body without the spirit is dead, so faith without works is dead also*, v.26. The best works, without faith, are dead; they lack their root and principle. It is by faith that anything we do is really good. Faith is the root, good works are the fruits, and we must see to it that we have both. We must not think that either, without the other, will justify and save us.

November 2

Unshakable assurance

Romans 8:38–39

For I am persuaded . . . , v.38,39. This denotes a full, strong, and affectionate persuasion, arising from the experience of the strength and sweetness of the divine love. And here the apostle enumerates all those things which might be supposed likely to separate Christ and believers, and concludes that it could not be done.

Neither death nor life—neither the terrors of death on the one hand nor the comforts and pleasures of life on the other, neither the fear of death nor the hope of life. Or, we shall not be separated from the love either in death or in life.

Nor angels, nor principalities, nor powers. Both the good angels and the bad are called principalities and powers. And neither shall separate us from that love. The good angels will not, the bad shall not; and neither can.

Nor things present, nor things to come—neither the sense of troubles present nor the fear of troubles to come. Time shall not separate us, eternity shall not.

Nor height, nor depth—neither the height of prosperity and preferment, nor the depth of adversity and disgrace; nothing from heaven above, no storms, no tempests; nothing on earth below, no rocks, no seas, no dungeons.

Nor any other creature—anything that can be named or thought of. It will not, it cannot, *separate us from the love of God, which is in Christ Jesus our Lord*. It cannot cut off or impair our love to God, or God's to us; nothing does it, can do it, but sin. This is the ground of the steadfastness of the love; because Jesus Christ, in whom he loves us, is the same yesterday, today, and for ever.

November 3

In humble adoration

Romans 11:33–34

Here the apostle adores with great affection and awe the secrecy of the divine counsels: *O the depth of the riches of the wisdom and knowledge of God*, of the whole mystery of the gospel, which we cannot fully comprehend. He confesses himself at a loss in the contemplation, and, despairing to find the bottom, he humbly sits down at the brink, and adores the depth. Those that know most in this state of imperfection cannot but be most aware of their own weakness and short-sightedness.

The depth of the riches: men's riches are shallow, you may soon see the bottom; but God's riches are deep. There is not only depth in the divine counsels, but riches too, and that passing knowledge.

The riches of the wisdom and knowledge of God. His seeing all things—that all is naked and open before him: there is his knowledge. His ruling and ordering all things and bringing about his own purposes in all; this is his *wisdom*.

How unsearchable are his judgments! that is, his counsels and purposes: and his *ways*, that is, the execution of these counsels and purposes. We know not what he has in view; it is *past finding out*. Secret things belong not to us. We cannot give a reason of God's proceedings. The apostle speaks this especially with reference to that strange turn, the casting off of the Jews, and the entertainment of the Gentiles, with a purpose to take in the Jews again in due time.

It follows, v.34, *For who hath known the mind of the Lord?* Is there any creature made of his cabinet-council? Is there any to whom he has imparted his counsels, or that is able to know the way that he takes? *For who hath known the mind of the Lord?* And so, though we know not the mind of the Lord, yet if we have the mind of Christ

(1 Corinthians 2:16) we have enough.—*Or who has been his counsellor?*
It is nonsense for any man to prescribe to God, or to teach him how
to govern the world.

November 4

How great thou art!

Romans 11:35–36

The apostle adores with great affection and awe the sovereignty of
the divine counsels. In all these things God does what he will,
because he will, and yet there is no unrighteousness with him.

He challenges any to prove God a debtor to him, v.35: *Who hath
first given to him?* Who is there of all the creatures that can prove God
is under obligation to him? All the duties we can perform are not
requitals, but rather restitutions. The apostle here proclaims, in
God's name, that payment is ready: *It shall be recompensed to him
again.* It is certain God will let nobody lose by him; but never
anyone yet dare make a demand of this kind.

The apostle resolves all into the sovereignty of God, v.36: *For of
him, and through him, and to him, are all things,* that is, God is all in all.
Of God as the spring and fountain of all, through Christ, as the
conveyance, to God as the ultimate end. If all be of him and through
him, there is all the reason in the world that all should be to him and
for him. To do all to the glory of God is to make a virtue of
necessity; for all shall in the end be to him, whether we will or not.

And so he concludes with a short doxology: *To whom be glory for
ever, Amen.* Paul had been discoursing at large of the counsels of God
concerning man, but, after all, he concludes with the
acknowledgment of the divine sovereignty, as that into which all
these things must be ultimately resolved.

Whatever are the premises, let God's glory be the conclusion.
Especially when we come to talk of the divine counsels and actings,
it is best for us to turn our arguments into awful and serious
adorations.

[263]

My grace is sufficient

2 Corinthians 12:7-10

Here observe the methods God took to prevent the apostle being lifted up *above measure*. The apostle was pained with a thorn in the flesh, and buffeted with a messenger of Satan, v.7. We are much in the dark what this was. Some think it was an acute bodily pain or sickness.

The design of this was to keep the apostle humble, v.7. If God loves us, he will hide pride from us, and keep us from being exalted above measure. This thorn in the flesh is said to be a messenger of Satan, which he did not send with a good design, but with ill intentions. But God overruled it for good.

The apostle prayed earnestly to God for the removal of this sore grievance. If an answer is not given to the first prayer, nor to the second, we must hold on, and hold out, till we receive an answer. As troubles are sent to teach us to pray, so they are continued to teach us to continue in prayer.

My grace is sufficient for thee. Though God accepts the prayer of faith, yet he does not always answer it in the letter; as he sometimes grants in wrath, so he sometimes denies in love. It is a great comfort to us, whatever thorns in the flesh we are pained with, that God's grace is sufficient for us.

Grace signifies two things: the goodwill of God towards us, which is sufficient to strengthen and comfort us, and the good work of God in us. Christ Jesus will proportion the remedy to our malady.

Observe the use which the apostle makes of this dispensation: *He gloried in his infirmities*, v.9, and took pleasure in them for Christ's sake, v.10. They were fair opportunities for Christ to manifest the power and sufficiency of his grace resting upon him. When we are weak in ourselves, then we are strong in the grace of our Lord Jesus Christ.

Christ's life and work

Luke 4:18–19

Here we have a full account of Christ's undertaking and the work he came into the world to do. Observe how he was qualified for the work: *The Spirit of the Lord is upon me.* All the gifts and graces of the Spirit were conferred upon him, not by measure, as upon other prophets, but without measure.

Notice how he was commissioned: *Because he has anointed me, and sent me.* His being anointed signifies both his being fitted for the undertaking and called to it.

He was qualified and commissioned:

(1) to be a great *prophet. He was anointed to preach*; that is three times mentioned here. Observe *to whom* he was to preach: to the *poor*, to those that were poor in the world; to those that were poor in spirit, to the meek and humble, and to those that were truly sorrowful for sin. Observe *what* he was to preach. In general he must preach *the gospel.* He is sent to evangelize them; not only to preach to them, but to make that preaching effectual; to bring it, not only to their ears, but to their hearts.

He is to preach: *deliverance to the captives*: the gospel is a proclamation of liberty, like that to Israel in Egypt and in Babylon; *recovering of sight to the blind*: he came not only by the word of his gospel to bring light to them that sat in the dark, but by the power of his grace to give *sight* to them that were *blind*; *the acceptable year of the Lord,* v.19: He came to let the world know that the God whom they had offended was willing to be reconciled to them, and to *accept* them upon new terms. It alludes to the year of release, or that of jubilee, which was an *acceptable year.*

(2) to be a great *physician*; for he was sent *to heal the broken-hearted*, to give peace to those that were troubled and humbled for sins, and to bring them to rest who were weary and heavy-laden, under the burden of guilt and corruption.

(3) to be a great *Redeemer.* He not only proclaims liberty to the captives, but he sets at liberty them that are bruised. Christ as one having authority, as one that had *power on earth to forgive sins*, came to *set at liberty.*

November 7

Words of grace

Luke 4:20-22

Here is Christ's application of this text to himself, v.21: When he had read it, he rolled up the book, and gave it again *to the minister*, or clerk, that attended, and *sat down*, according to the custom of the Jewish teachers. Now he began his discourse thus, '*This day is this scripture fulfilled in your ears.*' It now began to be fulfilled in Christ's entrance upon his public ministry; now, in the report they heard of his preaching and miracles in other places; now, in his preaching to them in their own synagogue.

Here is the attention and admiration of the listeners: *The eyes of all them that were in the synagogue were fastened on him.* It is good in hearing the word to keep the eye fixed upon the minister by whom God is speaking to us; for, as the eye affects the heart, so, usually, the heart follows the eye, and is wandering, or fixed, as that is.

They all bore him witness and *wondered at the gracious words that proceeded out of his mouth*; and yet, as appears by what follows, they did not believe in him. Christ's words are words of grace. And these words of grace are to be *wondered at*; Christ's name was wonderful, and in nothing was he more so than in his grace, in the words of his grace, and the power that went along with those words. Their wonder increased as they said, '*Is not this Joseph's son?*' Some from this suggestion took occasion perhaps so much the more to admire his gracious words, concluding he must be taught of God, while others perhaps with this consideration corrected their wonder at his gracious words, and concluded there could be nothing really admirable in them, whatever appeared, because he was the son of Joseph.

November 8

Seed on the path

Matthew 13:4,19

In the parable of the sower and the seed, observe the characters of the different sorts of ground. First, the highway ground (*the wayside*), or path, v.4,19.

Observe what kind of hearers are compared to the *wayside*; such as *hear the word and understand it not*; and it is their own fault that they do not. They take no heed to it, take no hold of it; they do not come with any design to get good, as the wayside was never intended to be sown. They come before God as his people come, and sit before him as his people sit; but it is merely for fashion-sake, to see and be seen; they mind not what is said, it comes in one ear and goes out at the other, and makes no impression.

Observe how they come to be unprofitable hearers. The *wicked one*, that is, the devil, *cometh and catcheth away that which was sown*. Such mindless, careless, trifling hearers are an easy prey to Satan, who, as he is the great murderer of souls, is the great thief of sermons, and will be sure to rob us of the word, if we take not care to keep it: as the birds pick up the seed that falls on the ground that is neither ploughed before or harrowed after. If we break not up the fallow ground, by preparing our hearts for the word, and humbling them to it, and engaging our own attention; and if we cover not the seed afterwards, by meditation and prayer; if we give not a *more earnest heed to the things which we have heard*, we ae as the wayside.

The devil is a sworn enemy to our profiting by the word of God; and none do more befriend his design than heedless hearers, who are thinking of something else, when they should be thinking of the things that belong to their peace.

Stony ground

Matthew 13:5–6, 20–21

The *stony ground. Some fell upon stony places*, v.5,6, which represents the case of hearers who receive some good impressions of the word, but they are not lasting, v.20,21.

Observe how far they went. They *hear the word*; they turn neither their backs upon it, nor a deaf ear to it. They are *quick in hearing, forthwith it sprung up*, v.5, it sooner appeared above ground than that which was sown in the good soil. He *receiveth it straightway*, without trying it; swallows it without chewing, and then there can never be a good digestion.

They receive it with joy. There are many that are very glad to hear a good sermon, that yet do not profit by it. They *endure for a while*. Many endure for a while, that do not endure to the end, they did run well, but something hindered them.

Observe how they fell away, so that no fruit was brought to perfection. They have *no root in themselves*, no settled, fixed principles in their judgments, no firm resolution in their wills. It is possible there may be the green blade of a profession, where yet there is not the root of grace.

Times of trial come, and then they come to nothing. *When tribulation and persecution arise because of the word, he stumbles.* After a fair gale of opportunity usually follows a storm of persecution, to try who have received the word in sincerity, and who have not. When trying times come, those who have no root soon stumble; they first quarrel with their profession, and then quit it.

Thorny ground

Matthew 13:7,22

The thorny ground: *Some fell among thorns and the thorns sprung up*, which intimates that they did not appear, or but little, when the corn was sown, but afterwards they proved choking to it, v.7. This went further than the former, for it had root; and it represents the condition of those who do not quite cast off their profession, and yet come short of any saving benefit of it. Prosperity destroys the word in the heart, as much as persecution does; and more dangerously, because more silently.

Now what are these choking thorns?

First, *the cares of this world*. Care for another world would quicken the springing of this seed, but care for this world chokes it. Worldly cares are fitly compared to thorns; they are entangling, vexing, and scratching. These thorns choke the good seed.

Worldly cares are great hindrances to our profiting by the word of God. They eat up that vigour of soul which should be spent in divine things; divert us from duty, distract us in duty, and do us most harm of all afterwards; quenching the sparks of good affections, and bursting the cords of good resolutions.

Secondly, *the deceitfulness of riches*. Those who, by their care and industry, have raised estates, and so the danger that arises from care seems to be over, and they continue hearers of the word, yet are still in a snare; it is hard for them to enter into the kingdom of heaven: they are apt to rely upon riches, and to take an inordinate delight in them; and this chokes the word as much as care did.

November 11

The good soil

Matthew 13:8–9, 23

The good ground, v.18: *Others fell into good ground*, and it is pity but that good seed should always meet with good soil, and then there is no loss; such are good *hearers of the word*, v.23.

Now that which distinguished this good ground from the rest, was, in one word, fruitfulness. He does not say that this good ground has no stone in it, or no thorns; but there were none that prevailed to hinder its fruitfulness. Saints, in this world, are not perfectly free from the remains of sin; but happily freed from the reign of it.

The hearers represented by the good ground are:

(1) intelligent hearers; they *hear the word and understand it*; they understand not only the sense and meaning of the word, but their

own concern in it; they understand it as a man of business understands his business.

(2) fruitful hearers, which is an evidence of their good understanding: which *also beareth fruit*. We then bear fruit, when we practise according to the word, and we do as we are taught.

(3) not all alike fruitful: *some a hundredfold, some sixty, some thirty*. Among fruitful Christians, some are more fruitful than others: where there is true grace, yet there are degrees of it; all Christ's scholars are not in the same form. But if the ground is good, and the fruit right, those who bring forth but thirtyfold shall be graciously accepted of God, and it will be fruit abounding to their account.

Christ closes the parable with a solemn call to attention, v.9, *Who hath ears to hear, let him hear*. The sense of hearing cannot be better employed than in hearing the word of God.

November 12

Christ and Peter

Luke 22:31–34

Simon, Simon, Satan hath desired to have you, that he may sift you as wheat. 'Give me leave to try them,' said Satan, 'and Peter particularly.' He desired to have them, *that he might sift them,* that he might show them to be chaff, and not wheat.

Observe the particular encouragement he gave to Peter: '*I have prayed for thee*: thou wilt be most violently assaulted, *but I have prayed for thee, that thy faith fail not.*' Though there may be many failings in the faith of true believers, yet there shall not be a total and final failure of their faith. It is owing to the mediation and intercession of Jesus Christ that the faith of his disciples, though sometimes sadly shaken, yet is not sunk.

The charge he gives to Peter to help others is: '*When thou art converted, strengthen thy brethren*; when thou hast found thy faith kept from failing, labour to confirm the faith of others; when thou has found mercy with God thyself, encourage others to hope that they also shall find mercy.'

Here is Peter's declared resolution to cleave to Christ, whatever it cost him, v.33: *Lord, I am ready to go with thee, both into prison and to death.* This was a great word, and yet I believe no more than he meant at this time, and thought he should make good to.

And yet there comes Christ's express prediction of his denying him thrice, v.34: '*I tell thee, Peter, the cock shall not crow this day before thou even deny that thou knowest me.*' Christ knows us better than we know ourselves. It is well for us that Christ knows where we are weak better than we do, and therefore where to come in with grace sufficient.

November 13

Peter's denial

Luke 22:54–60

We have here the melancholy story of Peter's denying his Master. They *took him*, Christ, *and led him, and brought him*, which may intimate that they were in confusion. Struck with inward terror upon what they had seen and heard, they took him the furthest way about.

Peter's falling began in sneaking. He *followed Christ*; this was well. But he followed *afar off*. He thought to trim the matter, to *follow Christ*, and so to satisfy his conscience, but to follow *afar off*, and so to save his reputation. It proceeded in associating himself with the high priest's servants. The servants *kindled a fire in the midst of the hall* and *sat down together, Peter sat down among them*, as if he had been one of them.

His fall itself was disclaiming all acquaintance with Christ, because he was now in distress and danger. He was charged by a sorry, simple maid with being a retainer to this Jesus. She *looked earnestly* upon him as he sat by the fire: '*This man was with him*,' she said. And Peter, as he had not the courage to own the charge, so he had not the wit and presence of mind to turn it off, and therefore flatly and plainly denies it: '*Woman, I know him not.*' His fall was repeated a second time, v.58: *After a little while another saw him*, and said, '*Even thou art one of them.*' '*Not I*,' said Peter; '*Man, I am not.*' And a third time, *about the space of an hour after another* confidently affirms, strenuously asserts it. '*Of a truth this fellow also was with him*, let him deny it if he can, for you may all perceive he is a Galilean.' Peter now not only denies that he is a disciple of Christ, but that he knows anything of him, v.60: '*Man, I know not what thou sayest.*'

The Lord looks at Peter

Luke 22:60–62

The *cock crew* just as Peter was the third time denying that he knew Christ, and this startled him and put him thinking. Small accidents may involve great consequences.

The Lord turned and looked upon him. This circumstance we have not in the other evangelists, but it is a very remarkable one. Though Christ has now his back upon Peter, and was upon his trial, yet he knew all that Peter said. Christ takes more notice of what we say and do than we think he does. When Peter disowned Christ, yet Christ did not disown him. It is well for us that Christ does not deal with us as we deal with him.

Christ *looked upon Peter*, for he knew that, though he had denied him with his lips, yet his eye would still be towards him. He only gave him a look, which none but Peter would understand the meaning of. Christ turned, and looked upon him, as if he should say, 'Dost thou not know me, Peter?' It was a *remonstrating*, upbraiding look: 'What Peter, art thou he that disownest me now? Thou that wast the most forward to confess me to be the Son of God, and didst solemnly promise thou wouldest never disown me?' It was a *compassionate* look; he looked upon him with tenderness. 'Poor Peter! How art thou fallen and undone if I do not help thee!' It was a *significant* look: it signified the conveying of grace to Peter's heart. The crowing of the cock would not have brought him to repentance without this look. Power went along with this look to change the heart of Peter.

Peter remembered the words of the Lord. The grace of God works in and by the word of God, brings that to mind, and sets that home upon the conscience. Then *Peter went out, and wept bitterly*. One look from Christ melted him into tears of godly sorrow for sin.

November 15

Christt died for the ungodly

Romans 5:6–10

We were without strength, v.6, in a sad condition; altogether unable to
help ourselves out of that condition. Therefore, our salvation is here
said to come *in due time*. God's time to help and save is when those
that are to be saved are without strength. It is the manner of God to
help at a dead lift.

Christ died for the ungodly; not only helpless creatures, and therefore
likely to perish, but guilty, sinful creatures, and therefore deserving
to perish. Being ungodly, they had need of one to die for them. This
he illustrates (v.7,8) as an unparalleled instance of love; in this
God's thoughts and ways were above ours. One would hardly *die for
a righteous man*, that is one that is unjustly condemned; everybody
will pity such a one, but few will risk their own lives in his stead.
One might perhaps be persuaded to die for a good man, who is more
than barely a righteous man. Many that are good themselves yet do
but little good to others; but those that are useful commonly get
themselves well beloved. And yet observe how he qualifies this: it is
but some that would do so, after all, it is but *peradventure* (perhaps).

But Christ died for sinners, v.8, neither righteous nor good; not only
such as were useless, but such as were guilty. Now in this *God
commended his love*, not only proved but magnified it and made it
illustrious, not only put it past dispute, but rendered it the object of
the greatest wonder and admiration.

While we were yet sinners. He died to save us, not in our sins, but
from our sins; but we were still sinners when he died for us.

No, which is more, *we were enemies*, v.10, not only malefactors but
traitors and rebels. And that for such as these Christ should die is
such a mystery, such an unprecedented instance of love, that it may
well be our business to eternity to admire and wonder at it.

The fruits of Christ's death

Romans 5:9–11

Justification and reconciliation are the fruit of the death of Christ. We are justified by his *blood*, v.9, *reconciled by his death*, v.10. Sin is pardoned, the enmity slain, and end made of iniquity, and an everlasting righteousness brought in. Immediately upon our believing we are actually put into a state of justification and reconciliation.

Justified by his blood. Our justification is ascribed to the blood of Christ because *without blood there is no remission* of sins. In all the propitiatory sacrifices, the sprinkling of the blood was of the essence of the sacrifice.

And so salvation results from wrath: *Saved from wrath*, v.9, *saved by his life*, v.10. If God justified and reconciled us when we were enemies, much more will he save us when we are justified and reconciled. He that has done the greater, which is of enemies to make us friends, will certainly do the less, which is when we are friends to treat us in a friendly manner and to be kind to us. The apostle speaks of it with a *much more*. *We shall be saved from wrath*. It is wrath of God that is the fire of hell.

Reconciled by his death, saved by his life. His life here spoken of is not to be understood as his life in the flesh, but his life in heaven. We are reconciled by Christ humbled, we are saved by Christ exalted. The dying Jesus laid the foundation in satisfying for sin, and slaying the enmity, but it is the living Jesus that perfects the work.

All this produces a further privilege our *joy in God*, v.11. God is now so far from being a terror to us that he is our *joy*. *We are reconciled and saved from wrath. And not only so*, there is more in it yet, a constant stream of favours; not only get into harbour, but come in with full sail: *We joy in God*, finding relief and comfort in his love. And all this by virtue of the atonement, for by him we *received the atonement* (reconciliation).

The privilege of reconciliation

2 Corinthians 5:17–19

Observe here a thorough change of the heart: *For if any man be in Christ*, if any man be a Christian indeed, and will approve himself such, *he is*, or he must be, *a new creature*, v.17. Some read it, *Let him be a new creature*. This ought to be the care of all who profess the Christian faith, that they be new creatures; not only that they have a new name, and wear new clothing, but that they have a new heart and new nature.

And so great is the change the grace of God makes in the soul, that, as it follows, *old things are passed away*—old thoughts, old principles, and old practices, are passed away; and *all* these *things must become new*. Regenerating grace creates a new world in the soul; all things are new. The renewed person acts from new principles, by new rules, with new ends, and in new company.

Reconciliation is here spoken of as an unquestionable privilege, v.18,19. Reconciliation supposes a quarrel, or breach of friendship; and sin has made a breach, it has broken the friendship between God and man. The heart of the sinner is filled with enmity against God, and God is justly offended with the sinner. Yet, behold, there may be a reconciliation; the offended Majesty of heaven is willing to be reconciled. He has appointed the Mediator of reconciliation. He has reconciled us to himself by Jesus Christ, v.18. All things relating to our reconciliation by Jesus Christ are of God, who by the mediation of Jesus Christ has reconciled the world to himself, and put himself into a capacity of being actually reconciled to offenders, without any wrong or injury to his justice or holiness, and does not impute to men their trespasses.

The duty of reconciliation

2 Corinthians 5:20–21

Reconciliation is here spoken of as our indispensable duty, v.20. As God is willing to be reconciled to us, we ought to be reconciled to God. And it is the great end and design of the gospel, that word of reconciliation, to prevail upon sinners to lay aside their enmity against God. Faithful ministers are Christ's ambassadors, sent to negotiate with sinners on peace and reconciliation: they come in God's name, with his entreaties, and act in Christ's place, doing the very thing he did when he was upon this earth, and what he wills to be done now that he is in heaven.

Wonderful condescension! Though God can be no loser by the quarrel, nor gainer by the peace, yet by his ministers he beseeches sinners to lay aside their enmity, and accept the terms he offers, that they would be reconciled to him, to all his attributes, to all his laws, and to all his providences, to believe in the Mediator, to accept the atonement, and comply with his gospel, in all the parts of it and in the whole design of it.

And for our encouragement so to do the apostle adds what should be well known and duly considered by us, v.21, namely, the purity of the Mediator: *He knew no sin*; the sacrifice he offered: *He was made sin*; not a sinner, but *sin*, that is, a sin-offering, a sacrifice for sin; and the end and design of all this: that *we might be made the righteousness of God in him*, might be justified freely by the grace of God through the redemption which is in Christ Jesus.

As Christ, who knew no sin of his own, was made sin for us, so we, who have no righteousness of our own, are made the righteousness of God in him. Our reconciliation to God is only through Jesus Christ, and for the sake of his merit: on him therefore we must rely, and refer to his righteousness and his only.

What must I do to be saved?

Acts 16:29–30

The jailor is afraid he shall lose his soul. He was put into a great consternation. The Spirit of God, that was sent to convince, in order to his being a Comforter, struck a terror upon him. *He called for a light*, and *sprang in and came trembling to Paul and Silas*. In this consternation, he applied to Paul and Silas for relief. How reverent and respectful his address to them is: *he fell down before them*. It is probable that he had heard that they were *the servants of the living God, who showed to them the way of salvation*. He fell down before them, to beg their pardon, for the indignities he had done them, and to beg their advice, what he should do. He gave them a title of respect, *Sirs, lords, masters*; just now it was, *Rogues* and *villains*, and he was their master; but now, *Sirs, lords*, and they are his masters. Converting grace changes people's language.

Observe how serious his enquiry was: *What must I do to be saved?* His salvation is now his great concern, and lies nearest his heart, which before was the furthest thing from his thoughts. He does not enquire concerning others, what they must do; but concerning himself, *'What must I do?'* It is his own precious soul that he is in care about.

He is convinced that something must be done, and done by him too, in order to gain his salvation; that it is not a thing that will do itself. He asks not, 'What may be done for me?' but, 'What shall I do?' He is willing to do anything: 'Tell me what I must do, and I am here ready to do it. Sirs, put me into the right way, though narrow, and thorny, and uphill, yet I will walk in it.'

Believe in the Lord Jesus

Acts 16:31

Paul and Silas now directed the jailor in what he must do, v.31. Though they are cold, and sore, and sleepy, they do not adjourn this cause to a more convenient time and place, do not bid him come to them the next sabbath at their meeting-place by the riverside. They 'strike while the iron is hot', take him now when he is in a good mind, lest the conviction should wear off. Now that God begins to work, it is time for them to set in as *workers together with God*. They are glad to show him the way to heaven as the best friend they have. They gave him the same directions they did to others, *Believe in the Lord Jesus Christ*. Here is the sum of the whole gospel, the covenant of grace in a few words: *Believe in the Lord Jesus Christ, and thou shalt be saved, and thy house.*

The happiness promised: '*Thou shalt be saved*; not only rescued from eternal ruin, but brought to eternal life and blessedness. Though a persecutor, yet thy heinous transgressions shall be all forgiven; and thy hard embittered heart shall be softened and sweetened by the grace of Christ.'

The condition required: *Believe on the Lord Jesus Christ*. We must approve the method God has taken of reconciling the world to himself by a Mediator; and accept Christ as he is offered to us. This is the only way and a sure way to salvation. No other way of salvation than by Christ, and no danger of coming short if we take this way. It is the gospel that is to be preached to every creature: *He that believes shall be saved.*

The extension of this to his family: *Thou shalt be saved and thy house.* Be they ever so many, let them believe in Jesus Christ and they shall be saved.

November 21

The God who is near us

Acts 17:27-28

God *is not far from everyone of us*, v.27. He is everywhere present. He is an infinite Spirit, *that is not far from any of us*. If we are in a palace or in a cottage, in a crowd or in a corner, in a city or in a desert, in the depths of the sea or afar off upon the sea, this is certain, *God is not far from everyone of us*.

In him we live, and move, and have our being, v.28. We have a necessary and constant dependence upon his providence, as the streams have upon the spring, and the beams upon the sun. *In him we live*. It is not only owing to his patience that our forfeited lives are not cut off, but it is owing to his fatherly care that our frail lives are prolonged. If he were to suspend the positive acts of his goodness, we would die of ourselves.

In him we move. It is likewise by him that our souls move our bodies, as he is the first cause, so he is the first mover. *In him we have our being*; not only from him we had it at first, but in him we have it still; we were and still are of such a noble rank of beings, capable of knowing and enjoying God; and are not thrust into the meanness of brutes, nor the misery of devils.

We are God's offspring. The apostle here quotes a saying of one of the Greek poets, Aratus, a native of Cilicia, Paul's countryman, who, speaking of the heathen Jupiter, that is, in the poetical dialect, the supreme God, says this of him 'for we are also his offspring'. By this it appears not only that Paul was himself a scholar, but that human learning is both ornamental and of service to a gospel minister, especially for the convincing of those that are non-believers; for it enables him to beat them at their own weapons, and to cut off Goliath's head with his own sword. How can the adversaries of truth be beaten out of their strongholds by those that do not know them?

God's mercy and command

Acts 17:30-31

The times of this ignorance God winked at. They were times of great
ignorance. In the things of God the Athenians were grossly
ignorant. These times of ignorance God disregarded: understand it
as an act of divine patience and forbearance. He was not quick and
severe with them, but was long-suffering towards them, because
they did it ignorantly.

He now commandeth all men everywhere to repent—to change their mind
and their way. It is to turn with sorrow and shame from every sin,
and with cheerfulness and resolution to every duty. This is God's
command. It is his command to *all men, everywhere.* All men have
made work for repentance, and have cause enough to repent, and all
men are invited to repent, and shall have the benefit of it.

God commands us to repent, *because he hath appointed a day in which
he will judge the world in righteousness*, v.31. The God that made the
world will judge it. There is a day appointed for this general review
of all that men have done in time, a day of decision, a day of
recompense, a day that will put a final period to all the days of time.

The world will be judged in righteousness; for God is not
unrighteous. God will judge the world *by that man whom he hath
ordained*, who can be no other than the Lord Jesus, to whom all
judgment is committed.

God's raising Christ from the dead is the great proof of his being
appointed and ordained the Judge of quick and dead. God has *given
assurance unto all men*, sufficient ground for their faith to build upon,
both that there is a judgment to come and that Christ will be their
Judge. The consideration of the judgment to come, and of the great
hand Christ will have in that judgment, should engage us all to
repent of our sins and turn from them to God.

November 23

The response at Athens

Acts 17:32–34

We have here a short account of the issue of Paul's preaching at Athens. Few were the better: the gospel had as little success at Athens as anywhere. Some ridiculed Paul and his preaching. They heard him patiently till he came to speak of the resurrection of the dead, v.32, and then they mocked. If he spoke of a *resurrection of the dead*, though it is of the resurrection of Christ himself, it is altogether incredible to them. They had deified their heroes after their death, but never thought of their being raised from the dead. How can this be? This great doctrine, which is the saints' joy, is their jest. We are not to think it strange if sacred truths are made the scorn of profane wits.

Others are willing to take time to consider of it; they said, *We will hear thee again of this matter*. They would not at present comply with what Paul said, nor oppose it. Thus many lose the benefit of the practical doctrine of Christianity, by wading beyond their depth into controversy. Those that would not yield to the present convictions of the word thought to get clear of them by putting them off to another opportunity. Thus the devil defrauds them of all their time, by defrauding them of the present time. Paul thereupon left them for the present to consider of it, v.33: *He departed from amongst them*.

Yet there were some that were influenced, v.34. There were certain men that adhered to him and believed. Two are particularly named; one was an eminent man, *Dionysius the Areopagite*, one of that high court that sat in Areopagus, one of those before whom Paul was summoned to appear; his judge becomes his convert. The *woman named Damaris*. Though there was not so great a harvest gathered in at Athens, yet these few being influenced there, Paul had no reason to say he had laboured in vain.

November 24

The call to preach

Romans 10:13-15

Whoever shall call upon the name of the Lord shall be saved. Calling upon the name of the Lord is here put for all practical religion. What is the life of a Christian but a life of prayer? He that thus calls upon him shall be saved. It is but ask and have; what would we have more?

For the further illustration of this the apostle observes how necessary it was that the gospel should be preached to the Gentiles, v.14. This was what the Jews were so angry with Paul for. He shows how needful it was to bring them within the reach of the promise. *They cannot call on him in whom they have not believed.* Except they believe that he is God, they will not call upon him by prayer. The grace of faith is absolutely necessary to the duty of prayer; we cannot pray aright without it. He that comes to God by prayer must believe.

They cannot believe in him of whom they have not heard. Some way or other the divine revelation must be made known to us, before we can receive it and assent to it; it is not born with us. *They cannot hear without a preacher.* Somebody must tell them what they are to believe.

They cannot preach except they be sent. How shall a man act as an ambassador, unless he has both his credentials and his instructions from the prince that sends him? It is God's prerogative to send ministers. He only can qualify men for, and incline them to, the work of the ministry.

But the right of that qualification and the sincerity of that inclination must not be left to the judgment of every man for himself. This be submitted to the judgment of those who are presumed the most able judges, and who are empowered to set apart such as they find so qualified and inclined. And those that are thus set apart, not only may, but must preach, as those that are sent.

Confessing our sins to one another

James 5:16

Christians are here directed to *confess their faults one to another*, v.16. The confession here required is that of Christians to one another. Where persons have injured one another, acts of injustice must be confessed to those against whom they have been committed. Where persons have tempted one another to sin, or have consented in the same evil actions there they ought mutually to blame themselves and excite each other to repentance. Where crimes are of a public nature, and have done any public injury, there they ought to be more publicly confessed, so as may best reach to all who are concerned. And sometimes it may be well to confess our faults to some prudent minister or praying friend, that he may help us to plead with God for mercy and pardon.

But then we are not to think that James puts us upon telling everything that we are conscious is amiss in ourselves or in one another; but so far as confession is necessary to our reconciliation with such as are at variance with us, or for reparation of wrongs done to any, or for gaining information in any point of conscience and making our own spirits quiet and easy, so far we should be ready to confess our faults.

And sometimes also it may be of good use to Christians to disclose their peculiar weaknesses and infirmities to one another, where there are great intimacies and friendships, and where they may help each other by their prayers to obtain pardon of their sins and power against them. Those who make confession of their faults one to another should then pray with and for one another.

The power of prayer

James 5:16–18

The great advantage and efficacy of prayer are here declared and proved: *The effectual fervent prayer of a righteous man availeth much.* He who prays must be a righteous man, not loving nor approving of any known iniquity. Further, the prayer itself must be a fervent, well-wrought prayer. It must be a pouring out of the heart to God; and it must proceed from a faith unfeigned. Such prayer avails much.

The power of prayer is here proved from the success of Elijah. This may be encouraging to us even in common cases, if we consider that Elijah was *a man of like passions with us.* He was a zealous, good man and a very great man, but he had his infirmities, and was subject to disorder in his passions as well as others. In prayer we must not look to the merit of man, but to the grace of God.

Only in this we should copy after Elijah, that he prayed earnestly, or, as it is in the original, *in prayer he prayed.* It is not enough to say a prayer, but we must pray in prayer. Our thoughts must be fixed, our desires firm and ardent, and our graces in exercise; and, when we thus pray in prayer, we shall speed in prayer.

Elijah *prayed that it might not rain*; and God heard him in his pleading against an idolatrous persecuting country, *so that it rained not on the earth for the space of three years and six months. Again he prayed, and the heaven gave rain.* Thus you see prayer is the key which opens and shuts heaven.

This instance of the extraordinary efficacy of prayer is recorded for encouragement even to ordinary Christians to be urgent and earnest in prayer. If Elijah by prayer could do such great and wonderful things surely the prayers of no righteous man shall return void.

November 27

A praying people

1 Timothy 2:1–2

Here is a charge given to Christians to pray for all men in general, and particularly for all in authority. Paul does not send Timothy any prescribed form of prayer. Paul thought it enough to give the Christians general headings; they, having the scripture to direct them in prayer and the Spirit of prayer poured out upon them, needed not any further directions. The disciples of Christ must be praying people.

There must be prayers for ourselves in the first place; this is implied here. We must also pray *for all men.* See how far the Christian religion was from being a sect, when it taught men this diffusive love, to pray for all men.

Pray for kings, v.2; though the kings at this time were heathens, yet they must pray for them. *For kings, and all that are in authority.* We must give thanks for them, pray for their welfare and for the welfare of their kingdoms, that in the peace of the kingdoms we may have peace. He does not say, 'that we may get promotion under them, grow rich, and be in honour and power under them'; no, the summit of the ambition of a good Christian is to lead a quiet and peaceable life. We cannot expect to be kept quiet and peaceable unless we keep in all godliness and honesty.

Here we have our duty as Christians summed up in two words: *godliness*, that is, the right worshipping of God; and *honesty*, that is, a good conduct towards all men. There two must go together.

November 28

Touching the hem of his garment

Matthew 9:20–21

Here we have the healing of the poor woman's bloody issue. I call her a poor woman, not only because her case was piteous, but because, though she had had something in the world, she had *spent it all upon physicians*, for the cure of her ailment, and was never the better; which was a double aggravation of the misery of her condition, that she had impoverished herself for the recovery of her health, and yet had not her health either.

This *woman was diseased with a constant issue of blood twelve years*, v.20, a disease, which was not only weakening and wasting, but which also rendered her ceremonially unclean, and shut her out from the courts of the Lord's house; but it did not cut her off from approaching to Christ. She applied herself to Christ, and received mercy from him, by the way.

Observe the woman's great faith in Christ and in his power. Her disease was of such a nature, that her modesty would not permit her to speak openly to Christ for a cure, as others did, but she believed him to have such an overflowing fulness of healing virtue, that the very *touch of his garment* would be her cure. This, perhaps, had something of fancy mixed with faith; for she had no precedent for this way of application to Christ.

But what weakness of understanding there was in it Christ was pleased to overlook, and to accept the sincerity and strength of her faith. She believed she should be healed if she did but *touch the* very *hem of his garment*, the very extremity of it. There is virtue in everything that belongs to Christ. Such a fulness of grace is there in Christ, that *from it we may all receive*.

November 29

Your faith has made you well

Matthew 9:22

Observe Christ's great favour to this woman. He did not suspend his healing influences, but permitted this bashful patient to obtain the cure surreptitiously and unknown to anyone else, though she could not think to do it unknown to him. And now she was well content to be gone, for she had what she came for, but Christ was not willing to let her go so: the triumphs of her faith must be to her praise and honour. He *turned about* to see her, v.22, and soon discovered her. It is great encouragement to humble Christians, that they who hide themselves from others are known to Christ, who sees in secret their applications to heaven when most private.

[286]

Christ puts gladness into her heart, by that word, *Daughter, be of good comfort*. She feared being scolded for coming clandestinely, but she is encouraged. He calls her *daughter*, for he spoke to her with the tenderness of a father. He bids her *be of good comfort*. His bidding her be comforted, brought comfort with it, as his saying, *Be ye whole*, brought health with it.

He puts honour upon her faith. That grace of all others gives most honour to Christ, and therefore he puts most honour upon it: *Thy faith has made thee whole*. This woman had more faith than she thought she had. She was spiritually healed; that cure was brought about in her which is the proper fruit and effect of faith, the pardon of sin and the work of grace. Her bodily cure was the fruit of faith, of her faith, and that made it a happy, comfortable cure indeed.

November 30

Salvation in Christ's name

Acts 4:12

Neither is there salvation in any other. As there is no other name by which diseased bodies can be cured, so there is no other by which sinful souls can be saved. By him, and him only, by receiving and embracing his doctrine, salvation must now be hoped for by all.

Our salvation is our chief concern, and that which ought to lie nearest to our hearts—our rescue from wrath and the curse, and our restoration to God's favour and blessing. Our salvation is not in ourselves, nor can be obtained by any merit or strength of our own; we can destroy ourselves, but we cannot save ourselves.

There are among men many names that pretend to be saving names, but really are not so; many institutions in religion that pretend to settle a reconciliation and correspondence between God and man, but cannot do it. It is only by Christ and his name that those favours can be expected from God which are necessary to our salvation, and that our services can be accepted with God. This is the honour of Christ's name, that it is the only name whereby we must be saved, the only name we have to plead in all our addresses to God.

This name is *given*. God has appointed it, and it is an inestimable benefit freely conferred upon us. It is given *under heaven*. Christ has not only a great name in heaven, but a great name under heaven; for he has all power both in the upper and in the lower world. It is given *among men*, who need salvation, men who are ready to perish. We may be saved by his name, that name of his, *The Lord our righteousness*; and we cannot be saved by any other.

December 1

My Lord and my God!

John 20:28–29

Here we have Thomas's believing consent to Jesus Christ. He is now ashamed of his former incredulity and cries out, *My Lord and my God*, v.28. We are not told whether he did put his finger into the print of the nails. Christ says, v.29, *Thou hast seen, and believed*; seeing sufficed. And now faith comes off a conqueror. Thomas is now fully satisfied of the truth of Christ's resurrection. His slowness and backwardness to believe may help to strengthen our faith. He therefore believed him to be Lord and God, and we are to believe him so.

We must believe his deity—that he is God; not a man made God, but God made man. His mediation—that he is Lord, the one Lord, to settle the great concerns that lie between God and man, and to establish the correspondence that was necessary to our happiness.

Thomas consented to him as his Lord and his God. We must accept Christ to be that to us which the Father has appointed him. This is the vital act of faith, he is mine.

Thomas made an open profession of this. He says it to Christ, *Thou art* my Lord and my God; or, speaking to his brethren, *This is* my Lord and my God. Do we accept Christ as our *Lord God*? We must go to him, and tell him so, tell others so, as those that triumph in our relation to Christ. Thomas speaks with an ardency of affection as one that took hold of Christ with all his might, *My Lord and my God*.

Thomas, the believer

John 20:29

Christ owns Thomas a believer. Sound and sincere believers, though they are slow and weak, shall be graciously accepted by the Lord Jesus. No sooner did Thomas confess to Christ than Christ gives him the comfort of it, and lets him know that he believes.

He upbraids him with his former incredulity. He had been so backward to believe, and came so slowly to his own comforts. Those that in sincerity have expressed agreement with Christ see a great deal of reason to lament that they did not do it sooner. It was not without much ado that he was brought to believe at last. If no evidence must be admitted but that of our own senses, and we must believe nothing but what we ourselves are eye-witnesses of, how must the world be converted to the faith of Christ? He is therefore justly blamed for laying so much stress upon this.

He commends the faith of those who believe upon easier terms. Thomas, as a believer, was truly blessed; but rather *blessed are those that have not seen* Christ's miracles, and especially his resurrection; blessed are those that see not these, and yet believe in Christ. This may look forward to those who should afterwards believe, the Gentiles, who had never seen Christ in the flesh. This faith is more praiseworthy than theirs who saw and believed. It shows a better temper of mind in those that do believe. He that believes on that sight has his resistance conquered by a sort of violence; but he that believes without it is more noble. It is a greater instance of the power of divine grace. Flesh and blood contribute more to their faith that see and believe, than to theirs who see not and yet believe.

December 3

Doers of the word

James 1:21–22

We are here fully, though briefly, instructed concerning hearing the word of God. We are required to prepare ourselves for it, v.21, to get rid of every corrupt affection and of every prejudice and prepossession, and to lay aside those sins which pervert the judgment and blind the mind.

We are directed how to hear the word of God: *Receive with meekness the engrafted word, which is able to save your souls.* In hearing the word of God, we are to receive it—assent to the truths of it—and consent to the laws of it.

We must therefore yield ourselves to the word of God, with most submissive, humble, and tractable tempers: this is to *receive it with meekness.* Being willing to hear of our faults, and taking it not only patiently, but thankfully, desiring also to be moulded and formed by the doctrines and precepts of the gospel.

We are taught what is to be done after hearing, v.22: *But be you doers of the word, and not hearers only, deceiving your own selves.* Hearing is in order to doing; the most attentive and the most frequent hearing of the word of God will not avail us, unless we are also doers of it. If we were to hear a sermon every day of the week, and an angel from heaven were the preacher, yet, if we rested in bare hearing, it would never bring us to heaven. Therefore the apostle insists much upon it.

December 4

Looking at God's word

James 1:23–25

The apostle shows what is the proper use of the word of God, who they are that do not use it as they ought, and who they are that do make right use of it, v.23–25.

The use we are to make of God's word may be learnt from its

being compared to a glass, in which a man may *behold his natural face.* As a looking-glass shows us the spots and defilements upon our faces, that they may be remedied and washed off, so the word of God shows us our sins, that we may repent of them and get them pardoned; it shows us what is amiss, that it may be amended.

We have here an account of those who do not use this glass of the word as they ought, v.24. This is the true description of one who hears the word of God and does it not. How many are there who, when they sit under the word, are affected with their own sinfulness, misery, and danger, acknowledge the evil of sin, and their need of Christ; but, when their hearing is over, all is forgotten, convictions are lost, good affections vanish, and pass away like the waters of a land-flood: he *straightway forgets.* In vain do we hear God's word, and look into the gospel glass, if we go away, and forget our spots, instead of washing them off, and forget our remedy, instead of applying to it.

Those also are described, and pronounced blessed, who hear aright, and who use the glass of God's word as they should do, v.25: *Whoso looketh into the perfect law of liberty, and continueth therein.* The gospel is a law of liberty, or liberation, giving us deliverance from the Jewish law, and from sin and guilt, and wrath and death. The ceremonial law was a yoke of bondage; the gospel of Christ is a law of liberty.

It is a perfect law; nothing can be added to it. In hearing the word, we look into this perfect law; we consult it for counsel and direction; we look into it, that we may thence take our measures. Those who thus do, and continue in the law and word of God, are, and shall be, blessed in their deed.

December 5

Worthless religion

James 1:26

The apostle here informs us how we may distinguish between a vain religion and that which is pure and approved of God.

What is a vain religion: *If any man among you seemeth to be religious, and bridleth not his tongue, but deceives his own heart, this man's religion is vain.* In a vain religion there is much of show. When men are more concerned to seem religious than really to be so, it is a sign that their religion is but vain.

In a vain religion there is much censuring, reviling, and detracting of others. Bridling not the tongue is chiefly meant as not abstaining from these evils of the tongue. When we hear people ready to speak of the faults of others, or to censure them as holding scandalous errors, or to lessen the wisdom and piety of those about them, that they themselves may seem the wiser and better, this is a sign that they have but a vain religion. The man who has a detracting tongue cannot have a truly humble gracious heart. He who delights to injure his neighbour in vain pretends to love God; therefore a reviling tongue will prove a man a hypocrite. There is no strength nor power in that religion which will not enable a man to bridle his tongue.

In a vain religion a man deceives his own heart; he goes on in such a course of detracting from others, and making himself seem somebody, that at last the vanity of his religion is consummated by the deceiving of his own soul. When once religion comes to be a vain thing, how great is the vanity?

December 6

Pure religion

James 1:27

Pure religion and undefiled before God and the Father is this, v.27. It is the glory of religion to be pure and undefiled; not mixed with the inventions of men nor with the corruptions of the world. False religions may be known by their impurity and lack of love. But, on the other hand, a holy life and a charitable heart show a true religion. Our religion is not adorned with ceremonies, but purity and love.

True religion teaches us to do everything as in the presence of God; and to seek his favour, and study to please him in all our actions.

Compassion and love to the poor and distressed form a very great and necessary part of true religion: *Visiting the fatherless and widow in their affliction.* Visiting is here put for all manner of relief which we are capable of giving to others; and fatherless and widows are here particularly mentioned, because they are generally most apt to be neglected or oppressed: but by them we are to understand all who are proper objects of love, all who are in affliction. It is very remarkable that if the sum of religion be drawn up in two articles this is one—to be charitable and relieve the afflicted.

An unspotted life must accompany an unfeigned love and charity: *To keep himself unspotted from the world.* The world is apt to spot and blemish the soul, and it is hard to live in it, and have to do with it, and not be defiled; but this must be our constant endeavour.

December 7

Immortal, invisible, God only wise

1 Timothy 1:16–17

Having spoken of the mercy he had found with God, v.16, the apostle could not go on with his letter without inserting a thankful acknowledgment of God's goodness to him: *Now unto the King eternal, immortal, invisible, the only wise God, be honour and glory for ever and ever. Amen.* Those who are aware of their obligations to the mercy and grace of God will have their hearts enlarged in his praise. Here is praise ascribed to him, as *the King eternal, immortal, invisible.*

When we have found God good we must not forget to pronounce him great; and his kind thoughts of us must not at all abate our high thoughts of him, but rather increase them. God had taken particular cognizance of Paul, and shown him mercy, and taken him into communion with himself, and yet he calls him the King eternal.

God's gracious dealings with us should fill us with admiration of his glorious attributes. He is *eternal*, without beginning of days, or end of life, or change of time. He is the Ancient of days. He is *immortal*, and the original of immortality; he only has immortality, for he cannot die. He is *invisible*, for he cannot be seen with mortal eyes, dwelling in the light to which no man can approach, whom no man hath seen nor can see. He is *the only wise God*; he only is infinitely wise, and the fountain of all wisdom.

'*To him be glory for ever and ever,*' or, 'Let me be for ever employed in giving honour and glory to him, as the thousands of thousands do (Revelation 5:12,13).

December 8

You are highly favoured

Luke 1:26–29

Here we have the address of the angel Gabriel to Mary, v.28. He surprised her with this salutation, *Hail, thou that art highly favoured.* This was intended to raise in her a value for herself: in some, who like Mary pore only on their low estate, there is occasion for it and an expectation of great news, not from abroad, but from above. *Hail, thou, rejoice thou*; it was the usual form of salutation.

Mary is dignified: 'Thou art *highly favoured*. God, in his choice of thee to be the mother of the Messiah, has put an honour upon thee belonging exclusively to thyself.' She has the presence of God with her: '*The Lord is with thee.*' Nothing is to be despaired of, not the performance of any service, not the obtaining of any favour, though ever so great, if we have *God with us*.

Mary also has the blessing of God upon her: '*Blessed art thou among women*; not only thou shalt be accounted so by men, but thou shalt be so. Thou that art so *highly favoured* in this instance mayest expect in other things to be blessed.' She explains this herself, v.48. *All generations shall call me blessed.*

Observe now the consternation she was in upon this address, v.29. *When she saw him* she was *troubled* at it, as not conscious to herself of anything that either merited or promised such great things; and she *cast in her mind what manner of salutation this should be.*

December 9

He will be great

Luke 1:30–33

We come to the message itself which the angel had to deliver to her. He went on with his errand, v.30. To what he had said she made no reply; he therefore confirms it: '*Fear not, Mary, thou hast found favour with God* more than thou thinkest of, as there are many who think they are more favoured of God than really they are.' Does God favour you? Fear not, though the world frowns on you. Is he for you? If so, then it does not matter who is against you.

Though Mary is a virgin, she shall have the honour of being a mother: '*Thou shalt conceive in thy womb, and bring forth a son*, thou *shalt call his name Jesus*,' v.31.

Though Mary lives in poverty and obscurity, yet she shall have the honour to be the mother of the Messiah; her son shall be named *Jesus*—a Saviour. He will be very nearly allied to the upper world. He *shall be great*, truly great, for he shall be called the *Son of the Highest*. Those who are the children of God are truly great, and therefore are concerned to be very good.

He will be very highly preferred in the lower world; for, though appearing in the form of a servant, yet *the Lord God shall give unto him the throne of his father David*, v.32. He assures her that his kingdom shall be spiritual: he shall *reign over the house of Jacob*. It must therefore be a spiritual kingdom, the house of Israel according to promise, that he must rule over. He also assures her that his kingdom shall be eternal: he shall reign *for ever*, and *of his kingdom there shall be no end*.

December 10

The Holy Spirit will come upon you

Luke 1:34–38

'*How shall this be?*' v.34. Mary knew that the Messiah must be born of a *virgin*; and, if she must be his mother, she desires to know how. It is a satisfactory answer that is given to it. She shall conceive by the power of *the Holy Ghost*. A divine power will undertake it, the power of the Holy Ghost himself, v.35.

The child she shall conceive is a holy thing, and therefore must not be conceived by ordinary generation. He is spoken of emphatically, *that holy thing*, such as never was; and he shall be called *the Son of God*. His human nature must be so produced, as it was fit that should be which was to be taken into union with the divine nature.

It was a further encouragement to her faith to be told that *her cousin Elisabeth*, though enfeebled by age, was *with child*, v.36. Here is an age of wonders beginning. *This is the sixth month with her that was called barren. For with God nothing shall be impossible*, v.37, and if

[295]

nothing, then not this. No word of God must be incredible to us, as long as no work of God is impossible to him.

Observe Mary's acquiescence in the will of God concerning her, v.38. She owns herself a believing subject to the divine authority: '*Behold, the handmaid of the Lord*. Lord, I am at thy service.' She leaves the issue with God, and submits entirely to his will. She shows a believing expectancy of the divine favour. She is not only content that it should be so, but humbly desires that it may be so: *Be it unto me according to thy word*. We must, as Mary here, guide our desires by the word of God, and ground our hopes upon it.

December 11

My soul magnifies the Lord

Luke 1:46–49

Here are the expressions of joy and praise in Mary's song of praise, and God alone is the object of the praise and centre of the joy. Observe how Mary here speaks of God:

(1) with great reverence of him as *the Lord*: '*My soul doth magnify the Lord*.' The more honour God has in any way put upon us, the more honour we must study to give it to him; and then only are we accepted in magnifying the Lord, when our souls magnify him, and *all that is within us*.

(2) with great delight in him as *her Saviour*: *My spirit rejoiceth in God my Saviour*. This seems to have reference to the Messiah, whom she was to be the mother of. She calls him *God her Saviour*; for the angel had told her that he should be the *Son of the Highest*, and that his name should be *Jesus, a Saviour*; this she fastened upon, with application to herself: *He is God my Saviour*. Even the mother of our Lord had need of an interest in him as her Saviour, and would have been undone without it.

Here are just causes assigned for this joy and praise upon her own account, v.48,49. Her *spirit rejoiced in the Lord*, because of the *kind things he had done for her. He has regarded the low estate of his handmaiden*. 'He has chosen me to this honour in spite of my great meanness, poverty, and obscurity.' He secures a lasting honour to her: '*From henceforth all generations shall call me blessed.*' Elisabeth had once and again called her *blessed*: 'But that is not all,' said she, 'all

[296]

generations of Gentiles as well as Jews shall call me so.' *He that is mighty has done to me great things.* A great thing indeed, that a virgin should conceive. A great thing indeed, that Messiah should now at length be born. It is the power of the Highest that appears in this. She adds, *and holy is his name.* He that is mighty, even he whose name is holy, has done to me great things.

December 12

Mercy to those that fear him

Luke 1:50-52

The virgin Mary, as the mother of the Messiah, has become a kind of public person, and therefore looks about her, looks before her, and takes notice of God's various dealings with the children of men.

It is a certain truth that God has mercy in store, mercy in reserve. But never did this appear so as in sending his Son into the world to save us, v.50: *His mercy is on them that fear him*; it has always been so. But he has manifested this mercy, so as never before, in sending his Son to bring in an everlasting righteousness, and work out an everlasting salvation for them that fear him, and this *from generation to generation*. In him mercy is settled upon all that fear God, pardoning mercy, healing mercy, accepting mercy, crowning mercy, *from generation to generation*, while the world stands.

It has been a common observation that God in his providence puts contempt upon the haughty and honour upon the humble. As God had, with his mercy to her, shown himself mighty also, so he had, with his *mercy on them that fear him,* shown strength likewise *with his arm.* In the course of his providence, it is his usual method to cross the expectations of men. Proud men expect to carry all before them, but he *scatters them in the imagination of their hearts,* and brings them low. The mighty think to secure themselves by might in their seats, but he *puts them down,* while, on the other hand, those of *low degree* are wonderfully *exalted.*

December 13

The hungry are filled with good things

Luke 1:53–55

The gospel grace is shown in the spiritual riches it dispenses, v.53. Those who see their need of Christ, he fills with good things, with the best things; he gives liberally to them, and they are abundantly satisfied. Those who are weary and heavy-laden shall find rest with Christ, and those who thirst are called to come to him and drink. Those who are rich, who, like Laodicea, think they have need of nothing, are full of themselves, and think they have a sufficiency in themselves, those he sends away from his door; he sends them *empty away*; they come full of self, and are sent away empty of Christ.

It was always expected that the Messiah should be the strength and glory of his people Israel, and so he is in a special manner, v.54: *He hath helped his servant Israel.* He has taken them by the hand *in remembrance of his mercy*. While this blessing was deferred, his people were often ready to ask, 'Has God forgotten to be gracious?' But now he made it appear that he had not forgotten, but remembered, his mercy.

This blessing is also in performance of his promise. It is a mercy not only designed, but declared, v.55; it was what he spoke *to our fathers*, and particularly to Abraham, that in *his seed all the families of the earth shall be blessed* with the blessings that are *for ever*.

December 14

The virgin Mary

Matthew 1:18

The mystery of Christ's incarnation is to be adored, not pried into. If we know not the way of the Spirit in the formation of ordinary people, nor how the bones are formed in the womb of anyone that is with child, much less do we know how the blessed Jesus was formed in the womb of the blessed virgin.

Here we have Mary's espousal to Joseph. Mary, the mother of our Lord, *was espoused to Joseph*, not completely married, but contracted. Christ was born of a virgin, but a betrothed virgin:

(1) to put respect upon the marriage state, and to recommend it as *honourable among all*. Who more highly favoured than Mary was in her espousal?

(2) to save the credit of the blessed virgin, which otherwise would have been exposed. It was fit that her conception should be protected by a marriage, and so justified in the eye of the world.

(3) that the blessed virgin might have one to be a help-meet for her. Some think that Joseph was now a widower, and that those who are called the brethren of Christ (Matthew 13:55) were Joseph's children by a former wife. Joseph was a *just man*, she a *virtuous woman*. We may also learn, from this example, that it is good to enter into the married state with deliberation, and not hastily: it is better to take time to consider before than to find time to repent after.

Observe her pregnancy of the promised seed; *before they came together*, she *was found with child*, which really was *of the Holy Ghost*. Now we may well imagine what a perplexity this might justly occasion to the blessed virgin. She herself knew the divine origin of this conception; but how could she prove it? She would be dealt with as a harlot. Never was any daughter of Eve so dignified as the virgin Mary was, and yet in danger of falling under the imputation of one of the worst of crimes; yet we do not find that she tormented herself about it; but, being conscious of her own innocence, she kept her mind calm and easy, and committed her cause to *him that judgeth righteously*.

December 15

The righteousness of Joseph

Matthew 1:19

We have here Joseph's perplexity, and his care what to do in this case. He is loth to believe so ill a thing of one whom he believed to be so good a woman; and yet the matter, as it is too bad to be excused, is also too plain to be denied.

Observe the extremity which he studied to avoid. He was *not willing to make her a public example*. How good is it to *think on things*, as Joseph did here! Were there more of deliberation in our censures and judgments, there would be more of mercy and moderation in them.

Some people of a rigorous temper would blame Joseph for his clemency: but it is here spoken of to his praise; because *he was a just man*, therefore he was not willing to expose her. He was a religious, good man; and therefore inclined to be merciful as God is, and to forgive as one that was forgiven. It becomes us, in many cases, to be gentle towards those that come under suspicion of having offended.

Notice the expedient he found out for avoiding this extremity. He was *minded to put her away privily*, that is, to give a bill of divorce into her hand before two witnesses, and so to hush up the matter among themselves. The necessary censures of those who have offended ought to be managed without noise. Christian love and Christian prudence will *hide a multitude of sins*, and great ones, as far as may be done without having fellowship with them.

December 16

Born of the Holy Spirit

Matthew 1:20

While he thought on these things and knew not what to determine, God graciously directed what to do, and made him easy. Those who would have direction from God must *think on things* themselves, and consult with themselves. It is the thoughtful, not the unthinking whom God will guide.

The message was sent to Joseph by an angel of the Lord. How far God may now, in an invisible way, make use of the ministration of angels, for extricating his people out of their straits, we cannot say; but this we are sure of they are all *ministering spirits* for their good. This angel appeared to Joseph *in a dream* when he was asleep. When we are most quiet and composed we are in the best frame to receive the notices of the divine will.

Joseph is here directed to proceed in his intended marriage. It was requisite to put this poor carpenter in mind of his high birth: 'Value thyself. Joseph, thou art that son of David through whom the line of the Messiah is to be drawn.' We may thus say to every true believer,

'Fear not, thou son of Abraham, thou child of God; forget not the dignity of thy birth, thy new birth.' *Fear not to take Mary for thy wife*; so it may be read.

He is here informed concerning that *holy thing* with which his espoused wife was now pregnant. That which is conceived in her is of a divine original. He is told that she had conceived by the power *of the Holy Ghost*; not by the power of nature. The Holy Spirit, who produced the world, now produced the Saviour of the world, and prepared him a body. He is the Son of God, and yet so far partakes of the substance of his mother as to be called *the fruit of her womb*.

December 17

The name Jesus

Matthew 1:21

And she shall bring forth a son and thou shalt call his name Jesus, a Saviour. Jesus is the same name with Joshua, the termination only being changed, for the sake of conforming it to the Greek. Christ is our Joshua; both the *captain of our salvation*, and the *high priest of our profession*, and, in both, our Saviour—a Joshua who comes in the stead of Moses, and does that for us which *the law could not do, in that it was weak*. Joshua had been called Hosea, but Moses prefixed the first syllable of the name Jehovah, and so made it Jehoshua, to intimate that the Messiah, who was to bear that name, should be *Jehovah*; he is therefore *able to save to the uttermost*, neither is there *salvation in any other*.

For he shall save his people from their sins. Those whom Christ saves he saves from their sins; from the guilt of sin by the merit of his death, from the dominion of sin by the Spirit of his grace. In saving them from sin, he saves them from wrath and the curse, and all misery here and hereafter. Christ came to save his people, not in their sins, but from their sins; to purchase for them, not a liberty to sin, but a liberty from sins, to redeem them from all iniquity, and so to redeem them from among men to himself. Those who leave their sins, and give up themselves to Christ as *his people*, are interested in the Saviour, and the great salvation which he has brought.

[301]

December 18

Emmanuel, God with us

Matthew 1:22–24

Here the Old Testament prophecies had their accomplishment in our Lord Jesus. Now the scripture that was fulfilled in the birth of Christ was that promise of a sign which God gave to King Ahaz (Isaiah 7:14), *Behold a virgin shall conceive*; where the prophet directs the people of God to look forward to the Messiah, who was to come of the people of the Jews, and the house of David. The sign given is that the Messiah shall be *born of a virgin*. *A virgin shall conceive*, and, by her, he shall be manifested in the flesh.

The truth proved by this sign is, that he is the Son of God, and the Mediator between God and man: for *they shall call his name Emmanuel*. *Emmanuel* signifies '*God with us*'; a mysterious name, but very precious; God incarnate among us, and so God reconcilable to us, at peace with us, and taking us into covenant and communion with himself. The people of the Jews had *God with them* in types and shadows, dwelling between the cherubim; but never so as when the *Word was made flesh*.

In this consists the salvation he has accomplished, in the bringing of God and man together; this was what he designed, to bring *God* to be *with us*, which is our great happiness, and to bring us to be with God, which is our great duty.

Observe Joseph's obedience to the divine precept, v.24: *Being raised from sleep* by the impression which the dream made upon him, *he did as the angel of the Lord had bidden him. He took unto him his wife.* God has still ways of making known his mind in doubtful cases, by hints of providence, debates of conscience, and advice of faithful friends; by each of these, applying the general rules of the written word, we should take direction from God.

December 19

Zacharias' prophecy

Luke 1:76–80

Zacharias here blesses God for the work of preparation for salvation, which was to be done by John the Baptist, v.76: *Thou child* shalt be called *the prophet of the Highest.* Jesus Christ is *the Highest.* John the Baptist was his prophet. John's business was to prepare people for the salvation: *Thou shalt go before the face of the Lord to prepare his ways.* Let everything that may obstruct his progress be taken away. His work was also to give people a general idea of the salvation, for the doctrine he preached was that the *kingdom of heaven* is at hand.

There are two things in which you must know that this salvation consists:

(1) the forgiveness of what we have done amiss. It is salvation *by the remission of sins,* v.77. John the Baptist gave people to understand that, though their case was sad, it was not desperate, for pardon might be obtained *through the tender mercy of our God.*

(2) direction to do better for the time to come. The gospel salvation sets up a clear and true light, by which we may order our steps aright. In it *the dayspring hath visited us from on high,* v.78; and this also is owing to the *tender mercy of our God.*

We gave as much reason to welcome the gospel day as those have to welcome the morning who had long waited for it. The gospel is discovering; it is to *give light to them that sit in darkness, the light of the knowledge of the glory of God in the face of Jesus Christ.* It is also reviving; it brings light to them that sit *in the shadow of death,* as condemned prisoners in the dungeon, to bring them the tidings of a pardon, at least of a reprieve and opportunity of producing a pardon. How pleasant is that light! It is directing; it is to *guide our feet in the way of peace.* It guides us into the way of making our peace with God; that way of peace which as sinners we have wandered from and have not known, nor could ever have known of ourselves.

December 20

The Word made flesh

John 1:14

The Word was made flesh, v.14. This expresses Christ's incarnation: we see here the human nature of Christ with which he was veiled. *Forasmuch as the children* who were to become the sons of God, *were partakers of flesh and blood, he also himself likewise took part of the same.* He subjected himself to the miseries and calamities of the human nature. Flesh speaks of man tainted with sin, and Christ appeared *in the likeness of sinful flesh*, and was made *sin for us*, and *condemned sin in the flesh*. The Word of the Lord, who was made flesh, endures for ever; when made flesh, he ceased not to be the Word of God.

He *dwelt among us*. Having taken upon him the nature of man, he put himself into the place and condition of other men. He dwelt among us, us that were corrupt and depraved, and revolted from God. When we look upon the upper world, how lowly and contemptible does this flesh, this body, appear, which we carry about with us, and this world in which our lot is cast. But that the eternal Word was *made flesh*, and dwelt in this world as we do should make us willing to abide in the flesh while God has any work for us to do.

He dwelt among the Jews. Though the Jews were unkind to him, yet he continued to dwell among them. He dwelt among us. He was in the world, not as a wayfaring man that tarries but for a night, but he dwelt among us. The original word is observable, he dwelt *as in a tabernacle*, which intimates that he dwelt here in very mean circumstances, as shepherds that dwell in tents. We see that his stay among us was not to be perpetual. He dwelt here as in a tent, not as at home.

December 21

We have seen his glory

John 1:14

The beams of his divine glory darted through this veil of flesh: *We beheld his glory, the glory as of the only begotten of the Father, full of grace and truth.* The sun is still the fountain of light, though eclipsed or clouded;

so Christ was still the brightness of his Father's glory. There were those that saw through the veil; who were the witnesses of this glory: *we*, his disciples and followers, we among whom he *dwelt*. They saw the glory of his divinity, while others saw only the veil of his human nature. Observe what evidence they had of it: *We saw it*. They had not their evidence by report, at secondhand, but were themselves eye-witnesses: *We saw it. The glory as of the only begotten of the Father*. The glory of the *Word made flesh* was such a glory as became the only *begotten Son of God*, and could not be the glory of any other. Jesus Christ is the only begotten of the Father.

Believers are the children of God by the special favour of adoption and the special grace of regeneration. They are in a sense *of a like nature*, and have the image of his perfections; but Christ is *of the same nature*. His divine glory appeared in the holiness and heavenliness of his doctrine; in his miracles; it appeared in the purity, goodness, and kindness of his whole way of life.

Notice what advantage those he dwelt among had from this. In the old tabernacle in which God dwelt was the *law*, in this was grace; in that were types, in this was *truth*. He was *full of grace and truth*, the two great things that fallen man stands in need of. He was full *of grace*, and therefore qualified to intercede for us; and full *of truth*, and therefore fit to instruct us.

December 22

The fulness of time

Galatians 4:4

When the fulness of time had come, the time appointed of the Father, when he would put an end to the legal dispensation, and set up another and a better in the room of it, *he sent forth his Son*. The person who was employed to introduce this new dispensation was no other than the Son of God himself, the only begotten of the Father, who, as he had been prophesied of and promised from the foundation of the world, so in due time he was manifested for this purpose.

He, in pursuance of the great design he had undertaken, submitted to be *made of a woman*—there is his incarnation; and to be *made under the law*—there is his subjection. He who was truly God for our sakes became man; and he who was Lord of all consented to come into a state of subjection and to take upon him the form of a servant; and one great end of all this was *to redeem those that were under the law*—to save us from that intolerable yoke and to appoint gospel ordinances more rational and easy.

He had indeed something more and greater in his view, in coming into the world, than merely to deliver us from the bondage of the ceremonial law; for he came in our nature, and consented to suffer and die for us, that in so doing he might redeem us from the wrath of God, and from the curse of the moral law, which, as sinners, we all lay under.

He was sent to redeem us, *that we might receive the adoption of sons*—that we might no longer be accounted and treated as servants, but as sons grown up to maturity, who are allowed greater freedoms, and admitted to larger privileges.

December 23

The fulfilling of God's promises

Luke 2:1–4

The *fulness of time* was now come when God would send forth his Son, and it was foretold that he should be born at Bethlehem. Now here we have an account of the time and place of it.

He was born in the days of Augustus Caesar, when the Roman empire extended itself further than ever before or since, including Parthia one way, and Britain another way; so that it was then called 'the empire of the whole earth', and here that empire is called *all the world*, v.1, for there was scarcely any part of the civilized world, but what was dependent on it.

He was born when Judaea was become a province of the empire, and tributary to it; as appears evidently by this, that when all the Roman empire was taxed, the Jews were taxed among the rest. Judaea was ruled by Cyrenius the Roman governor of Syria, v.2. This was the first taxing that was made in Judaea, the first badge of their servitude.

The place where our Lord Jesus was born is very observable. He was born at Bethlehem; so it was foretold (Micah 5:2), the scribes so understood it, so did the common people. The name of the place was significant. Bethlehem signifies the house of bread; a proper place for him to be born in who is the bread of life, the bread that *came down from heaven*. Bethlehem was the city of David, where he was born, and therefore there he must be born who was the *Son of David*. Zion was also called *the city of David*, yet Christ was not born there; for Bethlehem was that city of David where he was born in lowliness to be a shepherd; and this our Saviour chose for the place of his birth; not Zion, where he ruled in power and prosperity.

December 24

The Saviour is born

Luke 2:3-7

Now when the virgin Mary was with child, and near her time, providence so ordered it that, by order from the emperor, all the subjects of the Roman empire were to be *taxed*; that is, they were to be registered and enrolled, according to their families.

In his birth, Christ was under some abasements in common with other children; he was *wrapped in swaddling clothes*, as other children are when they are new-born, as if he could be bound, or needed to be kept straight.

He was born *at an inn*. Christ was born in an inn, to intimate that he came into the world but to sojourn here for awhile, as in an inn. An inn receives all comers, and so does Christ. He hangs out the banner of love for his sign, and whoever comes to him, he will in no wise cast out.

He was born in a stable; so some think the word signifies which we translate *a manger*. Because there was *no room in the inn*, and for want of convenience, no, for want of necessaries, he was laid *in the manger*, instead of a cradle. His being born in a stable and laid in a manger was an instance:

(1) of the poverty of his parents. Had they been rich, room would have been made for them.

(2) of the corruption and degeneracy of manners in that age. If there had been any common humanity among them, they would not have turned a woman in travail into a stable.

(3) of the humiliation of our Lord Jesus. We were become by sin like an outcast infant, helpless and forlorn; and such a one Christ was.

They fell down and worshipped him

Matthew 2:10–11

What a transport of joy these wise men were in, upon this sight of the star. Now they had reason to hope for a sight of *the Lord's Christ* speedily, of *the Sun of righteousness*, for they see *the Morning Star*. We should be glad of everything that will show us the way to Christ. This star was sent to meet the wise men, and to conduct them into the presence of the King.

See how they made their address to him when they had found him, v.11. We may well imagine what a disappointment it was to them when they found a cottage was his palace, and his own poor mother all the retinue he had! However, these wise men were so wise as to see through this veil. They did not think themselves baulked or baffled in their enquiry; but, as having found the King they sought, they presented themselves first, and then their gifts to him.

They presented themselves to him: they *fell down and worshipped him*. We do not read that they gave such honour to Herod, though he was in the height of his royal grandeur; but to this babe they gave this honour, not only as to a king, but as to a God. All that have found Christ fall down before him; they adore him, and submit themselves to him.

They presented their gifts to him. In the eastern nations, when they did homage to their kings, they made them presents. With ourselves, we must give up all that we have to Jesus Christ. Nor are our gifts accepted, unless we first present ourselves to him living sacrifices. The gifts they presented were *gold, frankincense, and myrrh*, money, and money's-worth. Providence sent this for a seasonable relief to Joseph and Mary in their present poor condition.

These were the products of their own country; what God favours us with, we must honour him with. They offered him *gold*, as a king, paying him tribute; *frankincense*, as God, for they honoured God with the smoke of incense; and *myrrh*, as a Man that should die, for myrrh was used in embalming dead bodies.

Glory to God in the highest!

Luke 2:10-14

Here we have the message which the angel had to deliver to the shepherds, v.10-12. '*Fear not,* you need not fear your enemies, and should not fear your friends.' He furnishes them with abundant matter for joy: 'Behold, I *evangelize to you great joy.* It shall bring *joy to all people*; that *unto you is born this day a Saviour which is Christ the Lord, in the city of David,*' v.11. 'The Saviour *is born this day*; and, since it is a matter of *great joy to all people*, you may proclaim it. He is born in the place where it was foretold he should be born, in the *city of David*; and he is born *to you*; to you Jews he is sent in the first place, to bless you, to you shepherds, though poor and lowly in the world.'

Unto us a child is born, unto us a son is given. This is matter of joy indeed to all people, great joy. Long-looked for is come at last. He gives them a sign for the confirming of their faith in this matter. 'You will find him by this token: he is lying in a *manger*, where surely never any new-born infant was laid before. You will find him wrapped in *swaddling clothes*, and *laid in a manger.*

The angels' doxology to God, and congratulations of men, upon this solemn occasion is recorded, v.13,14. The message was no sooner delivered by one angel than suddenly there was with that angel *a multitude of the heavenly host praising God.* Let God have the honour of this work: *Glory to God in the highest; Glory to God*, whose kindness and love designed this favour, and whose wisdom contrived it. Other works of God are for his glory, but the redemption of the world is for his *glory in the highest*. Let men have the joy of it: *On earth peace, goodwill toward men.*

The shepherds visit the baby

Luke 2:15–20

While the angels were singing their hymn, the shepherds could attend to that only; but, *when they were gone away from them into heaven*, the *shepherds said one to another, let us go to Bethlehem*. These shepherds do not speak doubtfully, 'Let us go see whether it be so or no'; but with assurance, *Let us go and see this thing which is come to pass*; for what room was left to doubt of it, when the Lord had thus made it known to them?

They immediately made the visit, v.16. They lost no time, but *came with haste* to the place, and there *they found Mary and Joseph*, and the *babe lying in the manger*. Observe the care which the shepherds took to spread the report of this, v.17: *When they had seen it* they made *known abroad* the whole story of what was *told them*, both by the angels, and by Joseph and Mary, *concerning this child*, that he was the Saviour, even *Christ the Lord*, that in him there is *peace on earth*. What impression did it make upon people? Why truly, *All they that heard it wondered at those things which were told them by the shepherds*, v.18. They wondered, but never enquired any further about the Saviour, but let the thing drop as a nine days' wonder.

But we see the use which those made of these things, who did believe them. The virgin Mary made them the matter of her private meditation. She said little, but *kept all these things, and pondered them in her heart*, v.19. As she had silently left it to God to clear up her virtue, when that was suspected, so she silently leaves it to him to publish her honour, now when it was veiled; and it is satisfaction enough to find that, if no one else takes notice of the birth of her child, angels do. The truths of Christ are worth keeping; and the way to keep them safe is to *ponder them*. Meditation is the best help to memory.

The shepherds made them the matter of their more public praises. If others were not affected with those things, yet they themselves were, v.20: *They returned, glorifying and praising God*. They praised God for what they had heard from the angel, and for what they had seen, the babe in the manger, as it had been spoken to them.

December 28

Go therefore . . .

Matthew 28:18–19

Here we observe the commission which our Lord Jesus received himself from the Father. *All power is given unto me in heaven and in earth.* He has *all power.* It was given him, by a grant from him who is the fountain of all being, and consequently of all power. As God, equal with the Father, all power was originally and essentially his; but as Mediator, as God-man, *all power* was *given him.*

He has this power in *heaven and earth,* comprehending the universe. He is Lord of all. He has all power in heaven. He has power of dominion over the angels. He has power of intercession with his Father, he intercedes not as a suppliant, but as a demandant: *Father, I will.* He has *all power on earth* too; he prevails with men, and deals with them as one having authority, by the ministry of reconciliation.

The commission he gives to those whom he sent forth: *Go ye therefore.* This commission is given to the apostles primarily, the architects that laid the foundation of the church. It is given to their successors, the ministers of the gospel, whose business it is to transmit the gospel from age to age, to the end of the world in time.

Observe how far his commission is extended: to *all nations.* Go, and disciple *all nations.* Now this plainly signifies it to be the will of Christ, that the covenant of exclusiveness made with the Jews, should now be cancelled and disannulled. Whereas the apostles, when first sent out, were forbidden to go into the way of the Gentiles, now they were sent to *all nations.* This also shows us that salvation by Christ should be offered to all, and none excluded that did not by their unbelief and impenitence exclude themselves.

Discipling all nations

Matthew 28:19-20

Observe what is the principal intention of this commission; to *disciple* all nations. Christ the Mediator is setting up a kingdom in the world, bring the nations to be his subjects; setting up a school, bring the nations to be his scholars; raising an army, enlist the nations of the earth under his banner.

Here we have their instructions for executing this commission. They must admit disciples by the sacred rite of baptism: 'Go into all nations, preach the gospel to them, work miracles among them, and persuade them to come in themselves, and bring their children with them, into the church of Christ, and then admit them and theirs into the church, by washing them with water.' This baptism must be administered *in the name of the Father, and of the Son, and of the Holy Ghost.* That is by authority from heaven, and not of man; for his ministers act by authority from the three Persons in the Godhead; and by calling upon the name of the Father, Son, and Holy Ghost. Everything is sanctified by prayer, and particularly the waters of baptism.

It is into the name of *Father, Son, and Holy Ghost*; this was intended as the summary of the first principles of the Christian religion. By our being baptized we solemnly profess our assent to the scripture-revelation concerning God, the Father, Son, and Holy Ghost, and our consent to a covenant-relation to God, *the Father, Son, and Holy Ghost.*

Those that are thus baptized, and enrolled among the disciples of Christ, must be taught, v.20: *Teaching them to observe all things, whatsoever I have commanded you.* This denotes two things. The duty of disciples, of all baptized Christians; they must *observe all things* whatsoever Christ has commanded, and, in order to achieve that, must submit to the teaching of those whom he sends.

I am with you always

Matthew 28:20

Here is the assurance Christ gives his disciples of his spiritual presence with them in the execution of this commission: *And lo, I am with you always, even unto the end of the world.*

Observe the favour promised them: *I am with you.* Not, *I will be* with you, but *I am.* He was now about to leave them; his bodily presence was now to be removed from them, and this grieved them; but he assures them of his spiritual presence, *I am with you;* that is, 'My Spirit is with you, the Comforter shall *abide with you.* I am with you, and not against you: with you to take your part, to be on your side. I am with you, and not absent from you, not at a distance; I am a very present help.' Christ was now sending them to set up his kingdom in the world.

He promises them his presence with them to carry them on through the difficulties they were likely to meet with and to succeed in this great undertaking: 'Lo, *I am with you,* to make your ministry effectual for the discipling of the nations.' They shall have his constant presence: *always, all days,* every day. 'I will be with you on sabbath days and weekdays, fair days and foul days, winter days and summer days.' They shall have his perpetual presence, even to *the end of the world.* This is hastening towards its period; and even till then the Christian religion shall, in one part of the world or other, be kept up, and the presence of Christ continued with his ministers. I am with you *to the end of the world.*

There is one word more remaining, which must not be overlooked, and that is Amen; which is not a cipher, intended only for a concluding word, like *finis* at the end of a book. It speaks of Christ's confirmation of this promise, *Lo, I am with you.* It is his *Amen,* in whom all the promises are *Yea and Amen.* Our *Amen* to Christ's promises turns them into prayers.

Come, Lord Jesus!

Revelation 22:20–21

We have now come to the conclusion of the whole, and that in three things:

(1) Christ's farewell to his church. He parts with his people on earth in great kindness, and assures them it shall not be long before he comes again to them: *Behold, I come quickly.* If any say, 'Where is the promise of his coming, when so many ages have passed since this was written?' let them know he is not slack to his people, but long-suffering to his enemies: his coming will be sooner than they are aware, sooner than they are prepared, sooner than they desire; and to his people it will be in season.

He will come quickly: let this word be always sounding in our ear, and let us give all diligence that we may be found of him in peace, *without spot and blameless.*

(2) the church's hearty echo to Christ's promise, declaring her firm belief of it: *Amen, so it is*, so it shall be and expressing her earnest desire of it: *Even so, come, Lord Jesus*; make haste, my beloved, and be thou like a roe, or like a young hart on the mountains of spices. Thus beats the pulse of the church, thus breathes that gracious Spirit which actuates and informs the mystical body of Christ; and we should never be satisfied till we find such a spirit breathing in us, and causing us to look *for the blessed hope, and glorious appearance of the great God and our Saviour Jesus Christ.*

(3) The apostolical benediction, which closes the whole: *The grace of our Lord Jesus Christ be with you all, Amen.* Nothing should be more desired by us than that the grace of Christ may be with us in this world, to prepare us for the glory of Christ in the other world. It is by his grace that we must be kept in a joyful expectation of his glory, fitted for it, and preserved to it; and his glorious appearance will be welcome and joyful to those that are partakers of his grace and favour here; and therefore to this most comprehensive prayer we should all add our hearty *Amen.*